Proceedings
Comparative Literature Symposium
Texas Tech University
Volume X

# IBERO-AMERICAN LETTERS IN A COMPARATIVE PERSPECTIVE

Edited by
*Wolodymyr T. Zyla*
*Wendell M. Aycock*

Texas Tech Press
Lubbock, Texas
1978

860.9
C737L

Proceedings of the Comparative Literature Symposium result from annual symposia organized by Texas Tech University's Interdepartmental
Committee on Comparative Literature. *Ibero-American Letters in a
Comparative Perspective* is the proceedings of a symposium held on 26 to
28 January 1978. Copies of the Proceedings may be obtained on an exchange basis from, or purchased through, the Exchange Librarian,
Texas Tech University Library, Lubbock, Texas 79409.

81-5361

ISSN: 0084-9103
ISBN: 0-89672-061-6
Library of Congress Catalog Card Number: 78-52067
Texas Tech Press
Texas Tech University, Lubbock, Texas 79409
Printed in the United States of America

# Contents

# Preface

The emergence of Ibero-American literature is, without doubt, one of the most extraordinary literary events of our time. Today this belletristic phenomenon is represented by a true and real achievement of many noteworthy writers who began to appear in that part of the world, which, until three or four generations ago, had made little or no contribution to the world's literature. This achievement is the result of the publication in recent decades of a great number of outstanding works that represent almost the whole of Latin America. Moreover, outside Latin America the prestige of its leading writers has probably never been higher than at the present time. The recent translations of two important works, Carlos Fuentes' historical novel *Terra Nostra* and Gabriel García Márquez's *The Autumn of the Patriarch*, both of which received wide international attention, offer further proof of the significant literary developments that we are witnessing in Latin America. Furthermore, this literature appears to many critics as a single literature, in spite of the fact that it comes from various countries belonging to differing ideologies, sometimes incompatible regimes, different cultural traditions and divergent national characteristics.

On 26, 27, and 28 January 1977, Ibero-American scholars and devotees from various parts of the United States and Canada assembled at Texas Tech University to participate in the Tenth Annual Comparative Literature Symposium. The theme of the symposium was "Ibero-American Letters in a Comparative Perspective." The symposium examined selected aspects of Ibero-American letters—the boldness of its many writers, the stubbornly experimental nature of some of their works, its obvious youth, and its tangible tradition with roots in the immediate past of Latin American culture.

The first day of the symposium activities began with opening remarks by Glenn E. Barnett, Executive Vice President of Texas Tech University. Musical performances of "Varita de Canela," "Reversible," "Oración," and "La Canción de la Pilmana" by William G. Hartwell, baritone, and Lora Deahl, pianist, created an atmosphere appropriate to the theme of the symposium. The speech of dedication of the symposium to Boyd G. Carter, in recognition of his outstanding contribution to the study of Spanish American literature, was made by Wolodymyr T. Zyla. "The New World as Creator and Catalyst of Culture," by Boyd G. Carter, The University of Iowa, was the keynote address presented that day. In his address Carter offered probably the most characteristic statement of the whole symposium, saying: "In a comparative perspective, Ibero-American Letters have demonstratively come of age and taken their place in world literature as a positive reality. In the kaleidoscope of historical perspective Ibero-American Letters offer multiple attractions to scholars as areas for study and research. In the kaleidoscope of optimist projection, Ibero-American Letters beckon as an oasis of promise to comparatists of all languages and countries."

In the first lecture of the symposium, "Mexican Fiction of the Seventies: Author, Intellect, and Public," John S. Brushwood, The University of Kansas explained that the outstanding characteristics of the Mexican novel since 1967 are technical virtuosity and a tendency toward metafiction. He maintained that "these characteristics, while interesting to the cognoscenti, seem to alienate many readers" and puzzle some who "may be reacting as Auerbach reacted when confronting *Ulysses.*" Frank Dauster, Rutgers College, The State University of New Jersey, in his paper entitled "Social Content and Revolutionary Form: Spanish American Drama Today," pointed out that "within a society which is increasingly polarized between the restless demands of the impoverished and the frantic defense of privilege, the theater in Latin America has become perhaps the most politicized of the arts, in large measure because the drama is a living art and much more difficult to control and censor." He went on to say that the Spanish American dramatists, "convinced that commitment without craftsmanship becomes a meaningless exercise in amateurism . . . experiment continuously in dramatic form, accepting such European tendencies as the absurd, Brecht or Artaud, each in turn, while seeking an original expression capable of communicating the unique reality they perceive in their sector of the Third World."

Angela B. Dellepiane, The City University of New York, gave a lecture on "Fiction of Southern South America: A Comparison," in which she said that "the southern narrative, with the exception of that of Paraguay, does not deviate from the general tendencies of the rest of the continent, although it shows some unique characteristics." Seymour Menton, University of California, Irvine, in his presentation, "Periodization and Typology of the Novel of the Cuban Revolution," pointed out the following: "The novel, because it reflects society more directly than the other literary genres, has been particularly susceptible to official changes in government policy." He maintained that "the production of Cuban novels may be divided into four clearly discernible chronological periods: 1959-1960, 1961-1965, 1966-1971, 1972-1977." He went on to say: "Although the degree of adherence to the regime varies from one chronological group of novels to the next, some individual variations make the establishment of a typology more complicated than the periodization."

Robert J. Morris, Texas Tech University, in his paper on "Isaacs' *María* and Its Neoplatonic Legacy," indicated that "until now no one has approached Isaacs' novel as a product of the humanistic environment in which his genius was nurtured and as a reflection of his personal interests, particularly his lifelong devotion to the classic and neoclassic literatures." He stressed "Isaacs' indebtedness to the neoplatonic tradition" especially when his "novel is compared with Spain's best known pastoral novel, *La Diana* by Jorge de Montemayor." Gregory Rabassa, The City University of New York, in his lecture, "A Comparative Look at the Literatures of Spanish America and Brazil: The Dangers of Deception," maintained that there is a great superficial resemblance between the literatures of Spanish America and Brazil, but this similarity inevitably grows dim under a close scrutiny. Furthermore, he said: "For reasons that are most likely historical, Brazilian literature settled down into a more orderly pattern of development with the establishment of definable movements and schools which corresponded closely to the European scene, while Spanish America seemed to be afflicted with a chaotic kind of drumbling and wambling. In recent times, however, there has, indeed, been a marked similarity between literary works from the two areas, and the problem for interpretation is how this converging of directions came about."

Daniel R. Reedy, University of Kentucky, presented "The Hidden Goddess in Julio Cortázar's *Hopscotch*." Reedy argued that "Cortázar's use of mythic structures in several of his earlier works makes plausible our assumption that a similar technique has been employed" in *Hopscotch*, "which because of the nature of the sexual act, most critics have either avoided or have interpreted as convincing proof of the absurd nature of the protagonist's existence. The ritualistic nature of the scene, when examined in light of Lucian's (Lucian of Samosata, author of *De Dea Syria*) commentaries and our knowledge of the symbolic meaning of other religious rituals, strongly suggests that rather than being an unnecessary, absurd interpretation, it is one of the pivotal occurrences in the novel and constitutes a significant aspect of its interior structure." Sabine Ulibarrí and Dick Gerdes, The University of New Mexico, in their paper on "Mexican Literature and Chicano Literature: A Comparison," stressed that "the Mexican heritage of Chicano literature also includes Hispanic influences which—since the Conquest, through the Colonial period, and up to the present century—had all but been lost in Chicano history, art and literature. But in the same way that the Mexican Revolution created a new spirit in art for the Mexican then, rediscovered Hispanic and Mexican values have influenced the Chicano Renaissance of today."

The luncheon speaker, Harley D. Oberhelman, Texas Tech University, in his presentation, "Faulknerian Techniques in Gabriel García Márquez's Portrait of a Dictator," maintained that "brilliant literary style is the real achievement of both William Faulkner and Gabriel García Márquez. They are regional writers who deal with universal problems. Faulkner views his created world with a sense of moral judgment. Likewise, García Márquez, in what may be the best of the current vogue of novels of dictatorship, attempts to wipe away the repugnant, dictatorial past and allow the inhabitants of his fictional nation to celebrate the arrival of a new day of moral justice."

The symposium lectures were followed by panel discussions and comments from the audience. The symposium panel discussion members were Angela B. Dellepiane, Gregory Rabassa, Daniel R. Reedy, guest speakers; Jim M. Baker, Lubbock Christian College, Robert G. Collmer, Baylor University, Fred P. Ellison, The University of Texas at Austin, Mary J. Gill, West Texas State University, Carlos H. Monsanto, University of Houston, Bart L. Lewis, Texas A&M University, Leon F. Lyday, III, Pennsylvania State University, John L. Marambio, McMurry College, and Berta Savariego, Richland College and El Centro College in Dallas, guest panelists; and Norwood H. Andrews, Jr., Wendell M. Aycock, Gonzalo Cartagenova, Sydney P. Cravens, Edmundo García-Girón, Sheldon C. Klock, Jr., Henry J. Maxwell, Robert J. Morris, Lorum H. Straton, faculty members at Texas Tech University; and Luis F. Badell, Richard L. Brown, Rodolfo Rocha, and Ann C. Tavenner, graduate students at Texas Tech University. In all its sessions the symposium was attended by approximately 1,470 persons, including faculty members, graduate students, and undergraduates from Texas Tech University and from forty-two universities and colleges.

In addition to the lectures, the symposium program included theatrical and musical performances and three exhibits. *Los Caminantes* of Lubbock Christian College presented in Spanish *Juicio Final* by José de Jesús Martínez and *El Ausente* by Xavier Villaurrutia. These performances were directed by June Bearden and Jim M. Baker of Lubbock Christian College. There was also a symposium concert with performances of Wind Orchestra and Texas Tech University Concert Band. The concert, co-sponsored by the Twenty-Sixth Symposium of Contemporary Music and the Tenth Annual Comparative Literature Symposium, presented "Concerto for Piano and Wind Orchestra," a major composition by John Beall, a young American composer. This work received the Howard Hanson Prize in 1973 and was premiered by pianist Carol Allen Beall and the Eastman Wind Ensemble in 1974.

The University Bookstore featured a display of visiting lecturers' works, and the Univeristy Library presented "Other Americas' Belles-lettres." The main symposium exhibit, "Ibero-American Literature: Rare Books and Letters," was on display in the Museum of Texas Tech University. There were also two television programs devoted to the symposium theme and presented on Texas Tech Educational Television Station (KTXT-TV).

This volume of the Proceedings is divided into three parts: A Dedication and Keynote Address, Symposium Lectures, and Luncheon Presentation and Looking Back Remarks. The lectures appear in alphabetical order. The cover for this work is based on the artistic design of the symposium poster, created by Jerry D. Kelly. This volume contains a photograph of Boyd G. Carter and several photographs of the symposium activities. An exchange publication, this volume is placed in various libraries throughout the world in order to stimulate the growth of comparative literature studies.

In conclusion I should like to express my deep gratitude to the distinguished guest speakers, speakers from the University, guest panelists, and panelists from Texas Tech, who made this symposium possible. Appreciation is due to all guests from other universities and colleges who attended this symposium. I thank the Department of Music, The Museum of Texas Tech University, The University Library and the University Bookstore for their helpful cooperation. I am indebted to the Lubbock Visitors and Conventions for their help in registration. Thanks are due to all colleagues at Texas Tech University who helped in this symposium by working on various committees. My sincerest thanks go to those who served as chairpersons of various symposium meetings: Glenn E. Barnett, Ann A. Daghistany, Robert W. Deahl, Donald T. Dietz, Lawrence L. Graves, Carl Hammer, Jr., Charles S. Hardwick, J. Knox Jones, Jr., Marion C. Michael, Harley D. Oberhelman. I am especially grateful to M. Cecil Mackey, President of Texas Tech University, and J. Knox Jones, Jr., Vice President for Research and Graduate Studies, for their generous support of the comparative literature symposium project.

Wolodymyr T. Zyla

# A Dedication and Keynote Address

# Dedication

To Boyd G. Carter, teacher and scholar, we dedicate this issue of the Proceedings of the Comparative Literature Symposium in sincere recognition of his outstanding contributions to the study of Spanish American literature. As an inspiring teacher and a significant scholar, Boyd G. Carter is regarded as the initiator of a long line of brilliant critics in this field who flourish at the present time in the United States. Carter's works are intricate and profound; they combine true Spanish American motifs with philosophical thought and careful analysis. They therefore will have a lasting impact upon Spanish American scholarship.

Boyd G. Carter

# The New World as Catalyst and Creator of Culture

Boyd G. Carter

### ABSTRACT

Ibero-American literature draws its content from a vast reservoir of unique material rooted in the unusual experience of diverse ethnic groups, immigrants, political exiles and adventurers, in the New World's multiple exotic geographical environments with their diverse flora and fauna. With evident and inevitable variations from country to country, and especially in regard to Brazil, Ibero-American literature falls roughly into the following periods and thematic categories: Precolumbian; the Conquest; Colonial; Independence; Post Independence (Romanticism and *Costumbrismo*, Anti-Slavery literature, Gaucho literature, Satire); *Modernismo* and Vanguardism; *Criollismo*; literature of the Mexican Revolution, of social protest and of the land. Since World War II, Ibero-American literature has reflected the thought and events of the period in both traditional and vanguardistic writings.

The major preoccupations of writers previous to *Modernismo* (roughly from 1876 to 1916) were regionalistic or nationalistic with the role of the author as that of observer-catalyst. With *Modernismo* content equates with form to constitute an esthetic experience of cosmopolitan or universal appeal. The author becomes less a catalyst than a creator and recreator. With recent fiction Spanish American literature has come of age internationally in prose as it already had with *Modernismo* in poetry.

Today, Ibero-American letters offer multiple attractions to scholars and beckon to comparatists of all languages and cultures. (BGC)

*The New York Evening Post*, in the 17 April 1915 issue of the *Literary Digest*, deplored United States' readers' neglect of Spanish American Literature. "Our chilling indifference," the writer comments, "was illustrated recently when her greatest poet, Rubén Darío, paid a visit to New York and the public, the press and even literary and artistic circles took almost no notice.... Our indifference to the work of Latin Americans rises less from their poverty in original writers than from our ignorance of the special features of their life."

15

In January 1967, Tom Streichorst and his camera crew checked into the Gran Hotel of Managua the day I did but not, as I had at first assumed, to cover the week of activities and the program sponsored by the Nicaraguan government to celebrate the centennial anniversary of Rubén Darío. In spite of my urging and picking up checks for several rounds of drinks and sending a cablegram to NBC, I could not persuade the crew to make a single move. Streichorst said he would like to but couldn't without authorization, and we never got it. They were only there to cover the election, and, although they were around for several days before it was held, to my knowledge NBC's camera crew never took a single picture nor did this network report on the event.

This illustrates, I think, that although Ariel still hovers and, as illustrated by this Symposium, sometimes perches on pinnacles of appreciative recognition, the slob Caliban, bounded in narrow shallows of utilitarianism, is still ubiquitously around and slovenly vigilant.

* * *

My topic is so vast, so complex and so open to dissenting interpretations that it invites disaster to start. The title itself is a verbal noose despite its elusive vagueness. Why the "New World" instead of "Spanish America," "Ibero-America" or "Latin America"? Obviously because there is also an "Indoamerica," an "Afroamerica," an "Angloamerica," an "Oriental America" and other Americas.

Even the terms "creator" and "catalyst," which the dictionary defines with reasonable clarity, may become opaque in the context of this topic. The boundary in literature and in art between creation as invention and creation as renascent discovery or ingenious imitation is always mobile and its contours webbed in subtleties and filigreed overlappings.

The word "catalyst" presupposes as coefficient the word "assimilation" which of necessity precedes any act of creativity in art and literature. But whereas assimilation involves incorporation and digestion, catalysis precipitates or modifies without being changed in the process. In this sense the New World exists as a catalyst that modifies and processes imported cultural experience and the experience of migrants, emigrants, exiles and travelers while maintaining the fundamental continuity of its own basic and peculiar features, contours and attributes.[1]

Culture, whether spelled with the letter $K$ in German or with $C$ in English and in the Romance languages, is a treacherous word, protean, kaleidoscopic and opportunistic, a shield for vagueness, a verbal bureaucrat and yet, withal indispensably necessary. In the nineteenth century the words "literario" and "científico" gave tone and dignity to titles of periodicals. In the twentieth, "Culture" is the in-word whose canopy of connotations is all embracing.

Ibero-American literature draws its content from more different sources and from a wider range of human experience and expression than probably any other: native Indian cultures and the New World's variegated physical environment with its extraordinary flora and fauna; Africans forcibly abducted from their homeland; immigrants in exile fleeing from dictators; voluntary expatriates seeking new experiences and opportunities; ethnic and social groups such as criollos, mestizos, negroes, gauchos and others; invaders and interventionists, English, French, North Americans. This vast reservoir of unusual material and of unique human experience had the good fortune to be viewed, observed, assimilated and processed in literary form in two of the great Romance languages, Spanish and Portuguese.

For the first time in recorded history apparently, a mature culture encountered a previously unknown and unheard of new culture already amazingly mature in organization and in artistic and literary achievements, and heralded it in written reports that grip and strain the imagination. Cortés, for example, reports in his *Cartas de Relación* that the buildings of Tenochtitlán, the Aztec word for Mexico City, were as good as those being built in Spain at the time and that Aztec goldsmiths were second to none.

It is doubtful that the incidence of total impact of the Incas and their welfare state on the thinking of ideologues and utopian oriented writers has been sufficiently assessed, even to this day. *Los comentarios reales* (1609; 1617) of El Inca Garcilaso de la Vega, which deal with the origins, history, customs and achievements of the Incas, directly or indirectly contributed to the formulation of philosophical and sociological concepts that ennobled Indians and made them sympathetic characters in much Romantic literature. Among notable Europeans whose works deal or reflect preoccupation with the New World's inhabitants, we recall the names of Lope de Vega, Montaigne, Montesquieu, Rousseau, Voltaire, Chateaubriand and the French Utopian Socialist Charles Fourier.

The events of the Conquest and experiences of the participants produced chronicles of high literary merit, the great epics, *La Araucana* of Ercilla and *Os Lusíadas* of Camões, and inspired a quantity of good poetry and prose. Unfortunately, the zeal to evangelize and to hispaniolize contributed to the relative neglect of Indo-American literature until this century.

Cervantes and Lope de Vega, contemporaries of Alonso de Ercilla, as well as Voltaire and other Europeans, praised Ercilla's epic, *La Araucana* (1569, 1578, 1589) which dramatizes the heroic struggle of the Araucos of Chile to retain their freedom. These Indians, like the inhabitants of Numancia (1585) in Cervantes' play by this name preferred death to surrender and servitude.

*La Araucana* is the New World's closest approach to a genuine epic poem. Works in English such as John G. Neihardt's *A Cycle of the West* and Longfellow's *Hiawatha* and *Evangeline*, while epic in tone and dealing with life and death aspects of cultural clash and shock, lack the formal dignity, tragic scope and dramatic density of the Chilean epic.

The *Popol Vuh*, Bible of the Mayas, the Inca drama *Ollantay*, the poetry of Netzahualcóyotl, contemporary of François Villon with whose poetry his own has a notable thematic identity, the copious two volume *Historia de la literatura Náhuatl* by Angel María Garibay K., *Trece poetas del mundo azteca* by Miguel León Portilla and *Literaturas aborígenes de América* by Abraham Arias-Larreta—all these works and numerous others attest to the existence of a vast body of precolumbian literature largely disregarded or unknown outside of the country of origin.

A major area, therefore, for the comparatist to explore is the Indian as represented in literature, the Indian as a creator of literature and the collateral impact of the Indian on aspects of literary creativity.

The cultural clash, conflict and shock that accompanied the Conquista was mainly with firmly rooted native cultures. The advent of slavery which uprooted Africans and made them unwilling foreigners in conquered lands added new, novel and vital elements of culture to the New World's own native cultures. From "La Rebelión de Enriquillo" as told by Fray Bartolomé de las Casas in *Historia de las Indias*, and the adventures of the negro Estebanico with Alvar Núñez Cabeza de Vaca in their trek through the Southwest into Mexico, to the novels on slavery by Cuban writers of the last century to the modern poetry of Nicolás Guillén[2] or Luis Palés Matos and in the United States of Langston Hughes[3]—the negro, his experience, his destiny and his contributions to the New World have been the substance of a copious and significant body of literature.

The negro as creator and theme of literature, now that a nationalistic Africa is emerging with French as its principal language, becomes increasingly important as an area of investigation for the comparatist.[4] The field is also relatively wide open in Brazil, in Spanish America, in French America and in English America. The principal difficulty is linguistic, likewise an obstacle for beginning students of *Indigenista* and gaucho literature.

Georges Clemenceau observed that in France there was a continuous struggle "entre la société civile qui veut vivre et la société cléricale qui ne veut pas mourir."[5] The same kind of struggle developed in Latin America after Independence, more so in some countries than in others, but particularly in Mexico. By analogy, there has been dissention on the cultural level between those writers who champion *nationalism* in letters (also called *americanismo, Indianismo, telurismo, localismo, costumbrismo* and other names), and those who opt for *cosmopolitanism, exoticism, internationalism, vanguardism, transculturation*. The writer's religion is not necessarily a determining factor in his choice of camps.

The literary nationalists propose to feed the raw materials of historic event and public aspiration, of indigenous reality and social conflict, of cultural graftings and telluric uniqueness into Ibero-American literature with emphasis on authenticity in presenting types, groups, social problems, legends, customs and features of the environment. Writers with this orientation are more interested in what they say than in how they say it, in representation than in creation, in social problems than in esthetics and in particulars than in universals. It should not be inferred, however, that because of major preoccupation with content the writings of nationalists necessarily lack form. On the contrary, the form normally used, adapts appropriately to the content and conveys it well, as in *Martín Fierro*, the great gaucho poetic narrative. The point is that the nationalist writer is a catalyst-observer rather than being a re-creator, via techniques, of what he has assimilated.

The cosmopolitans' view of literature and of the writer's rôle in creating it varies considerably from that of the literary nationalist. For the latter, universality, when achieved, is a by-product of a work written about specific people, things and events, often with a definite pragmatic purpose and intended for a specific public.

The cosmopolitan writer, by contrast, sets priority on adding dimensions of universality to the raw material of content by the manner in which he conceives and processes it structurally and artistically. His relation to his content is that of catalyst re-creator and his goal the production of a work of art that is and exists on its own as an invented reality. Such residue of national essence as it may have, will be, therefore, a by-product of an artistic realization and not a pragmatic result deliberately sought and contrived.

The strictly nationalist current of literature would obviously have less to offer the comparatist than would works by authors whose cultural interests and realizations are cosmopolitan in scope.

Cosmopolitan attitudes towards literature stimulate foreign language learning, cultural importations, translations, vanguardistic experimentations in linguistic techniques, emphasis on innovative renovations and focus on personal problems and intimate concerns of individuals. Thus *nationalism* falls within the literary mode that Amado Nervo calls *hacia afuera*,[6] "outwards," in which the author serves as catalyst and observer-creator; and *cosmopolitanism* within the tendency of *hacia adentro*, "inwards," with the author involved experimentally as catalyst-assimilator and re-creator.

When the writer succeeds in jelling the substance of national reality in a structure and style uniquely suited to the purpose, there is a confluence of the two streams and the result can be a work of art of both national and universal appeal.

Several works by Mexican writers based in the substantive reality of the Mexican Revolution or subsequently in its collateral and fractional impacts on Mexican society reflect and illustrate this kind of creative synthesis. Some examples of this synthetic result are: *Los de abajo* (1915, The Underdogs) of Mariano Azuela, *El Aguila y la Serpiente* (1928, The Eagle and the Serpent) of Martín Luis Guzmán, *El Resplandor* (1937, The Dazzling Glare) of Mauricio Magdaleno, *Al filo del agua* (1947, The Edge of the Storm) of Agustín Yáñez, *Pedro Páramo* (1955) of Juan Rulfo, *La muerte de Artemio Cruz* (1962, The Death of Artemio Cruz) of Carlos Fuentes. It is to be noted in these novels that, beginning with Mauricio Magdaleno, the technique of the author becomes increasingly more important as a creative adjunct to content.

Polarization and synthesis in the sense that concerns us here are well exemplified in the works of Poe and Whitman.[7] Both writers created works of universal appeal especially appreciated in Europe and in Ibero-America, Whitman within and Poe primarily outside the currents of national experience.

Whereas it strains credulity to conceive of Whitman writing *Leaves of Grass* elsewhere than in this country, I have no difficulty at all in imagining Poe writing "The Raven" or "Ulalume" in London, Berlin, Paris, Madrid or in any city in the Hispanic and Portuguese New World.

Mexico's Sor Juana Inés de la Cruz (1648-1695) by any criterion is one of the world's great literary geniuses. This extraordinary woman, born within sight of the volcanoes Popocatépetl and Iztaccíhuatl, who made her debut at the viceroy's court at thirteen and entered a convent at fifteen, where she spent her life, is one of the most distinguished, lovable and intriguing personalities in all literature. Although she was involved in the national experience of her country, as is reflected by her life, in her prose and in much of her occasional poetry ("obrillas de circunstancias"), written sometimes for humorous effect in macaronic verse, náhuatl, negro dialects and Portuguese, the fact is that in regard to theme, conceptualization and execution, she could just as well have written her major compositions in Madrid and Rome as in Mexico City. But even though her writing reflects the baroque spirit and tendencies of the time and the influence of Góngora and of her Taxco born compatriot Ruiz de Alarcón, her Art has about it a distinctive savor of originality, for she saw her corner of nature and slice of life, as Zola expresses it, through the eyes of a Mexican with a personality that is unique to the world of letters.[8] And because of its universality of theme, the whimsical graciousness of its poignancy and humor, and irreversibility of language, Sor Juana's poetry is probably even more appreciated today than when it was written.

In contrast to the deductive procedure of Sor Juana, which sets an illustration, a reflection, an anxiety within a thematic generality, Ramón

López Velarde proceeds by "induction" from an inventory of representative aspects and details. His "Suave patria," considered by many as a national poem, is a sensuous assessment of things loved and cherished by Mexicans. The composition communicates a sense of identity, even to foreigners with some knowledge of Mexico, because it establishes a spirit of nostalgic communion with one's own place of origin, the "Pago chico," and reenforces pride in the cultural endowments of the nation. "Suave patria" attains its status of meta-national appeal because it defines the feelings of people everywhere who love their country and its way of life.

Chile's Nobel Prize winner, Gabriela Mistral, like López Velarde, works from a base of intimate reality rooted in her environment, her career as a teacher and her personal life. But unlike López Velarde, whose literary prism is uniquely nationalistic, Gabriela's devotion is to humanity and to love in its multiple manifestations. The patterns and coincidences of her personal and regional experience motivate and condition the release of emotional tensions and idealistic concerns for people in synthetic language, compassionate in connotation, that speaks to hearts and minds above politics, above religion, above political nationalism.

Thus, these three poets, each with a different point of departure, have succeeded in adding dimensions of universality to their compositions: Sor Juana by choice of theme, illustration and language; López Velarde by endowing aspects of national life with the substantive intimacy of generic communication; Gabriela Mistral by the apostolic mission of transmuting her experience into love in all of its expressions.

No poet of stature fits snugly in a category of total inclusion. The poetry of Octavio Paz is both Mexican and cosmopolitan in inspiration and universal in synthetic connotation.

"Altazor" of Vicente Huidobro appears to be a symbol of human destiny in falling transit from birth in the universe to a crazy planet of gibbering puppets bouncing in anguish while waiting to be reintegrated into eternity. Huidobro's "creacionismo," a concept of literature as an esthetic process of invention deliberately initiated to produce something new, as for example the image of a "bird's nest in a rainbow," would be the antipode of the view that literature has a social function and must be written to fulfill it.

Is poetry of social protest anti-poetry by virtue of its didacticism, political partisanship and ideological orientation? How do writings of social protest in both poetry and prose differ from satire?

The answer to the first question will depend, of course, on the conception one has of what poetry is.[9] If, as Andrei Siniavsky affirms, "Art always begins by transforming reality into something exotic,"[10] then, theoretically, poetry could be created in any thematic context in which this occurs. But if with Octavio Paz we think of poetry as "something

Symposium Keynote Address: From left to right Boyd G. Carter (guest speaker) and Glenn E. Barnett (chairperson of the session). (Photographed by Sheldon C. Klock, Jr.)

Texas Tech University administrators and faculty members. From left to right Wolodymyr T. Zyla, M. Cecil Mackey, Charles S. Hardwick, J. Knox Jones, Jr , and Norwood H. Andrews, Jr. (Photographed by Sheldon C. Klock, Jr.)

irrevocably said,"[11] then we are dealing with a reality unalterably created and sufficient unto itself.

The choice of invectives for a poet of social protest to use in attacking an opponent, a government or a system are many, but there is only one way to write a poem or for that matter to bring off any individual work of art. Thus, according to these concepts, Pablo Neruda, Chile's other Nobel Prize winner; Peru's César Vallejo; Mexico's José Revueltas, Efraín Huerta, Jesús Arellano and Miguel Bustos Cerecedo; Cuba's Nicolás Guillén and Roberto Fernández Retamar; Nicaragua's Ernesto Cardenal, these and others[12] within the orbit of fixed or semi-jelled ideological orientations will only succeed as poets whenever they escape the temporality of partisanship by transforming reality into something exotic and something irrevocably said. Great poets, of course, who become addicted to political invariables, may still produce good poetry but to do so they need to avoid, in the particular, the parochialism of emotion paralyzed in ideology.

The indignation of narrow political partisanship may sometimes produce a masterpiece of the quality of Esteban Echeverría's "Slaughter-house" (*El Matadero*) but more often the great or successful works of social protest—like *Uncle Tom's Cabin*, *Les Misérables*, *Grapes of Wrath*, *War and Peace*, Jorge Icaza's *Huasipungo*, José Hernández' *Martín Fierro*, Rómulo Gallegos' *Doña Bárbara*, Heriberto Frías' *Tomochic*, José Mármol's *Amalia*—are potent dramatizations of injustices and of uncivilized behavior and attitudes that rape the inherent dignity of people in general and deny them the right to be, to become and to endure.

Within the orbit of Spanish American vanguardism, as was the case in Europe, politics and social concerns may overlap preoccupations with pure esthetics and the elaboration of literature as a personal experience. Such overlapping occurs in José Carlos Mariátegui's vanguardist review, *Amauta* (1926-1930), in Peru; in the *Revista de Avance* (1927-1930), in Cuba; and decisively in the writings of the *estridentistas* in Mexico during the years 1926-1927. On the other hand, *Proa* (1922-1923) and *Martín Fierro* (1924-1927), in Argentina and *Contemporáneos* (1928-1931), in Mexico, project a profile of cosmopolitan literary intent and of brilliant accomplishment without deliberate disregard or rejection of national realities.[13]

*Vanguardismo* in both North and South America is still a vital phenomenon whose experimental, stylistic and ideological impact on contemporary writing, especially on fiction, has not yet been sufficiently explored. Vanguardist writings, particularly by surrealists, served as models that nourished the style and structure of Nobel Prize winner Miguel Angel Asturias' *El señor Presidente* (1946), of Agustín Yáñez' *Al filo del agua* (1947) and of Juan Rulfo's *Pedro Páramo* (1955), all three landmark novels. Their innovations in style and structure had an impact on Carlos

Fuentes and on the extraordinary explosion of creativity in fiction in the sixties, known as "The Boom."[14]

Western hemisphere fiction of the United States in the twenties and thirties–Faulkner, Hemingway, Fitzgerald, Dreiser, Steinbeck–was the best of its time. Today the Spanish American novel, continuing in the directions pioneered by Rivera, Onetti, Sábato, Asturias, Yáñez and Rulfo still rides uncertainly on the crest of international popularity. The works of Carlos Fuentes, Gabriel García Márquez, Mario Vargas Llosa, Julio Cortázar, Jorge Luis Borges and others are translated and read by world-wide audiences and reviewed by the world's critics impressed by the versatile craftsmanship of these sophisticated writers who involve the substance and peculiarities of national events and experience in strange adventures with peculiar characters with fascinating results and seek to involve their puzzled and harassed readers as unpaid collaborators.

Although New World literature in Spanish has made it all the way, the same concerns continue to be voiced and the same questions debated: literature as raw content in disregard of form versus rarified verbalizations of form in quest of content; literature obsessedly preoccupied with national realities or national realities artistically processed to create literature of international appeal; literature for the sake of literature or literature "al servicio del pueblo." Nowhere do these basic concerns, which constantly challenge students of comparative literature, emerge in better focus within documented contexts of discerning critical scrutiny than in two recent books fundamental to the study of Spanish American literature: *The Spanish American Novel: A Twentieth Century Survey* (1975) by John S. Brushwood, and *Prose Fiction of the Cuban Revolution* (1975) by Seymour Menton.

Several paragraphs back, we left a question suspended relating to satire which Dr. Johnson defines as "a poem in which wickedness or folly is censured." The term designates both a genre of literature and an attitude or tone that may be present or dominant in other genres. In general, the satirist wishes to correct and reform; the writer of social protest wants to demolish and substitute.

Our century is not only an age of alienation. It has also been the age par excellence of exiles: political and cultural exiles abroad and morally and culturally alienated people in exile in their own countries.[15]

In a very real sense we live in a world in which to be creative necessarily means to be alienated. Only alienated people are creative in that creativity is the result of frustration energized to close the gap between discontent and aspiration, absurdity and sense, ideal and reality, goal and attainment.

In the time remaining, and within the general scope of alienation and exile in geographical space and of alienation within one's own country and culture, I should like to comment briefly on the following literary manifestations of Ibero-America: satire, the picaresque, romanticism, the Argentine *proscriptos, modernismo* and an aspect of *vanguardismo* in Brazil.[16]

The volume of satire in Ibero-American literature is not commensurate in quantity with all that needs to be or could be satirized. Even so, there is a copious amount of it and much of it good: Sor Juana's castigation of would-be don Juans; Chilean Juan de Valle Caviedes' and Mexico's Fernández de Lizardi's ridicule of quack doctors; Mexican Juan Bautista Morales' *El Gallo Pitagórico*; Argentina's José Mármol, poetic executioner ("verdugo poético") of Juan Manuel Rosas; Ecuadorean Juan Montalvo's verbal floggings of dictator Gabriel García Moreno; Mexican ridicule in periodical literature of Maximilian, his henchmen and his empire; Manuel Gutiérrez Nájera's irony in his "Plato del día" series that deals with nearly everything Mexican and Mexican related of his epoch.

The *pícaro* as an outsider in exile within his own society, as "an unheroic protagonist caught up in a chaotic world,"[17] has reemerged as a type in a considerable amount of modern fiction. Ulrich Wicks devotes several pages of his recent study, in *Mosaic*, titled "Onlyman" to José Rubén Romero's "Pito Pérez," anti-hero of *The Useless Life of Pito Pérez* (*La vida inútil de Pito Pérez*). Incidentally the Spring (1975) number of this review has the subtitle of *The Literature of Exile*. In his extensive study of the picaresque, Wicks makes no mention at all of *El Periquillo Sarniento*, "The Mangy Parrot," generally recognized as Spanish America's first novel, published in 1816 in the midst of the Struggle for Independence. Neither does he mention Lesage's *Gil Blas* which probably had a greater influence on José Joaquín Fernández de Lizardi's novel than *Lazarillo de Tormes* or *Guzmán de Alfarache*. It is likely that Wicks thinks of Gil Blas and El Periquillo as young bourgeois of good families who duped or got duped because of naiveté or lack of character and are therefore not really alienated. Besides, El Periquillo's adventures, like those of Candide's, are programmed to illustrate, inform and reform. The picaresque in the literature and life of Ibero-America, on all levels, needs to be studied thoroughly for its aspects of uniqueness.

The aspirations of the newly independent nations to create new national literatures encountered drubbing obstacles in political instabilities, in foreign interventions, in the high rate of illiteracy, in the lack of publishing outlets and in the excessive use of translations. As a rule a poem originally in German, for example, came into Spanish through French as an almost new composition. The study of translations by linguistics oriented comparatists would be most revealing, fascinating and useful.

Romanticism at its worst in Spanish America is a hash of sentimental verbiage about faded flowers, trysts in grottoes, unfortunate love, untimely death and the like. At its best, it produced poets of the quality of José María Heredia, born in Cuba like his first cousin of the same name, who wrote in French;[18] Esteban Echeverría of Argentina; Manuel Acuña and Jorge Isaacs, author of *María*, a novel of durable and intriguing quality.

Heredia's "In the Temple of Cholula" ("En el Teocalli de Cholula"), written in 1820, is considered by many as the first romantic poem in Spanish. In 1951 I came across a partial translation of this poem in *La Revue des Deux Mondes*, made in 1853, by Jean Jacques Ampère, in which he plays tricks with Mexican geography.[19] Cholula is a town situated between the volcano Orizaba to the East and the volcanoes Popocatépetl and Iztaccíhuatl to the West. Ampère in his translation has the sun set behind Orizaba!

All three poets were alienated in one way or another: Heredia from Cuba and Echeverría from Argentina, as political exiles; Acuña from his childhood faith as a Catholic, yet unable to accept the positivistic philosophy of his time as a substitute.

An extensive comparative study would document some apparent differences between European and Ibero-American romanticism, notably in the rôle of nature and identification of romanticism with social progress.

Nature in Heredia is dramatic, awesome, intimate; in Echeverría, violent, hostile, destructive; in Sarmiento, vast, numinous, intimidating, indifferent; in Isaacs, lush, idyllic, beautiful.

Pedro Pablo Figueroa lists seventy distinguished Argentinians in his *Diccionario biográfico de extranjeros en Chile*[20] who lived there for varying periods of time during the years of Rosas tyranny 1835-1852. Among those destined to become influential and illustrious were Juan Bautista Alberdi, Juan María Gutiérrez, Vicente Fidel López and Domingo Faustino Sarmiento. José Mármol and Esteban Echeverría lived and wrote in Montevideo. Bartolomé Mitre produced the first novel written and published in Bolivia. Others went to Brazil and France.

Whereas in Argentina the number of periodical publications decreased from thirty-three in 1833 to never more than one or two during the Rosas dictatorship, the country's exiles founded not less than twenty-five periodicals abroad and had a vigorous rôle in animating the development of national literatures wherever they went. In the words of Ricardo Rojas,[21] the nation's exiles took its ideals with them to Montevideo, Bolivia, Chile, Brazil and France. Rojas characterizes this somber period of Argentina's political history as "el más sólido de nuestra literatura."[22] Thus, we have here an extraordinary example of a national literature conceived, produced and published abroad by a country's writers in exile.

It was in Chile that Sarmiento wrote and published, serially, in 1845, in *El Progreso*, a paper he founded, *Facundo: Civilización y barbarie*. The thirty-four page review[23] of the book by Charles de Mazade in France's prestigious *Revue des Deux Mondes*, in 1846, brought world-wide recognition to the future author of a book on Lincoln, who was an admirer of Horace Mann and the President of Argentina from 1868 to 1874.

The well publicized polemic between Sarmiento and Andrés Bello on Romanticism and Classicism took place in Chile in 1842. For Sarmiento, Classicism was impotent, had the odor of rancid bacon (tocino rancio) and was static and outmoded. To espouse Romanticism on the other hand was to believe in progress, to believe that "man, society, language and nature itself are on the march towards a state of perfectibility."[24] In this statement he echoes the utilitarian views on Democracy expressed by Echeverría in his Asociación de Mayo and reveals awareness of the postulates and doctrines of the French ideologues and of the concept of dialectical change and of "werden" of Hegelianism. But Sarmiento goes further. He affirms that Romanticism was useful as an instrument to destroy but ineffective as an agent to create and therefore it, too, had become outmoded. Its successor would be *socialismo*. "Hemos sido siempre i seremos eternamente socialistas, es decir, haciendo concurrir el arte, la ciencia, la política, o lo que es lo mismo, los sentimientos del corazón, las luces de la inteligencia i la actividad de la acción, al establecimiento de un gobierno democrático . . . ."[25]

Perhaps comparatists, deterred by generalities and the emotive rhetoric of much Hispanic Romanticism, have insufficiently studied the total impact of Sarmiento's view of Romanticism as a preparatory stage for socialism within the ideological fabric of some areas of Spanish American literature and political orientations.

*Modernismo* is an infelicitous term to designate the literary movement that brought innovative esthetic maturity and international recognition to Ibero-America's literature.[26] Although relative in meaning, bound to the ephemeral in time, and a slave to faddy nowism, in the perspective of Spanish American letters the term designates the dominant literature, art and music produced in Ibero-America between 1876, date of Gutiérrez Nájera's essay, "El Arte y el Materialismo"[27] and of the innovative critical and esthetic writings in the same period of José Martí, and 1916, the date of Rubén Darío's death.

There is still a tendency to group the major writers of the modernist period together as literary knitters from the same ball of esthetic yarn and to view them collectively as escapists, as effete imitators of the French, as thematic refugees from national realities, or as unpatriotic mugwumps and mavericks more interested in elegant living than in their country and its problems. Nothing could be further from the truth. Martí and Gutiérrez Nájera, journalists who lived by their pen, were honest men of principle, of vast cosmopolitan culture and deep national loyalties; Chocano and Lugones, swashbuckling adventurers of vacillating political affiliations and convictions; Valencia, a conservative politician; Darío and Nervo career diplomats; Casal, Silva and Herrera y Reissig, like Poe, wounded idealists and aliens in their own culture; Jaimes Freyre, career academician and historian. The principal thing they had in common was poetry and in varying degrees an insatiable interest in foreign literature. Thanks to them Ibero-America began to dilute its rôle as telluric catalyst and to take its place in world culture as creator-catalyst via assimilation and cross-fertilization. With *modernismo* Spanish American writing and especially poetry attained European recognition as literature of universal appeal.

Gutiérrez Nájera as early as 1885 made this comment: "Hoy no puede pedirse al literato que sólo describa los lugares de su patria y sólo cante las hazañas de sus héroes nacionales. El literato viaja, el literato está en comunicación íntima con las civilizaciones antiguas y con todo el mundo moderno . . . ."[28]

In defense of cross-fertilization[29] in literature and in refutation of charges that nationalism and cosmopolitanism are irreconcilable opposites, this same writer comments in one of his satirical essays in the "Plato del día" series that roastbeef is roastbeef whether one eats it in London or Mexico and that good taste admits of good food anywhere in the world. He says: "Se puede tener, *verbi gratia*, mucho patriotismo, y no tomar forzamente en cada comida mole verde, pulque blanco y mole colorado, con el fin de enarbolar en el estómago la bandera nacional."[30]

For the purpose of this paper, I have followed a zig-zag course hopscotching in time and geography, in order to pinpoint some of the distinct characteristics, differentiating aspects, literary currents and specific achievements of Spanish American literature. By necessity I have been selective and therefore heinously guilty of some serious omissions: the theater, the short story, the essay, bibliography, periodicals, Brazilian literature.

Fortunately, for the theater we have present for this Symposium, Frank Dauster,[31] Leon Lyday and Robert Morris, for the short story Seymour Menton,[32] who are maximum authorities on these genres and their ramifications. As for the essay, bibliography[33] and periodicals, most of us at one time or another have worked in these important areas. Not so long ago bibliography[34] and periodicals[35] were neglected stepchildren of Spanish American letters. Today, these resources are considerably more ample but still conspicuously lacking in many areas, fragmentary and unreliable in others.

In regard to periodicals, great surprises await patient and persistent comparatists of sound lungs not allergic to book dust. As one who, along with Jefferson Rea Spell, Sturgis Leavitt and John Englekirk has sniffed, snuffed and sneezed pounds of rancid dust from ancient tomes, I still thrill in spite of it to the curiosity of wondering what the next page that I turn

29

of a periodical may reveal. All I have ever needed to do to restore my
battered spirits, when ignored or harassed by academic bureaucrats,
bugged by colleagues or badgered by students was to go to the library and
peruse a periodical!

In conclusion, I apologize for not sticking more tightly in my comments to the thematic intent of this Symposium as stated in the title:
"Ibero-American Letters in a Comparative Perspective." In the first place,
I would feel uneasy in this center of emphasis on Portuguese language and
literature, even to generalize on a topic about which I have more intuitive
awareness than assimilated information.[36] The presence of Gregory
Rabassa, Fred Ellison and Norwood Andrews offers further assurance that
the letters of Portugal and of Brazil are amply and ably represented at this
Symposium. In the second place, I chose to take advantage of the preroga-
tive accorded me to broaden the comparative perspective of my approach
sufficiently to indicate some peripheral areas of Western Hemisphere cultural presence and cross-breeding.

Don José Vasconcelos first postulated the theory, and then rejected it
as unrealistic, that the people born in the New World of mixed racial
parentage, mestizos, mulatos, zambos and others, would be the *Raza
cósmica* of the future. Even though Ibero-America may never evolve a
*Raza cósmica*, it does have a *cultura cósmica* in its present which will
become increasingly important in its future.

In a comparative perspective, Ibero-American letters have demonstratively come of age and taken their place in world literature as a positive
reality. In the kaleidoscope of historical perspective Ibero-American letters
offer multiple attractions to scholars as areas for study and research. In the
kaleidoscope of optimistic projection, Ibero-American letters beckon as an
oasis of promise to comparatists of all languages and countries.

*The University of Iowa* (Visiting Professor, Spring, 1977)
*Texas Tech University* (Scholar in Residence and Adjunct Professor,
1977-1978)

NOTES

[1] A recently published work containing material on the periphery of this theme
is *Tradition and Renewal: Essays on Twentieth-Century Latin American Literature
and Culture*, ed. Merlin H. Forster (Urbana, Ill.: Univ. of Illinois Press, 1975).

[2] Angel Augier, "La Revolución cubana en la poesía de Nicolás Guillén," *Plural*,
5, No. 11 (August 1976), 47-61.

[3] Edward J. Mullen, "Presencia y evaluación de Langston Hughes en Hispanoamérica," *Comunidad Latinoamericana de Escritores*, No. 15 (1974), pp. 16-21; "The
Literary Reputation of Langston Hughes in the Hispanic World," *Comparative Literature Studies*, 13, No. 3 (September 1976), 254-69.

[4] A Conference and Symposium announced as "First Congress of Negro Culture
in the Americas," sponsored by the "Centro de Estudios Afro-Colombianos" of the

"Fundación Colombiana de Investigaciones Folclóricas" will be held in Bogotá, 24-28 August 1977. The organizer of the "Congreso" is Manuel Zapata Olivella, novelist, essayist, teacher, editor of the review, *Letras Nacionales*, and zealous promoter of cultural awareness of the Negro in Colombia and in the Americas. Marguerite C. Suárez-Murias devotes an article to "Black Literature in Latin America in Translation" as an interdisciplinary area, in *Latin American Literary Review*, 4, No. 7 (Fall-Winter 1975), 49-56.

[5] Alphonse V. Roche, *Les Idées traditionalistes en France de Rivarol á Charles Maurras* (Urbana, Ill.: Univ. of Illinois Press, 1937), p. 30.

[6] Amado Nervo, "El Modernismo," *La Aurora*, 1, No. 20 (15 September 1907), 4.

[7] For bibliographies of these writers and studies of their works in Spanish America, see John E. Englekirk, *Poe in Hispanic Literature* (New York: Instituto de las Américas, 1934); Fernando Alegría, *Walt Whitman en Hispano América* (México: Ediciones de Andrea, 1954).

[8] An article titled "Mexicanía de Sor Juana Inés de la Cruz" by Fina García Marruz is scheduled for publication in a future number of *Sin Nombre*.

[9] The nature of poetry in this context is amply and eruditely discussed in the *Princeton Encyclopedia of Poetry and Poetics*, ed. Alex Preminger et al. (Princeton: Princeton Univ. Press, 1965). See "Theories of Poetry," pp. 639-49.

[10] Andrei Siniavsky (Abram Tertz), "Exile and Writer" (as told to Michael Beausang), *Mosaic*, 8, No. 3 (Spring 1975), 18.

[11] "Introduction" by Octavio Paz to *Anthology of Mexican Poetry*, comp. Octavio Paz with Preface by C. W. Bowra, trans. (poetry) Samuel Beckett (Bloomington, Ind.: Indiana Univ. Press, 1959), p. 42.

[12] For an article on "Pablo de Rokha, poeta del pueblo," by Pablo Muñiz, see *Plural*, 5, No. 12 (September 1976), 20-29.

[13] For comment and analysis of the political and esthetic orientation of Spanish American vanguard publications, see John S. Brushwood, *The Spanish American Novel: A Twentieth Century Survey* (Austin and London: Univ. of Texas Press, 1975), pp. 59-60; Boyd G. Carter, "Vanguardismo en Hispanoamérica: ala estética; Vanguardismo; ala izquierdista," *Historia de la literatura hispanoamericana a través de sus revistas* (México: Ediciones de Andrea, 1968), pp. 98-121.

[14] See Brushwood, pp. 211-13, 287, 334; Juan Loveluck, "La vieja novedad del 'Boom,'" *El Urogallo* (Madrid), 6, Nos. 35-36 (September-December 1975), 79-84.

[15] *Mosaic*, 8, No. 3 (Spring 1975) is devoted to "Literature in Exile." Among articles that focus especially on alienation, exile and the writer are the following: the interview of Michael Beausang with Andrei Siniavsky (Abram Tertz), 15-20; Ulrich Wicks, "Onlyman" (the pícaro in modern fiction), 21-47; Erica Harth, "The Creative Alienation of the Writer: Sartre, Camus, Simone Beauvoir," 177-86; Erdmute Wenzel White, "Return of the Artist: The Quest for Authenticity in Brazilian Literature," 187-92. See also Ivan A. Schulman, "Casal's Cuban Counterpoint of Art and Reality," *Latin American Research Review*, 11, No. 2 (1976), 113-28.

[16] See note 36.

[17] Wicks, p. 22. The author devotes pages 28-33 of his study to *La vida inútil de Pito Pérez* by José Rubén Romero. His quotations are from the translation of William O. Cord, *The Futile Life of Pito Pérez* (Englewood Cliffs, N.J.: Prentice-Hall, Inc., 1966). For a comparative study of this novel, see Henryk Ziomek, "El Lazarillo de Tormes y La Vida inútil de Pito Pérez: dos novelas picarescas," in Carlos H. Magis, *Actas del Tercer Congreso International de Hispanistas* (México: El Colegio de México, 1970), pp. 945-54. As additional evidence of the eternal modernity of the

picaro and the picaresque, see Margaret Paula Sommers, "D'Aubigné's Baron de Faeneste: Courtier, Matamore, pícaro," *The French Review*, 50, No. 1 (October 1976), 6-11.

[18] For a study of these writers, see Max Henríquez Ureña, "Poetas cubanos de expresión francesa," *Revista Iberoamericana*, 3 (May 1941), 317-25.

[19] Boyd G. Carter, "Traducciones francesas de José María Heredia, en *La Revue des Deux Mondes*," *Revista Iberoamericana*, 17, No. 34 (January 1952), 315-30.

[20] Pedro Pablo Figueroa, *Diccionario biográfico de extranjeros en Chile* (Santiago: Imprenta Moderna, 1900), pp. 299-301.

[21] The nation's idealism, Rojas writes, "fue entonces, con sus grandes proscritos, a refugiarse en Montevideo, en Bolivia, en Chile, en Brasil, en Francia; y es allá donde debemos estudiarlo." *Obras*, I, 40.

[22] Ibid.

[23] Charles de Mazade, "De l'américanisme et des Républiques du Sud . . . Vida de Juan Facundo Quiroga por Domingo F. Sarmiento," *La Revue des Deux Mondes*, 16 (October-December 1846), 625-60.

[24] "Nosotros creemos en el progreso, es decir, creemos que el hombre, la sociedad, los idiomas, la naturaleza misma, marchan a la perfectibilidad." Sarmiento, *Obras*, I ([critical and literary articles], 1841-1842; rpt. Paris: Belin Hermanos, 1909), 253-54.

[25] Ibid., p. 318. The quote continues as follows: . . . "al establecimiento de un gobierno democrático *fundado en bases sólidas en el triunfo de la libertad i de todas las doctrinas liberales, en la realización, en fin, de los santos fines de nuestra revolución.*"

[26] Apparently Rubén Darío was the first to use the term in a literary context, in his article, "La literatura en Centroamérica," *Revista de Arte y Letras* (Chile), 12 (1887), 601. See also Allen W. Phillips, "Rubén Darío y sus juicios sobre el modernismo," *Revista Iberoamericana*, 24, No. 47 (January-June 1959), 41-64.

[27] Published in *El Correo Germánico* (1876), Nos. 3, 4, 11, 13, 16; 5, 8, 24, 26 August and 5 September. Reproduced in *Manuel Gutiérrez Nájera. Estudio y escritos inéditos* by Boyd G. Carter, with *prólogo* by E. K. Mapes (México: Ediciones de Andrea, 1956), pp. 113-44; also in Manuel Gutiérrez Nájera, *Obras*, investigación y recopilación de E. K. Mapes; edición y notas de Ernesto Mejía Sánchez; introducción de Porfirio Martínez Peñaloza, *Crítica literaria*, I (México: Centro de Estudios Literarios, Universidad Nacional Autónoma de México, 1959), 49-64.

[28] In *El Partido Liberal*, I, No. 135 (2 August 1885), 1. Reprinted in M. G. Nájera, *Obras. Crítica literaria*, I, under the title "Literatura propria y literatura nacional," 83-87.

[29] Manuel Gutiérrez Nájera, in an article titled "El cruzamiento en literatura" in the *Revista Azul*, I, No. 19 (9 September 1894), attributes the decadence of poetry in Spain to cultural isolation and lack of crossbreeding. He admonishes and warns: "Conserve cada raza su carácter substancial; pero no se aísle de las otras ni las rechace, so pena de agotarse y morir . . . . Mientras más prosa y poesía alemana, francesa, inglesa, italiana, rusa, norte y sudaméricana etc., importe la literatura española, más producirá y de más ricos y más cuantiosos productos será su exportación" (p. 289). Nájera opines that the renaissance of the novel in Spain is due to the abundance of translations published of works of Balzac, Flaubert, Stendhal, George Eliot, Thackeray, Tolstoi and others. In summary, he says: "No quiero que imiten los poetas españoles; pero sí quiero que conozcan modelos extranjeros; que adapten al castizo estilos ajenos; que revivan viejas bellezas, siempre jóvenes; en resumen, que su

poesía se vigorice por el cruzamiento" (p. 290). This article was reprinted in *Obras.* *Crítica literaria*, I, 101-06.

[30] Published with the title, "Las leyes de sombrero ancho" in the series of satirical essays, "Plato del día," in *El Universal*, 28 November 1893. Reprinted in *Manuel Gutiérrez Nájera. Escritos inéditos de sabor satírico: "Plato del día."* Estudio, edición y notas de Boyd G. Carter y Mary Eileen Carter (Columbia, Missouri: Univ. of Missouri Press, 1972), pp. 83-84.

[31] Frank N. Dauster, *Historia del teatro hispanoamericano. Siglos XIX y XX.* 2ª edición muy ampliada; in the series *Historia literaria de Hispanoamérica* (México: Ediciones de Andrea, 1973); and *Ensayos sobre teatro hispanoamericano* (México: SepSetentas, No. 208, 1975).

[32] Seymour Menton, *El cuento hispanoamericano. Antología crítico-histórica*, 2 vols. (1964, 1965, 1970; rpt. México: Fondo de Cultura Económica, 1972).

[33] The most important overall bibliographical, historical-literary initiative undertaken up to this time and still in progress is the eight volume *Historia literaria de Hispanoamérica*, directed by Dr. Pedro F. de Andrea, director of Ediciones de Andrea, Mexico. Volumes already published are: Tomo I: *Historia de la novela hispanoamericana* by Fernando Alegría; Tomo II: *Historia del cuento hispanoamericano* by Luis Leal; Tomo III: *Historia del teatro hispanoamericano (época colonial)* by José Juan Arrom; Tomo IV: *Historia del teatro hispanoamericano (XIX-XX)* by Frank N. Dauster; Tomo V: *Historia de la literatura hispanoamericana a través de sus revistas* by Boyd G. Carter; Tomo VI: *Historia del ensayo hispanoamericano* by Peter G. Earle and Robert G. Mead; Tomo VII: *Historia de la poesía hispanoamericana* by Merlin H. Forster is in press; Tomo VIII: *Bibliografía de la literatura hispanoamericana* by Pedro F. de Andrea is in an advanced stage of preparation.

[34] An important addition to Hispanic bibliography in a hitherto neglected area is *Russian Literature in the Hispanic World: A Bibliography / La literatura rusa en el mundo hispánico: Bibliografía* (Toronto: Univ. of Toronto Press, 1972), XLVI, 312 pp.

[35] J. R. Spell, "Mexican Literary Periodicals of the Nineteenth Century," *PMLA*, 52 (1937), 272-312; "Mexican Literary Periodicals of the Twentieth Century," *PMLA*, 54 (1939), 835-52. Sturgis E. Leavitt, Madaline W. Nichols, Jefferson Rea Spell, *Revistas hispanoamericanas. Indice bibliográfico 1843-1935* (Santiago de Chile: Fondo Histórico y Bibliográfico, José Toribio Medina, 1960). Indices to 56 reviews. John E. Englekirk, "La literatura y la revista literaria en Hispanoamérica," *Revista Iberoamericana*, 26, No. 51 (January-June 1961), 9-79; 27, No. 52 (July-December 1961), 219-79; 28, No. 53 (January-June 1962), 9-73; 29, No. 55 (January-June 1963), 9-66. Boyd G. Carter, *Las revistas literarias de Hispanoamérica* (Mexico: Ediciones de Andrea, 1959); *Historia de la literatura hispanoamericana a través de sus revistas* (México: Ediciones de Andrea, 1968).

[36] Probably the most novel expression of cultural revolt and vanguardistic renovation in Ibero-America was that of Oswald de Andrade of Brazil against all foreign influence. This writer, who in 1912 had wanted to create a Brazilian theatre by writing in French, in 1924 satirized imitation of Europe in any form and affirmed that "poetry should be found in the reality that surrounds us." In 1928 he went so far in his nationalism that he recommended a return to cannibalism because "the cannibal provocatively embodied the contrary of what humanism pretended to stand for, everything western culture had mutilated in man." The Revolution of Getulio Vargas in 1930 and the Depression put an end to Andrade's pseudo-cannibalism as a program of cultural renewal in Brazil. See Erdmute Wenzel White, "Return of the Artist: The Quest for Authenticity in Brazilian Literature," *Mosaic*, 8, No. 3, 187-92.

# Symposium Lectures

# Mexicans Fiction in the Seventies: Author, Intellect, and Public

John S. Brushwood

ABSTRACT

The image of the contemporary Mexican novel may be described by reference to four writers: Carlos Fuentes, Sergio Galindo, Gustavo Sainz, and Salvador Elizondo. Respectively, they represent the "boom," the character novel, the "onda," and an approximation of the *nouveau roman*. The outstanding characteristics of the Mexican novel since 1967 are technical virtuosity and a tendency toward metafiction. These characteristics, while interesting to the cognoscenti, seem to alienate many readers. This latter reaction may be related to the function of the novel. Puzzled readers may be reacting as Auerbach reacted when confronting *Ulysses*. However, the reason may not be simply a craving for mimesis. If the function of the novel is thought of in terms of a communication act (extrapolating the ideas of Jakobson and Searle), someone is expected to be communicating something to someone else. However, insofar as a novel is a metafiction, the reader becomes the narrator with the result that the reader-narrator is communicating something to the narrator-reader—a literary act dangerously close to talking to oneself.

This phenomenon may do more than please a few readers and puzzle many. It may reflect a social condition in which technique (procedure) is considered more important than substance (result). However, there are some indications of a possible reaction, in very recent Mexican novels, against this exclusivism—expecially in the works of Sainz and of Ignacio Solares, and in the opinion of Salvador Elizondo. (JSB)

Recent fiction in Mexico might be described as fascinating, hard to read, technically intricate, elitist, sophisticated, intellectually stimulating, self conscious—and more. Since history has not yet placed contemporary literature in a perspective where we may view it comfortably, critics are often tempted to compensate by qualifying their statements too elaborately. On this occasion, in order to be clear as possible, I shall divide my observations into three sections: (1) a general view—the image—of Mexican fiction at this time, (2) the apparent function of the novel during the past nine or ten years, and (3) indications of possible changes taking place in very recent fiction.

## THE IMAGE OF THE CONTEMPORARY MEXICAN NOVEL

The image of the Mexican novel at this time may be described by commenting first on some writers and then on certain tendencies. Obviously, I am not planning to mention all the novelists who are active, but a selected few who may serve as indicators.

First, there can be no doubt that Carlos Fuentes is the best known. He has long been recognized as one of the novelists of the Spanish American "boom," and is also known for his speculation on the nature of fiction. His most recent work, *Terra Nostra* (1975), is a gigantic recasting of history in which Fuentes searches out the meaning of Spain in America. The novel is forbidding because of its size and the relative impenetrability of its narrative structure. On the other hand, it has to be regarded as a major work by a highly gifted writer. It is an important part of the author's identification of reality. He is and has always been obsessed by history. *Terra Nostra* is also a fiction that is about fiction because it interrelates established fictional characters—e.g., Don Juan, Celestina—with Fuentes' own invented characters and transformations of historical personages.

Fuentes is, by now, one of Mexico's older novelists. If we look among younger writers for someone with a substantial body of work, an established reputation, and a promising future, we are likely to find Gustavo Sainz. Sainz, along with José Agustín, initiated the fiction of "la onda"—the younger generation of the 1960's whose members flaunted their disrespect for conventionalities, and especially for the inhibitions placed on language by social custom. His four novels are quite different from each other in many ways, but they do share two constants: the author's sensitivity to language and an equally sharp awareness of the city as his home. He is a novelist of the city—not in the sense of a writer who has come from the provinces and discovered the exotic and disturbing ways of the capital, but in the sense of a writer for whom Mexico City is the native region, the place where he grew up and in which his identity is rooted.

The novels of Fuentes and Sainz are particularly noteworthy for their innovations in narrative technique, and they sometimes inspire questions about whether or not there are more familiar types of novels in Mexico. Without going into the very complicated issue suggested by this query, I can probably say that there are indeed books in Mexico that would be readily identified as "character novels," with no disturbing caveats added. Sergio Galindo is one of several novelists who may be included here. To place this information in a context that permits a rough comparison, I may say—I hope without creating grave misconceptions—that if Fuentes and

Sainz might correspond to Thomas Pychon or John Barth, Galindo and others like him might correspond to Graham Greene or Bernard Malamud. Certainly the authors of "character novels" are much less generally known than their more innovative contemporaries. However, it would be dangerous to assume a correlation between innovation and high profile, because there are some very strange Mexican novels written by relatively little known authors. I think of Salvador Elizondo as an example. One way of describing the work of these writers is to say that certain notions form the basis of their novels, and what we remember after reading one of them is the development of the notion rather than the development of characters. However, if we extend slightly the boundaries around this group, it would be possible to say that their production ranges from an approximation of the French "noveau roman" to a metafiction suggestive of John Barth's *Chimera*.

If we think in terms of tendencies in the novel, rather than of authors, it may be possible to point out the distinguishing characteristics of the genre during the past decade. I will often mention technical innovation, but I do not mean that this kind of inventiveness belongs only to the last ten years. Indeed, the fiction of Jaime Torres Bodet and others—some of it written almost a half-century ago—uses techniques that have been present in fiction since Proust and Joyce but are still considered, occasionally, to be new. It is also apparent that Agustín Yáñez's *Al filo del agua*, in 1947, reasserted the novelist's right to create rather than paint a true-to-life portrait of a social condition. From approximately 1962, the novel of the "boom" certainly uses a wide variety of narrative techniques and obviously enjoys playing with language. Nevertheless, it seems to me that the tendency does not stop at this point. By 1967, technical wizardry reached the level of virtuosity where the narrative procedure dominated all other aspects of some works. Such virtuosity was accompanied by a tide of allusions, many of them necessarily unfamiliar to a large number of readers. The result is an "in" type of novel that makes a few readers feel very cozy and the larger public very unwelcome.

The exclusiveness of these novels emphasizes the authors' interest in observing the art of creating fiction. Claude Fell, a French critic of Latin American literature, noted this characteristic, in 1970, among new tendencies of the novel, and cited Salvador Elizondo's *El hipogeo secreto* (1968) as an example.[1] The authors' fascination (it is Fell's word) need not refer only to novels in which the phenomenon is as dominant as in Elizondo's novel. There are many in which it is apparent to varying extents. These books are fictions that are about fictions. We may call them metafictions; but it is well to remember that a novel may have a metafictional aspect along with other characteristics, and the relative importance of the metafictional aspect may vary from one work to another.

38

## THE FUNCTION OF THE NOVEL DURING THE PERIOD 1967-1977

When we recognize these tendencies as characteristic of Mexican fiction during the last ten years, it is possible to point out some very recent developments that may indicate a different function of the novel. However, we cannot deal with these developments clearly without examining first some aspects of the meaning of the novel during the period 1967-1975. I shall divide this section of my comments into three parts: (1) the ambivalent reaction of readership, (2) the function of the novel as an artistic experience, and (3) the effect of the novel on readership after the book has been read.

The novel has been following an exclusivistic route that delights a select group of readers and displeases many others. Why does this conflict exist? I am not concerned here with the problem of how large an audience art should seek. Rather, I am simply recognizing an obvious fact—that many people who enjoyed reading new novels a few years ago do not read new novels anymore. Corollary to this fact is the presence, in bookstores, of large numbers of books often referred to as "non-fiction." These treatises explain how to do something, or promise solutions to the problems of the world or of individuals. They may or may not keep the promise, but many copies are sold. More stimulating to the imagination are biographies, memoirs, and essays on strange natural or historical phenomena. Thinking of the works of "non-fiction" in general, I suspect that readers seek in them some assurance of stability, some promise that they may discover a right way, some identification with other humans who have "made it."

There must be a relationship between this preference and the frequent references to "traditional" novels or to "understandable" novels. These terms are heard in the remarks of quite literate people. I am not searching out the reactions of people who do not enjoy reading. The problem has to do with the representation of reality. More than thirty years ago, an eminent scholar, Erich Auerbach, wrote a book, *Mimesis*, that deals with the representation of reality in western literature.[2] Toward the end of this work, he has to take account of Joyce's *Ulysses* and other novels in which various aspects of reality are so fragmented that, for a reader attuned to the nineteenth-century novel, they seem to offer no representation of reality at all. Chronologically, *Ulysses* is a long way from the recent Mexican novels I have been referring to; but it may be considered the beginning of the problem I am dealing with now.

Auerbach notes the relationship of this kind of fiction to the nature of social reality following the first World War. Reality was itself fragmented, disjointed, hard to comprehend. Although he recognizes this relationship of the new fiction to the new reality, Auerbach is so concerned for an older kind of representation that he cannot let the Joyce-type novel go without censure. His exact words are important:

There is something confusing, something hazy about them, something hostile to the reality which they represent. We not infrequently find a turning away from the practical will to live, or delight in portraying it under its most brutal forms. There is hatred of culture and civilization, brought out by means of the subtlest stylistic devices which culture and civilization have developed, and often a radical and fanatical urge to destroy.[3]

Frustrated or weary readers of recent fiction frequently make statements similar to Auerbach's—usually in a less elegant fashion. It is worth noting, however, that Auerbach's discomfort is caused not only by the narrative technique, but by the author's attitude as well. Or if we assume that this attitude reflects reality, he does not like reality. It is impossible to estimate the extent to which readers in the seventies may dislike the *kind* of reality recent fiction portrays.[4] On the other hand, it is easy to see that they, like Auerbach, often find novels confusing and hazy.

The objection seems to be composed of three interrelated factors: (1) the change from nineteenth-century realism forces readership into unfamiliar territory, (2) some post-Realism novels make use of many allusions that may be unfamiliar to some readers either because they are recondite or because they belong to the intimate world of the author and his friends, and (3) the reader is expected to commit himself to the work in ways that cause him to participate more and observe less than in a novel of realism. Obviously, the narrative techniques of the post-Realist novel do provide a special kind of experience, and it is equally apparent that part of the objection may be explained by the fact that change requires a period of adjustment. *Ulysses* no longer evokes the outcry of fifty years ago. *Pedro Páramo* is an old standby. Multiple narrative voices in *The Sound and the Fury* still make interesting analyses possible, but the phenomenon is no longer disconcerting. Nevertheless, in all these novels, the reader is required to participate, in some way, in the organization of the material. The degree of such participation, the frequency with which fiction-reading requires it, and the skill of the author in evoking it—these three seem to be the factors that govern the intensity of reaction to such novels.

With respect to the function of the novel, Scholes and Kellogg have said that "we can hazard the notion that stories appeal primarily because they offer a simulacrum of life which enables an audience to participate in events without being involved in the consequences which events in the actual world would inevitably carry with them."[5] Such appeal indicates the appreciation of an experience which the reader may live vicariously, or reject, or even judge. However, in the metafictional novels, the reader's relationship to the narrative situation changes substantially. It is important to point out that the reader is not always involved by subtle means. He may be overtly challenged to write the novel. In *Lapsus* (1971), Héctor Manjarrez interrupts the narration to suggest that the reader might wish to write a certain kind of episode at that point. After suggesting a source of inspiration for such a contribution, the narrator continues: "Even better, the reader may, if he wishes, imagine any kind of episode he might like, so long as he doesn't leave Huberto goofing off in his easy chair."[6] Obviously, this contact between narrator and reader plays havoc with the experience described by Scholes and Kellogg. It suggests a feigned detachment on the part of the storyteller. However, it is equally possible that he may be confronting a vital problem in contemporary fiction. Let us consider a statement by Pere Gimferrer in an essay on Fuentes' *Terra Nostra* (1975). The critic says that the essential question that paralyzes narrative in our time is: why narrate this rather than that, or simply, why narrate? [7] He also says that one of Fuentes' major achievements is the incorporation of this question into the very structure of the novel. Something similar might be said with respect to José Emilio Pacheco's *Morirás lejos* (1967), in which the interrelationship of alternatives becomes most important and thus subordinates theme and obliterates character identity.

My comments on these novels are not intended to be derogatory. The point is to demonstrate that their function is different from the function anticipated by many readers whose reactions I know. In any conceiveable communication act, someone sends a message to someone else. If the person who receives the message becomes also the one who sends the message, we have the equivalent of someone talking to himself. In terms of the novel, if the reader becomes the narrator, he is making the fiction for himself, inventing the happening which he wishes to experience vicariously.[8] There is no reason why such a procedure cannot happen; however, I am not persuaded that many people wish to participate in it more than once or twice.

Awareness of fiction-in-the-making is most intense in novels where the story is actually the creation of the story. We might say that the perfect fiction is one that generates a subordinate fiction in such a way that both the primary fiction and the subordinate fiction have the same outcome. John Barth apparently thinks along this line in the writing of *Chimera*. Elizondo's *El hipogeo secreto* might be described as a novel in which the narrator and the reader gradually become one. Vicente Leñero's *El garabato* (1967) deals with inventions inside inventions that all lead in the same direction. Interesting fictional constructions, but are they about anything? Of course, they are about creating fictions.

There is a difference between the experience of reading a novel and the effect of the novel on a reader after the book is read. The latter amounts to a kind of interpretation of the work. In general, what we remember of metafiction novels is the clever idea—or maybe only the technique itself. Such emphasis on technique, extrapolated to the world in which the reader lives, immediately suggests the enormous number of "how-to" books that are available. Even closer to us who are gathered in this academic situation is the practice of spending hours on procedural matters—in committees, assemblies, senates, conferences—hours spent on how to do something that seem quite out of proportion to the hours spent in taking substantive action.

If narrative techniques may be related to worldly reality in this regard, it is equally interesting to explore the significance of a two-step invention, or the invention of invention.[9] One step is the transformation of the anecdotal material—the development of the basic material into plot. If this basic material is related in any way to the reality in which the novelist lives, his narrative act transforms that reality into a literary experience. However, if a subordinate fiction is invented within this act of transformation, it is a creative act removed by an additional step from the basic material. This procedure may well correspond to a tendency in society to invent a subordinate problem that will absorb our attention and protect us from facing a basic problem that we cannot solve or may not wish to solve.

Lest we be tempted to put aside these possibilities as unlikely, let us recall that the novels are very real. They do exist, and it is impossible to demonstrate convincingly that any work of art is totally separated from the human milieu in which it is created. It is far easier to show that literature has sought to adjust its expression to accomodate changes in the reality that it has sought to represent. Erich Auerbach's study states the case eloquently. Even when he boggles before Joyce, Auerbach recognizes the possible correspondence of the new expression to a new reality. In fact, from the time of Joyce up to the present, we may observe a new reality, a new perception of reality, and a new way of expressing it. Like Auerbach, many may not wish to recognize that reality. On the other hand, we must not assume that alienation from contemporary fiction necessarily means flight from the fragmented reality of our time.[10] We have already noted certain narrative procedures that distort the generally accepted act of communication.

The most disturbing aspect of reader alienation is the lost of aesthetically creative activity. Hardly anyone would deny that we live in a situation that needs an increase of such activity, not a decrease. In the best imaginable reader-novel relationship, the kind of fiction I refer to probably enhances the creative participation of readers. However, if it reduces the number of readers, we must question its value to a society that needs help in expressing itself. Those who read metafiction profitably are those who are able to accept the unusual narrator-reader role—or at least suspend a negative reaction to it—and so enjoy the act itself rather than rely on a message of some kind. Others must find themselves abdicating a role (possibly less creative, but nonetheless important) that they may well have considered their right.

## INDICATIONS OF POSSIBLE CHANGES

More than a few people have asked me—and I am sure many others have been asked the same question—whether or not I expect a return to a more accessible kind of fiction. In the past two years, my response has tended to become affirmative. However, the question is not as straightforward as it seems, and an answer is not simple. In the first place, there is plenty of accessible fiction being written. Some of it is not very artistic, but much of it is quite recommendable. The other necessary clarification has to do with plot. When people complain about the absence of a story, it is hard to believe they are talking about recent fiction. Metafiction is nothing but story.

Jorge Luis Borges, one of the greatest storytellers of all time, has been a major influence in the renaissance of plot invention. However, concentration on fiction for the sake of making a fiction tends to decrease the importance of characterization with which the reader can identify. In fact, metafiction may reasonably be considered a reaction against the agonized character studies of a few years ago. Scholes and Kellogg, writing in the mid-1960's, call attention to the divergence of plot and character. They point out that novelists from Fielding to Tolstoy have resisted this tendency which has its roots in the substitution of psychology for myth. Nevertheless—in their words—"Serious works, in which the empirical is emphasized get the characters; adventure stories get the plots."[11] A suggested example of this division is the difference Graham Greene makes between his "novels" and his "entertainments." Since the mid-sixties, it is apparent that the divergence has grown into a dichotomy, any possible pejorative connotation has been removed from the "entertainment" side, and now a reintegration may have begun in Mexico. It would be impossible to deal with every suggestion of such a development. Therefore, I will describe two cases in some detail—one a well known novelist, Gustavo Sainz; the other a newcomer, Ignacio Solares.

Sainz's first novel, *Gazapo* (1965), is about people in Mexico City whom my children, at that time, would have referred to as "kids." It is a novel of "la onda"—the "in" thing. Interesting characters very shortly become apparent; fresh and humorously appropriate language is immediately attractive. The novel is technically innovative, and some readers have been put off by the repetition, in various forms, of a very simple story. Nevertheless, *Gazapo*'s immediate attractions provided enough interest for a large public, in spite of some reaction against its technique.

His second novel, *Obsesivos días circulares* (1969), in spite of being very carefully made, attracted far fewer readers. It does have story, and also character study, but they are cloaked in diversions and grotesqueries that lead many readers hopelessly astray. The novel's narrator-protagonist has trouble "getting it all together"—to use the words of his contemporaries in the United States. His characterization is a fine commentary on a social circumstance, but it could not honestly be called easily accessible.

Sainz realized that *Obsesivos días circulares* had somehow failed to meet his goal as a novelist. The nature of this goal became amply apparent when, in the fall of 1974, he was interviewed repeatedly in connection with the publication of his third novel, *La Princesa del Palacio de Hierro*. Basically, he believes that a novel should alter its readers' habits of perception. In order to accomplish this, Sainz the novelist expects to create recognizable characters, invent unusual but believable happenings, and shake up his readers—to give them butterflies in the stomach.[12]

With *La princesa . . .* , Sainz took no avoidable chances. Knowing well that Mexican publishers are not famous for imaginative advertising, he organized and carried out a campaign to attract readers. Beyond that, the book had to stand on its own. It is immediately attractive because Sainz again shows off his amazing sensitivity to the spoken language. However, analysis shows several characteristics that might turn out to be negative. The novel is a three-hundred-page monologue that is one side of a telephone conversation. The speaker is a woman in her thirties who recalls the adventures of her youth. She was a department store model, but her activities covered a rather wider range than modelling. We never know to whom she is talking. The narrator position is not perfectly consistent. The ordering of events reflects the "Princesa's" personality more accurately than it responds to the reader's sense of chronology. There are extraneous passages that may well be puzzling.

Why, then, is it that *La Princesa del Palacio de Hierro* is a more accessible novel than *Obsesivos días circulares*? Stated very simply, Sainz has been careful to make one level of experience easy to appreciate, even while making other levels available to those who wish to achieve them. Karen J. Hardy has explained this procedure quite clearly in her study of the book.[13] She defines the first level of experience as focussing on the narrator-protagonist and the validity of her perception of her own experience. Beyond that, Hardy defines three other levels, or readings, and analyzes each. It is important for our purpose here to notice a distinction claimed by Hardy for the Sainz novel. She says that, like many other contemporary novels, it "reveals new levels of meaning on each successive encounter or reading"; on the other hand, it is different because "it does not *demand* repeated readings before making accessible a complete experience."

The second case is *Puerta del cielo*, a first novel, published by Ignacio Solares in the summer of 1976. The story is perfectly clear and the people recognizable. A narrator using the third person tells the story of a middle

44

A moment between symposium lectures permits an exchange of ideas among (from left to right) Professors Wolodymyr T. Zyla (Texas Tech University), Boyd G. Carter, and John S. Brushwood (guest speakers). (Photographed by Sheldon C. Klock, Jr.)

class Mexican youth who has to leave school and take a job in order to bolster the family economy. His experiences at work and in his first love affair combine to form his exterior reality. In addition, there are episodes narrated in the first person, in which the protagonist sees and talks with the Holy Virgin. It is interesting to note at least three characteristics of the novel that would have been commented on extensively in an earlier period: (1) the shift of narrative voice, (2) the appearance of the Virgin in absolutely commonplace, non-contemplative circumstances, and (3) the anomalous plot situation which is both trite and inspired. Today, Solares' novel does not seem vanguardist at all. Indeed, it might be called "traditionalist," though it obviously is not so if we associate traditionalism with nineteenth-century Realism.

Let us consider the opinion of *Puerta del cielo* expressed by Salvador Elizondo, high priest of hermeticism in Mexican fiction:

> This novel by Ignacio Solares bursts forth like the sun at midnight, in the panorama of recent fiction. . . . It comes, I believe, as a prudent corrective to the excesses of a well documented but opaque type of narrative. . . . at a time when almost all novels are written excessively, [this] one has neither too much nor too little.[14]

This paper, of course, is not intended to evolve into prophecy. Present indications are best taken as one characteristic of recent fiction, as the latest phenomenon observable in Mexican fiction of our time. Going back, therefore, to the first part of this exposition, we now refer to four characteristics of Mexican fiction during the last decade: (1) technical virtuosity and specialized allusions, (2) the author's fascination with observing the act of creating fiction, (3) complete metafiction (unless this characteristic be subsumed under Number 2) and (4) a movement toward easier accessibility for more readers. These are characteristics, not categories. They do not indicate sub-periods of the decade, though there may be some barely discernible process in their variation. Finally, if the fourth characteristic seems reactionary, it is so only in terms of the other three. It does not signal a return to the past.

*University of Kansas*

## NOTES

[1] Fell's paper, "Destrucción y poesía en la novela latinoamericana contemporánea," was presented at the III Congreso Latinoamericano de Escritores, Caracas, July, 1970. The paper was published in a volume entitled *III Congreso Latinoamericano de Escritores* (Caracas: Ediciones del Congreso de la República, 1971), pp. 207-13. The particular reference is to p. 208 where the characteristic is described as "la fascinación frente a la creación creándose (como en *El hipogeo secreto* de Salvador Elizondo)."

[2] Erich Auerbach, *Mimesis* (1946; rpt. Princeton: Princeton Univ. Press, 1968).

[3] Ibid., p. 551.

[4] The difference between rejection of new techniques and concern created by an unwelcome perception of reality might be explored profitably by reference to Roland Barthes' *Writing Degree Zero*. His definition of and references to *écriture* create an interesting shift in the appearance of fiction's relationship to history. In addition, his discussion is relevant to what readers expect in a novel. The plurality and the meaning of "modes of writing" (écriture) became concerns around 1850, a date associated with Flaubert and with the beginning of the decline of the bourgeosie. It is interesting that Auerbach, when he points out the difficulty experienced by Joyce-type novelists in comprehending a fragmented reality, confesses that Flaubert was already having problems of this kind. For Barthes' views, see *Writing Degree Zero*, in a volume with *Elements of Semiology* (Boston: Beacon, 1970), especially pp. 1-18, 29-40, 55-61.

[5] Robert Scholes and Robert Kellogg, *The Nature of Narrative* (1975; rpt. London: Oxford, 1968), p. 241. The point here is made as an illustration of the "ineluctable irony" of a narrative situation. The point made in the quotation leads the authors to say that "our pleasure in narrative literature . . . can be seen as a function of disparity of viewpoint or irony." The point I am making is closely related, although I am not inclined to discuss irony. It is quite apparent, within the Scholes and Kellogg formulation, that insofar as the reader participates as narrator, his relationship to the "disparity of viewpoint" changes, and so does his experience of the work.

[6] Héctor Manjarrez, *Lapsus* (Mexico: Joaquín Mortiz, 1971), pp. 21-22. Translation mine.

[7] Pere Gimferrer, "El mapa y la máscara," *Plural*, V, 10 (julio 1976), 58-60. The specific reference is near the end of the third column on p. 58.

[8] The narrator-reader relationship is extremely complicated. One way of illustrating my point is to use Roman Jakobson's model of a communication act. It may be found in his essay entitled "Linguistics and Poetics," published in *Style and Language*, ed. Thomas A. Sebeok (Cambridge, Mass.: MIT Press, 1960) and reprinted in *The Structuralists From Marx to Lévi-Straus*, ed. Richard and Fernande DeGeorge (Garden City: Anchor Books, 1972). It takes this form:

$$\text{addresser} \underline{\qquad\qquad \begin{array}{c} \text{context} \\ \text{message} \\ \text{contact} \\ \text{code} \end{array} \qquad\qquad} \text{addressee}$$

Substituting appropriately and adding a step, I suggest the following:

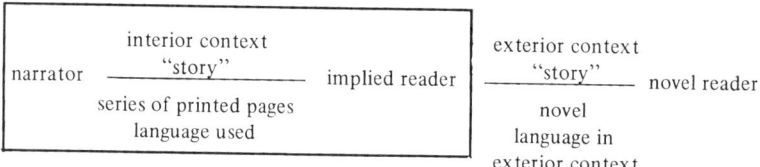

In this formulation, the communication act enclosed within the rectangle, taken as a whole, becomes the addresser who redirects the "story" to any one of millions of readers. The novel, now an object, is a *fait accompli*; but the communication act is not a *fait accompli*. The "story" remains the same insofar as the changed context and code will allow. However, if the novel reader acts as the narrator, he must necessarily be in an equivocal position because there are actually two narrator positions in the model—one (within the rectangle) in which the novel reader would address the implied reader, and another (in place of the rectangle) in which the novel reader would address himself. It seems that any creative satisfaction the novel reader might enjoy by being thrust into the narrator position would be negated by the uncertain nature of his new role, and by the ultimate sterility of talking to himself.

Many studies are relevant to this problem. The two most helpful on the particular point I am making are John R. Searle, *Speech Acts* (London: Cambridge, 1969), and Winifred Bryan Homer, *Text Act Theory: A Study of Nonfiction Texts* (Ph.D. dissertation, University of Michigan, 1975).

[9] I have mentioned this phenomenon in another context: "Literary Periods in Twentieth-Century Mexico: The Transformation of Reality," in *Contemporary Mexico*, ed. James W. Wilkie, Michael C. Meyer, and Edna Monzón de Wilkie (Los Angeles: UCLA Latin American Center, 1976).

[10] Robert Scholes, *Structuralism in Literature* (New Haven: Yale, 1974), pp. 180-90.

[11] Scholes and Kellogg, *The Nature of Fiction*, p. 237. It should be noted that the punctuation of this quotation is as it appears in the 1975 reprint, (see note 5). My reading inserts a comma between "emphasized" and "get."

[12] See, for example, Margarita García Flores, "Los secretos de una princesa," *La Onda*, supplement to *Novedades*, No. 71 (20 October 1974), pp. 6-7.

[13] The study by Karen J. Hardy, entitled "Gustavo Sainz's *La Princesa del Palacio de Hierro*: A Three-Hundred-Page Telephone Conversation," is unpublished at this writing.

[14] Inside the cover (front and back) of Ignacio Solares, *Puerta del cielo* (Mexico: Grijalbo, 1976).

# Social Content and Revolutionary Form: Spanish American Drama Today

Frank Dauster

ABSTRACT

Within a society which is increasingly polarized between the restless demands of the impoverished and the frantic defense of privilege, the theater in Latin America has become perhaps the most politicized of the arts, in large measure because drama is a living art and much more difficult to control and censor. The commercial theater continues to be the refuge of forms associated with escapism, but experimental and university groups, less subject to economic pressures and often physically mobile and thus less subject to other forms of intimidation, are committed to political ends. These traditional centers of social action have been joined by the review theaters, a movement whose spiritual and formal roots are in the German post-World War I theater, and by cooperative groups, frequently mutations of previously existing student groups or other small groups. Although quite different at times, both types are often little more than excuses for radical politics, although at their best they are striking. Despite this strong communal movement, there is a core of established dramatists who, like their counterparts in the novel, combine social commitment with artistic integrity. Convinced that commitment without craftsmanship becomes a meaningless exercise in amateurism, they experiment continuously in dramatic form, accepting such European tendencies as the absurd, Brecht or Artaud, each in turn, while seeking an original expression capable of communicating the unique reality they perceive in their sector of the Third World. (FD)

Within a society which is increasingly polarized between the restless demands of the impoverished and the frantic defense of privilege, the theater has become perhaps the most politicized of the arts. The commercial theater continues to be the refuge of forms associated with escapism, but experimental and university groups, sometimes less subject to economic pressures and often physically more mobile and less vulnerable to other forms of intimidation, are often committed to political ends. In contraposition to this commitment, we find in Spanish America today a

49

degree of technical competence, of craftsmanship, surpassing anything in its past. Further, we find, sometimes in opposition to the committed theater and sometimes closely related to it, another kind of commitment: the quest for formal renovation, for a theater which escapes the limitations of the commercial and the propagandistic.

The political thrust in Latin American drama is hardly a recent phenomenon; almost exactly a century ago, in 1876, Alfredo Bianchi used the theater to protest the Mexican government's iniquitous use of the military draft to rid itself of political protesters–he was jailed for his pains–and at almost exactly the same moment, in 1872, the Argentine Francisco Fernández was writing *Solané*, a rather heavy-handed romantic vision of the gaucho as the dispossessed and persecuted victim of society. Although little known, *Solané* is an important antecedent of the social motif which was a major factor in the theater of Argentina and Uruguay for a half century. Not coincidentally, Solané is a mestizo; equally important, he appears to have been a real figure. Bianchi, Fernández and others were using the theater to attack abuses of the prevailing social system.

But it is in the twentieth century that the two threads of social commitment and formal experimentation are most clearly defined and, at times at least, most clearly differentiated. However, this differentiation is often more apparent than real; it would be extremely misleading to regard the two strands as separate. Rather, they coexist within seemingly opposed contemporary groups, within different members of a movement or even, at times, within one author, although in the earlier part of the century this fusion is rarely achieved except at the expense of artistic merit. An example of this coexistence is visible in the two principal dramatists of the Teatro de Ahora group in Mexico in 1932, Mauricio Magdaleno and Juan Bustillo Oro. Magdaleno and Bustillo Oro were equally committed to a concept of the theater as an instrument of revolutionary change, and Magdaleno's works are little more than pamphlets, dogmatic and technically crude. Bustillo Oro, however, is quite a different matter. His *San Miguel de las Espinas* deals with three moments in the history of a rural village, but, instead of the routine violence so often used as a justification for revolutionary counterviolence, Bustillo Oro sought to give a mythic dimension to the suffering of the oppressed people for whom the Revolution had meant merely a change of master. The use of parallel dramatic structures, an effective chorus and, especially, the dramatic power of the omnipresent river which is the real master of the villagers' destiny, all transcend any propagandistic intention, even though the play loses none of its social impact.

At times this double thrust coexisted in different members of a same generation, as is the case with the two most distinguished Mexican playwrights of their time, Rodolfo Usigli and Xavier Villaurrutia. Villaurrutia was a confirmed innovator whose early works are experiments in dramatic form, and whose best play, *Invitación a la muerte*, is a provocative and ambiguous adaptation of *Hamlet* to Mexico and to Villaurrutia's own creative themes. He soon abandoned this kind of formal experimentation and devoted himself to creating realistic plays in a commercial idiom, in the belief that only in this way could he give the Mexican theater a much-needed lesson in professionalism. Villaurrutia is often considered a pure esthete, and the group with which he was long associated, the *Contemporáneos*, were mistakenly assailed for having turned toward Europe and abandoned national concerns and art forms. In contrast to this alleged aestheticism, Rodolfo Usigli's voluminous work has from the beginning attacked what he considers to be the multiple problems of Mexican society. Usigli is anything but simplistic; social abuses are, for him, the result of defects in the national character, and his best plays are frontal assaults on hypocrisy and other vices. In *Corona de sombra*, he presents an intuitive and original version of the significance for later Mexican history of the tragic empire of Carlota and Maximilian; in *El gesticulador*, he vigorously defines the abuses of post-Revolutionary opportunism. It has bothered Usigli not at all, apparently, that his stand has cost him a good deal of personal vilification and has kept many of his plays, in earlier days, from the productions they deserved. Usigli is clearly a reformer, a dramatist of social commitment. But these labels are inevitably false. In *Corona de sombra*, Usigli devised an ingenious method for the juggling of rapid chronological shifts without disrupting the dramatic unity. Usigli, the committed dramatist, is, when the mood takes him, also a dramatist of revolutionary form, just as Villaurrutia, the alleged formalist, offers to the perceptive reader considerable enlightenment about the nature and structure of the Mexican family on a particular level. Our rubrics, like all classifications, are only approximations, and this point will be increasingly true as we approach the postwar period.

The intricate interweaving we have seen is not always characteristic. In Cuba, the new movement which began about 1936 was essentially devoted to a cosmopolitan conception of art and a minority of the audience; although there were strongly committed, socially-oriented dramatists writing at the same time, these tended strongly toward a simplistic propaganda theater. The influences of Marx and the French poetic theater coexisted in a fashion not really satisfactory to either. In Puerto Rico at the same time, the opposite was true; the renovation, indeed the virtual rebirth of the theater in Puerto Rico is directly related to and springs from an examination of the national reality undertaken by a group of historians. For ten years, Puerto Rican theater was essentially naturalistic, committed to the exposure of such social evils as the long seasonal layoffs for agricultural workers. But despite the obvious and deliberate commitment we see in the works of the movement's leaders, they were also men of the theater who saw a distinction between propaganda and art. Manuel Méndez Ballester's desolate visions of rural suffering always had a dramatic dimension, and his later work ranges from the techniques of classical tragedy to the theater of the absurd, although frequently retaining the social vision.

The clearest example of the social dimension, even a forthright political thrust, is Argentina, where the independent theater movement, a reaction against an outworn tradition of commercial rural melodrama, began in a series of anarchist workers' centers. Such important groups as Teatro del Pueblo, Teatro Juan B. Justo and Teatro La Máscara, all had strong radical affiliations and were militantly opposed to the conservative government. Much of their work was overtly aimed at the various sectors of the establishment, and there was a conscious use of theater to indoctrinate the working-class audience, but there was also a strong emphasis on professionalism, on interaction with the audience, on workshop and tour and search for new authors, all the characteristics which would lead to the flourishing of the Argentine theater twenty years later.

In these various movements then, seen as local or national endeavours, there is no single dominant pattern. But what I suggest is that it is an error to regard these movements as exclusively local. It is surely not coincidence that so many Latin American nations experienced a considerable and productive burst of theater activity during the 1930's. There may have been little contact between nations—indeed, there appears to have been virtually none—but in each area there was awareness of European and American models. Each region, in its fashion, responded to a complex set of external models and added its regional flavor, and if we observe the whole pattern, rather than dividing it into tiny fragments responding to national boundaries which are often historical accidents or geographic irrelevancies, we see the pattern of interwoven strands: the commitment to social reform, often in the most revolutionary sense, and the commitment to a new theater. Each of these sought to do away with the shackles of an older way, and often the two commitments were intermingled.

The true flourishing of the Latin American theater is a post-World War II phenomenon. The factors are many and complex; surely, among them were the final breakdown of the virtual isolation of much of Latin America, the crucial influence of European émigrés, the rapid expansion of American popular culture. After World War II, Latin America became a part of the world in the fullest sense, and its art forms—never as isolated as the masses of the poor in any case—participated fully in world currents. The dramatists who appeared just after the war were by far the most cosmopolitan and technically skilled generation in the history of Spanish America; at the same time, they were almost universally committed to social change of a drastic nature. More than any earlier group, they are world travelers in a literal sense, and this experience has exposed them both to the currents of world theater and to the struggle for political and social change which so characterizes our world today. It is symptomatic that several of the most important Mexican members of this generation consciously undertook to write plays under the direct influence of Arthur Miller, an influence at least as strong in the moral as in the technical sense. There are, as I see it, three major strands in this generational fabric: the influence of a number of foreign dramatists, most notably Brecht and a rather broad interpretation of the epic theater; the creation of a set of politicized or at the very least socially sensitive variations on the theater of the absurd; and the effort to revitalize traditional forms and at the same time to use them as vehicles for social commentary.

The influence of Brecht is obvious; there are inferior imitations on all sides. Several dramatists, however, have used Brechtian techniques in novel and effective ways. Among those who have followed most closely Brecht's theories is the Argentine Osvaldo Dragún, in *Heroica de Buenos Aires*, modelled on *Mother Courage*, and *Y nos dijeron que éramos inmortales*. These plays utilize the whole gamut of Brechtian effects: short scenes, interruption of the action, sardonic song, and speeches directed at the audience, aimed at forcing them to think seriously rather than permitting themselves to be absorbed into the illusion. There is even one splendid moment in *Y nos dijeron* ... when the two major characters are in a shooting gallery and take dead aim at the audience. The end result of all of these Brechtian effects, however, is rather curious, since Dragún is a very different sort of dramatist from Brecht. Both are committed in a political sense, both are men of the theater, but there the resemblance ends. Brecht was primarily a writer; Dragún writes only when any group with which he is affiliated happens to find itself without a dramatic text. Brecht approached the theater from a theoretical point of view—or at least maintained that he did—while Dragún sees the theater from the point of view of actor and director. His plays are acting plays, vehicles for representation, with the paradoxical result that the alienation-effect has in Dragún a reverse impact. In *Y nos dijeron* ... the interruptions of the action serve not to destroy the audience's identification with the character, but rather to enhance it. The lead role of Jorge is a difficult and demanding one, and the actor is on stage throughout the entire play. As his anguish and alienation deepen, the Brechtian song and commentary jolt the audience into a comprehension of the significance behind his suffering, but they never destroy the audience's insight into him as a human being, a person rather than a vehicle for the author's theories.

The Columbian Enrique Buenaventura is among the most politically committed of Latin American dramatists. Although his Teatro Experimental de Cali was one of the hemisphere's most active and imaginative theater groups, Buenaventura left it and renounced governmental subvention because of his profound personal disagreement with the policies and actions of the national government. Since then, Buenaventura has become increasingly involved in political theater and has now adopted a rigorously Marxist conception of the nature and purpose of the stage. He fits only rather peripherally into the category of Brechtian; as with many dramatists, he has used techniques developed by Brecht without really becoming a disciple. His earliest plays were efforts to create an epic theater on a vast scale, which would reveal the colonial substructure of Spanish American civilization; the subject matter was drawn from folklore or the lives of such historical figures as Henri Christophe or Father Las Casas. Since the mid-1960's, Buenaventura has been working directly in a political idiom; with each play he approaches more closely a purely agitational theater. Some of these works are perilously close to cliche, others contain powerful dramatic statements. *La denuncia* is a good example of the possibilities of political theater. Based on the 1928 massacre of banana plantation workers made infamous by García Márquez in *Cien años de soledad, La denuncia* is fast moving, imaginative in its staging and has considerable immediacy of impact. It also raises serious questions; historically important figures are skimped for what appear to be political reasons. Buenaventura appears to be at the outer edge of political theater; having evolved from a position fairly close to Brecht, he has now made the ultimate step in the confusion of politics with art by taking them to be the same. His conception of the theater as a political weapon of an agitational nature has been extended to the functioning of the group with which he is associated; Buenaventura was one of the few established dramatists to become involved in collective creation. His most recent plays are the result of joint effort by actors, director and author, words which really have no meaning within this framework. Theater is considered to be of and for the masses; the artist is a member of the masses who happens to work in the theater, but the same extreme notion of the equality of capacities prevails. It is, therefore, all the more intriguing to note the sign of Buenaventura in the most valid dramatic moments of the group's most recent creations.

The increased visibility of the Latin Americn theater in recent years has led to the debut as dramatists of several writers best known in other genres, such as Carlos Fuentes. Fuentes' plays betray the error of the assumption that writing for the theater is in some way much the same as writing novels, and requires no special preparation. *El tuerto es rey* and *Todos los gatos son pardos* both possess considerable dramatic potential, but both are brought to abrupt endings without any real resolution of the dramatic conflicts, victims of Fuentes' predilection for pop culture. In *Todos los gatos son pardos*, Moctezuma and Cortés are brought toward what seems their inevitable confrontation, but the collision never takes place. Instead, we are given a rock band and a series of anti-American slogans. This play seems to indicate a radical misunderstanding of the import of Brecht and ultimately of the rejection of Aristotle within the anti-realistic theater. It is not enough to simply declare the play ended; whether it be of character, of action or of some other sort, the work must have its own particular unity, a truth understood far better by Brecht than by most of his followers in Latin America.

The theater of the absurd swept Latin America, as it did Europe and the United States, and everywhere it has left an indelible mark. Non-realistic conceptions of creation and staging dominate, and a number of quite remarkable plays have been written within the idiom of absurdism. However, very few have shared the philosophical negativism which characterized the initial vogue of Ionesco, Beckett and others; from the beginning, the absurdist techniques have been utilized for purposes which are nearly always social or overtly political. The best known play of this sort, of course, is José Triana's *La noche de los asesinos*, which has been translated into and staged in a variety of languages. The play is clearly within the conventions of the absurd: the lack of any apparent objective coherence, the sense of despair, the rapid shifting of roles, the rejection of the canons of orthodox realism. Unlike the most famous models, however, the play has a clear political relevance. This point is hardly startling given the fact that the play was premiered in Cuba only eight years after the fall of Batista, but it is startling indeed to examine the nature of this statement and some of the reactions to it. Apparently the work deals with three adolescents who are rehearsing their parents' murder; the parents are presented as vulgar examples of a materialistic world. But the presumptive murderers then play out their prospective trial and speak for the parents who become simply confused people unable to contend with an oppressive external world. The children are not deterred—the play ends as they prepare to begin once more this dreadful ritual—but the play is far from a simple condemnation of them and, through them, of a previous order of society. *La noche de los asesinos* dissects the structure of the family, but it does so dramatically, without falling into propaganda. Ironically, at the first production of the French translation in Paris, a number of radical sympathizers with the Revolution stormed out of the theater during the play, denouncing it as insufficiently radical.

The best known absurdist dramatist and the one who has remained closest to the esthetic tenets of the form is the Chilean Jorge Díaz, whose earliest plays are very close to the French absurd, although leavened by a personal humor. *El cepillo de dientes* is a splendid example of the comic possibilities inherent in the form, but its resolute irreverence left unsuspecting audiences perplexed. The discerning detected in it, however, an ironic vision of our need for interpersonal relationships and the impossibility of achieving them. In succeeding plays, Díaz has attacked routing popular morality, the dehumanization of modern man and a series of diverse aspects of modern society. Long residence in Spain, motivated at least in part by the Chilean political situation, seems to have brought to a temporary halt Díaz' creative career, but in two recent works he has reaffirmed his absurdist affiliations in a curious fashion. *La orgástula* is a brief duet composed entirely of invented words, a vivid comment on the problem of stagnating dialogue which menaces every dramatist and every school; *La pancarta* utilizes a plot reminiscent of *Waiting for Godot* to make some atypically obvious sociopolitical points. In this return to the primal concerns of the absurd, the universe without discernible meaning and the need to reinvent language each time it is used or risk its loss entirely, Díaz may be pointing out the ultimate restrictions of a form within which he appears to have come full circle.

More typical is the development of Griselda Gamabro of Argentina, who has evolved from absurdist forms to a seemingly more realistic form which is, in fact, an ambiguous expression of man's capacity for evil. In *El desatino* and *Los siameses* she treats the inhumanity of those most closely connected; in the former, a man's whole family subjects him to humiliation, suffering and finally death out of their own insensitivity and self-centered egotism. *Los siameses* are twins incapable of working out the destiny which has united them; they are Cain and Abel, the two halves of each individual, the two components of the basic human situation. Both plays use nightmarish atmosphere and illogical plot and motivation, but the careful characterization and human concern give the plays a curiously convincing quality. In *El campo*, Gambaro abandons the absurdist form without renouncing its characteristic ambiguity in a tale of a concentration camp which is ultimately a metaphor of the human condition, in which we are all victims and all executioners. In *Sólo un aspecto* she combines this approach with the confrontation technique of *Los siameses*; torturer and tortured engage in an ambiguous relationship in which they finally reverse roles. It is not entirely fair to speak of Gambaro as a political dramatist; her examination of man's situation is always accompanied by a curious metaphysical objectivity, even when the plays seem to be angriest, as though she were hinting at depths of good and evil beyond such simplistic terms.

The Puerto Rican René Marqués has utilized absurd forms in several plays, always with a high degree of political commitment. But Marqués, like many members of his generation, has practiced a basically nonrealistic form of theater since very early in his career. In his best works, such as *Los soles truncos* and *Un niño azul para esa sombra*, he used complicated textures of flashback and lighting to contrast the present of Puerto Rico with its past and to create dramatic representations of these temporal levels. In *La casa sin reloj*, which the author subtitled "Comedia anti-poética en dos absurdos y un final razonable," he uses apparent realism to demonstrate what he considers to be the fundamental irrationality of the present situation of Puerto Rico. But the dramatic tension of the play, as in all Marqués' work, resides in the tension between two concepts of time: the political time which has transformed the island into an American colony, and the inner time which incessantly corrodes the individual with age and guilt.

Even such a work as *La muerte no entrará en palacio*, which may be considered a failed experiment in political tragedy, uses a number of non-realistic elements and techniques learned in such diverse sources as the absurdists, Brecht and conceivably Artaud. The play's greatest interest derives from the attempt to use a structure approximating that of classical tragedy, with elements of contemporary dramatic techniques, to treat a political subject: the betrayal of the ideal of independence by the leaders of that ideal. Ultimately, the play does not convince because its protago-nist does not convince as a human being; instead of the tragic process which might have made such betrayal comprehensible, we are given a man who is transformed, between acts, into something very close to a tyrant. The author's political commitment imposed upon him a structure which doomed his artistic purpose from the start. The play is, nevertheless, an interesting formal experiment, totally aside from questions of political validity.

There have been a number of similar attempts to revitalize the tragic form, frequently with strong political overtones. There have been versions of classical tragedies recast into terms of the Mexican Revolution and the civil wars of Argentina; recently there was published a version of Orestes by Carlos Esteban Deive, of the Dominican Republic, with considerable, although largely unrealized, comic potential. Leopoldo Marechal's *Antígona Vélez* is reasonably close to Sophocles' conception, although it is somewhat startling to find Creon defended and expounding the author's own Peronista political philosophy. One of the most provocative of these efforts is José Triana's *Medea en el espejo*, which transplants the play to a Cuban *solar*, converting it into an ironic commentary on Cuban society. In *La muerte del Ñeque*, Triana uses tragic structures without the classical trappings to trace the rise and fall of a criminal political leader; in its somber power and daring use of game as dramatic metaphor, it is one of the best plays of this sort. Another Cuban drama, *Los siete contra Tebas* of Antón Arrufat, led to a major political and artistic polemic within Cuba and was a factor in a considerable tightening-up of controls. An adaptation and at moments a virtual translation of the Aeschylan model, Arrufat's play was attacked as counterrevolutionary, by which was meant, presumably, that it did not condemn Polyneices, who was seen as a symbol of the invasion of the Bay of Pigs. It is probably correct that Arrufat intended this fraternal slaughter to suggest the tragedy of Cuba, but the play is hardly counterrevolutionary; it is rather a tragic vision of the struggle of Eteocles and the Cuban people whom he represents, against the dilemma of injustice on one side and violence on the other. Ironically, the play offers a clear vision of redemption for a society which must suffer this last tragic onslaught in order that there be no more.

Two plays, written by close friends and collaborators, the Mexican Emilio Carballido and Luisa Josefina Hernández, serve to contrast different conceptions of the tragic form. Carballido is a confirmed experimentalist; he has written *Te juro Juana* using the various characters as a composer might handle musical themes, and in one superb scene they are orchestrated in much the same fashion as the "Sextet" from *Lucia*, or the first-act curtain from *West Side Story*. His plays show that he has assimilated the theories of Brecht and Artaud, among others, and in *Medusa* he presents the classical myth of Medusa and Perseus from Athena's presentation of the magical shield and sword, to Perseus' return to Seriphus with Andromeda, having rescued her from the dragon. However, the myth is altered drastically by having Medusa and Perseus fall in love; her death at his hands is the result of their mutual recognition that such love is impossible, that corruption corrupts without remedy or appeal. Further, the whole classical world is presented with a skewed vision. The Gorgons sell information and advice much like the oracles, or itinerant palm readers; Athena's intervention is simply a case of reprisal for economic competition. Too many clients of the oracles have been lost. There are a few crucial anachronisms: a slave who sells the equivalent of pornographic postcards, another who sings a *corrido* of Perseus' deeds, just enough so that the gap between the two worlds disappears. The world of gods is suddenly cheapened and vulgarized, much like our own. Perseus the hero is a dehumanized murderer, and noble deeds are done for sordid economic motives. The world of classical myth is as corrupt as ours, and ours as corrupt as it. At the heart of a corrupt world, the tragic vision: the impossibility of love.

Luisa Josefina Hernández has taken a totally different approach to the problem of tragic form and the adaptation of tragic themes. *Los huéspedes reales* deals with a young woman who slowly realizes the real nature of her love for her father; the play ends with the father's suicide and the bleak perspective of an unending confrontation between mother and daughter as they live out blighted lives. The unwary reader might well stop here, but if we examine the work carefully, we see that it is in fact organized much like a Greek tragedy, without the intervention of the chorus. Rather than acts, it is composed of scenes, a series of confrontations in crescendo much like tragic agons, leading to the final agonic resolution. *Medusa* and *Los huéspedes reales* are, on the surface, totally different: one an apparently realistic work in a modern idiom, the other a somewhat oblique view of classical myth. But they both utilize principles of classical tragic construction; they are both versions of classical themes—Hernández was apparently inspired by the Electra myth—and they both partake in the tragic vision.

It is clearly legitimate to ask how much social commitment is visible in these plays, since I have posited such commitment as a virtual constant for this generation. For *Medusa*, the answer is obvious; the classical world, like our own, is organized around sordid economic principles which reduce human behaviour to a dehumanized level. Such a world is clearly unacceptable on any terms. In *Los huéspedes reales*, there is no social or political component; the play is a pure experiment in tragic form. In other works of Hernández, there has been a steady and visible commitment; her earlier plays are among the first in Latin America to treat the crushing repression of women in a totally male-oriented society. More recently, she has experimented with presenting a series of critical episodes from Mexican history in a form which avoids the cliches of patriotic drama but which is simultaneously accessible to untutored audiences.

Carlos Solórzano, a Guatemalan residing in Mexico, and the Chilean Luis Alberto Heiremans have turned to traditional forms in a search for new dramatic expression. Several of Solórzano's one-act plays are clearly absurdist, but in *Las manos de Dios* he was inspired in the medieval religious allegory. The play is conceived as an allegory of freedom and slavery, in a metaphysical or theological sense, and its protagonists are the Devil and the Priest, who battle for the soul of the village girl, Beatriz. The originality of *Las manos de Dios* lies in the inversion of roles: the Devil represents absolute and unlimited human freedom, the Priest is the spirit of repression, lackey of the unnamed but omnipresent Master. The play is hardly this schematic; there is a subtle dance of symbolic implications. Heiremans worked with the Nativity play, with elements from popular folklore. After early experiments in *Los güenos versos* and *Sigue la estrella*, in *Versos de ciego* he focussed on the theme of the Wise Men's search in the crude rural world, using the traditional structure and popular verse forms and themes. In *El abanderado*, Heiremans took the life of a rural bandit to explore the modern significance of Christ's passion and its meaning in the context of popular pagan survivals.

Our final example of the rejuvenation of a traditional form is the *sainete*, the local variant of the Spanish *género chico*, which was the dominant theater fare in Habana, Buenos Aires and other cities during the late nineteenth century. In Cuba, Argentina and Uruguay, decadent versions of the form continued to monopolize crude commercial theater until 1930. The potential of the *sainete* for political expression is considerable; it is basically the expression of the urban slum, constructed of a series of confrontations or melodramatic scenes rather than a sustained dramatic conflict. The characters tend strongly toward types, and the dialogue is urban and frequently incomprehensible to the outsider. There is often a musical background, and frequently the action stops in order for the principal characters to sing. The similarities to Brechtian theory are frankly startling; it is not accidental that the *sainete* should have been the vehicle for expressions of political resentment. A number of dramatists have seen the potential of the form today. Arrufat has used it as the framework for highly comic comments on the more ludicrous aspects of modern society, and Marechal's *La batalla de José Luna* is heavily theological. The virtually continuous political crises in Argentina have produced an inundation of nostalgia for presumably better times, and the *sainete* is the principal vehicle. The most effective work has been done by the Uruguayan Carlos Maggi in *El patio de la Torcaza*. In a grim inversion of values, the structure of the *sainete* is turned upside down: the heroine ends as a cheap prostitute, and her sweetheart and potential saviour—the *sainete* theme *par excellence*—is now her procurer. To an audience familiar with the *sainete* and with Uruguayan history, it is hardly secret that the *patio* is the whole nation; Maggi's vision of his country is acid indeed.

The generation of dramatists born about 1924 is, then, a politically oriented group, but one whose principal dramatic concern is formal: the adaptation of new theories, the revival of older structures. At the same time, these structures and theories are, in nearly every case, at the service of what might be called a political vision of existence. A younger group is emerging, more embittered, more politicized, more violent. It is not a chronological happenstance that their most typical works begin to be produced during the late 1960's. They are influenced less by Brecht or the absurd than by Peter Weiss or the theater of cruelty. Often their concerns in the theater are unrelated to the theater as such; rather it is seen as a vehicle for the expression of radical politics. More than anything else, they resemble the review theaters of central Europe after World War I. A typical form is the sketch or blackout, widely used as a means of political satire in many European nations today. One of the most interesting is *El avión negro*, a collaboration by Roberto Cossa, Germán Rozenmacher, Carlos Somigliana and Ricardo Talesnick, which presents a series of sketches treating the impact on various social levels of the rumored imminent arrival of the black airplane carrying Perón back to power. The acerbic attitudes are highly comic, but the underlying tone is of menace and violence. Patricio Esteve's *La gran histeria nacional* is more irreverent still, if less menacing; its sketches are only semirelated, having in common the view of Argentine history as a brothel.

Not all members of this younger group have entirely abandoned a more traditional form of theater, although almost invariably with considerable modification. Luis Rafael Sánchez of Puerto Rico adapts the classical theme in his *La pasión según Antígona Pérez*, but his version is totally politicized. Creon is a typical repressive dictator in a modern mold, using all the persuasive rhetoric of his kind, and Antígona is imprisoned, violated and murdered because of her refusal to betray a group of political activists. The dangers of such an approach are obvious; it is nearly impossible to handle such material without collapsing into rhetoric and propaganda. But Sánchez does the near impossible; *Antígona Pérez* is by far his best play. Its impassioned defense of freedom in the face of authoritarianism, the skillful handling of irony, the split staging with double levels of action, the chorus of corrupt newspapermen and the use of political slogans for dramatic effect, make *La pasión Según Antígona Pérez* a work of high quality.

Vincente Leñero of Mexico achieved initial recognition as a novelist, but his plays demonstrate a constant rethinking of the relations between form and subject matter. *Pueblo rechazado* is based on the famous attempt of Father Lemercier to use psychoanalysis as an element in the religious life; Leñero's sympathies are clearly with Lemercier, but he presents the dangers of the attempt in a skillful integration of varied levels of action, multiple choruses and a spare dialogue. *Pueblo rechazado* transcends the immediate plot to reflect the crisis of our institutions and the inner tensions which threaten the existence of Christianity. *Los albañiles* is an adaptation of Leñero's own novel dealing with a murder investigation which becomes a theological speculation and a reexamination of the role of Christ in modern society. Basically a deeply religious artist, in *El juicio* and *Compañero* Leñero sought to resolve troublesome theoretical problems inherent in political theater; the comprehension of the political figure in both human and political terms, and the search for historical and artistic truth. *Compañero* presents two Che Guevaras, two aspects of the one consciousness, two sides of one personality attempting to reconcile the conflicting demands of dogmatism, the need for action and the revulsion before violence. *El juicio* consists almost entirely of selections from the transcript of the trial for murder of the assassin of President Obregón; although technically documentary theater, the play gives surprisingly profound insights into the psychology of the murderers, as well as into the spirit of the time and the ambiguous plot itself.

One of the constant preoccupations of younger authors is that of identity, of human relationships and the playing of roles. This is a constant in the work of such established figures as Isaac Chocrón of Venezuela, but it is especially true of the young. One of the most intriguing versions is Guillermo Gentile's *Hablemos a calzón quitado*, in which the ambiguous sexual identity of the protagonist's father becomes a metaphor of a capitalist society gone mad. It would have been easy and tempting for the characters to become obvious political symbols, but the measure of his play is that both the son, roughly equivalent to today's youth, and the friend who would save him by pointing out salvation, roughly equivalent to the proper political course, are human beings beset by doubt and prone to error. Gentile deserves attention because he resists the simplistic and the obvious and insists on giving his characters human dimension. The same is true of Ricardo Monti, like Gentile an Argentine. Monti's *Una noche con el Sr. Magnus e hijos* is a grotesque vision of dehumanized capitalism presented within the framework of the theater of ritual and cruelty. The play is perhaps overlong and the dialogue not always convincing, but the play contains a harrowing dramatic nucleus. *Una noche con el Sr. Magnus e hijos* is a complex blend of ritual, game and theater-within-theater, which establishes a climate of hallucinated menace until the new order despatches the old.

The notion of collective creation currently has considerable importance in Latin America; even such established figures as Buenaventura have become converted to it. There is a visible relation to such American groups as the Living Theater: theater is conceived as a political weapon, the arm of the group within which all are equal and which frequently exist as communal living groups. All participate directly and equally in the creative activity. Many such groups originate directly from episodes of political repression, such as the group of Chilean and Argentine students at the Drama School of the University of Cordoba. Totally politicized by repressive violence, they spent several years traveling rural Latin America presenting their collective play, *El asesinato de X*. It is curious to note in the published version of the play how the group has progressively "purified" their text of theatrical elements in any traditional sense and has adjusted it to almost exclusively political criteria. What had been the drama of a murdered workers' leader has become a straightforward propaganda piece. Perhaps the most extreme version of this conception of theater is being practiced by Augusto Boal, the Brasilian currently based in Argentina. Boal's group plays out "scripts" in a unique way. For example, the members spread out along a series of bus stops, and enter the vehicle one or two at a time. As they enter, they make inflammatory political remarks or play out a prepared political argument. The purpose, of course, is to "liberate" the consciousness of the other passengers and convert them to Boal's point of view. Since the success of this kind of representation depends largely on the audience's never finding out that anything prepared is happening, it is debatable whether Boal's activities are theater in any sense. A theater which makes no pretense to any artistic value, which indeed rejects any such notion as irrelevant, is itself irrelevant as theater and must be judged on other bases.

Since World War II, Latin American theater has achieved an amount and level of activity beyond any possible expectation. Now, it faces the challenge of maintaining this level. Whether a nucleus of established playwrights and a promising group of younger writers can continue and develop this momentum will depend largely on whether the theater can transcend and absorb the current drive toward politicization, which in turn may depend on how well and how rapidly the world can right its grievous wrongs.

*Rutgers University*

# La narrativa del Cono Sur y el Paraguay: un panorama comparativo

Angela B. Dellepiane

SUMARIO

A fin de trazar un esquema comparativo de las diversas temáticas y de las estructuras de las formas narrativas en la prosa de ficción de los países del cono sur y del Paraguay, se organiza el material en una periodización generacional basada en grupos determinados por "sistemas de preferencias" los cuales objetivizan tipos diferenciales de sensibilidad. Dentro de los varios estratos generacionales de la época "contemporánea," se escogen los operantes a partir de los últimos 15 años (1960-1975) y, en cada uno de ellos y para cada país, se analiza el estrato del mundo narrado, el de los significados y el de la palabra. Se explora, asimismo, el concepto y la función de la literatura enunciado por algunos narradores jóvenes (argentinos y uruguayos, principalmente) y se discuten los nuevos derroteros marcados por ciertos narradores (particularmente en la Argentina y Chile). Se llega a la conclusión de que la narrativa del cono sur -y, con salvedades, la del Paraguay-, no se aparta de las tendencias generales del resto del continente, aun cuando muestra rasgos únicos. Tentativamente, puede decirse que la tendencia literaria predominante sigue siendo la narrativa; que la estructura del género continúa determinada por la postura del narrador -que es diversa- y que, en general, hay una concentración y hasta exasperación de todas las formas innovativas de la novela hispanoamericana contemporánea. Se pone especial énfasis en la "asincronía" de la literatura paraguaya *vis à vis* la de los países del cono sur y del continente. Finalmente, se plantea el interrogante de si ciertas direcciones observables en la narrativa del cono sur -semejantes a las de otras áreas de Hispano América- son manifestaciones de un nuevo "género" no conceptualizado aún por lo imperfecto de nuestra percepción actual dada la cercanía del fenómeno y su estado aún evolutivo. (ABD)

A fin de trazar el esquema comparativo de la narrativa de los países del cono sur -Chile, Argentina, Uruguay- y del Paraguay, de una manera significativa, el primer problema que se plantea -aparte el del volumen de la producción- es el de organizar el material en base a un criterio metodológico. El que he escogido elabora una clasificación dentro de categorías estrictamente literarias y, aunque discutible, es uno de los más serios para enfrentar el estudio de la literatura hoy. Me refiero a la periodización generacional que ha aplicado el profesor chileno Cedomil Goić en sus trabajos sobre la novela chilena e hispanoamericana.[1] Parte él de grupos humanos determinados por *"sistemas de preferencias"* los cuales objetivan "tipos diferenciales de sensibilidad." Cada cambio del sistema de preferencias determina una época. En la novela hispanoamericana, Goić ve dos épocas -la moderna y la contemporánea- con 1935 como el año que acusa claramente un cambio -o ruptura- fundamental: el de la posición del narrador. Dice Goić: "En relación a la figura personal del narrador de la novela moderna, dispensador de la perspectiva de comprensión del universo, de la disposición narrativa, señor de la presentación y sus modos y provisto de un lenguaje -una voz, un ritmo, una sintaxis, un temple- característicos, la novela contemporánea muestra: 1) una disminución o castigo de las dimensiones personales del narrador básico; 2) su material desintegración o desdoblamiento en varias personas, y 3) su completa anulación y desaparecimiento, sustituído por múltiples narradores."[2] Dentro del sistema de la época se producen cambios y/o variedades: éstos son los períodos. Las variaciones del sistema periódico constituyen las generaciones, el elemento más vivo y cambiante dentro del sistema histórico. Aun cuando se dan siempre casos que se escurren del encasillamiento generacional, este mismo hecho posibilita señalar quién y cómo trasciende su propia generación para integrarse al sistema de la generación siguiente. La generación es, pues, un fenómeno heterogéneo que actualiza una sensibilidad típica diferencial, una tendencia literaria (la de su período) y una estructura del género (la de la época) siendo siempre posibles "articulaciones transversales"[3] entre las generaciones.

Para la época contemporánea Goić señala cuatro generaciones:[4] la del 27, la del 42, la del 57 y la del 72 y las considera inscriptas en el único período que se da hasta el presente en la época, el período superrealista.[5] Las generaciones con las que trabajaré aquí son la del 57 y la del 72 ya que de sus filas salen los narradores que han ido surgiendo y consolidándose en los últimos 15 años (1960-1975), lapso a que limitaré mi observación. Se sobrentiende la importancia de la primera generación de la época contemporánea, la del 27 (o generación superrealista, según Goić),[6] a la que pertenecen, en los países que nos ocupan, Manuel Rojas, Jorge Luis Borges, Leopoldo Marechal, Roberto Arlt, Eduardo Mallea, Enrique Amorim; y de la segunda generación, la del 42 -neorrealista-,[7] en que se inscriben Carlos Droguett, Adolfo Bioy Casares, Julio Cortázar, Ernesto Sábato, Juan Carlos Onetti, Gabriel Casaccia y Augusto Roa Bastos.

En las tres repúblicas del cono sur -como en el resto de Hispanoamérica- la generación del 57[8] se comporta *cumulativamente* en relación a la tendencia del período, rescata la significación de los grandes autores de las dos generaciones precedentes, despersonaliza -por diversas maneras, como veremos- al narrador y configura por sus complejas ordenaciones narrativas de sentidos superpuestos, una imagen del ser ambigua y compleja. La efectividad de la expresión es lo más importante. El objeto de la representación es lo grotesco que se desprende de un mundo ambiguo y laberíntico y se exterioriza en formas o paródicas o imaginarias o fantásticas.[9]

Los autores que he elegido,[10] en esta generación, son: para Chile, José Donoso; para la Argentina, Antonio Di Benedetto y Manuel Puig y para el Uruguay, Mario Benedetti. Por razones que se explicarán más adelante, me ocuparé de la narrativa paraguaya aparte, una vez que haya recorrido las dos generaciones propuestas en los otros países australes.

José Donoso en *El obsceno pájaro de la noche*[11] escribe la más extraordinaria novela del despojamiento del ser humano por otros seres humanos y por un orden social, simbolizado, en última instancia, por el *imbunche*. Lo que confiere a la novela su polisemia es la estructura de un narrador-personaje y testigo a la vez, narrador totalmente despersonalizado ya que se lo oculta con máscaras y transformaciones o, mejor, con inversiones y trasvestimientos en secuencias narrativas que se niegan entre sí; con un protagonista -Humberto Peñaloza- que, castrado por su padre, por su patrón, por una mujer, por unos desechos humanos, se reduce finalmente a la nada, al *imbunche*, se cierra a la existencia en un mundo que lo ha marginado desde su nacimiento. Un sexo animal, un humor negro; una atmósfera claustrofóbica de degradación física, de vejez, de mugre, de seres que expían culpas de otros; un mundo dual -apolíneo pero momificado y demoníaco-mágico-, laberíntico, en suma; un lenguaje poético, literario-tradicional en cuanto es, por veces, modernista, barroco, pero asimismo coloquial con diversos niveles superpuestos y en colisión; pluralidad de tonos; indiferenciación de lo actuado y lo pensado y lo soñado, esto es, del nivel consciente y el alucinado, dicen de una visión subjetiva del mundo a partir de las obsesiones de Donoso. Una novela en que la imaginación creadora es absolutamente omnipotente y que contiene otras tres novelas: la que narra un nombre repetido 9300 veces en los 100 ejemplares de la biografía impresa de Jerónimo de Azcoitía; la que hace la crónica de *La Rinconada* concebida mentalmente pero no realizada y, finalmente, la relación del Mudito a la Madre Benita. En suma, pues, un texto que genera otros textos.

Junto a Donoso todos los otros autores chilenos de su generación[12] palidecen, aun cuando hayan hecho aportaciones tan originales como las de Hugo Correa,[13] el primer autor chileno de novelas de ciencia-ficción. Empero, Jorge Edwards y Enrique Lafourcade merecen atención especial, si no en relación con toda su obra publicada hasta hoy (lo que sería imposible por razones de tiempo), con dos libros de naturaleza peculiar. Edwards con *Persona non grata* ha escrito un libro que, basado en hechos reales vividos por el autor, se lee como una ficción casi hasta policial con un suspenso que no disminuye a pesar de conocerse el desenlace de los hechos narrados. Estamos aquí, como en algún relato de Skármeta y de Galeano,[14] frente a una forma no literaria, en sentido estricto, para cuyo estudio habrá que recurrir a determinantes genéricos y retóricos distintos de los que se manejan para las formas propiamente literarias que son el objeto de nuestra indagación. Dado el carácter autobiográfico del libro -su carácter catártico, en verdad-, está narrado en primera persona y aquí el narrador dista mucho de estar despersonalizado. Pero es que estamos frente a una tendencia secundaria en la generación, tendencia en la que lo específicamente literario se subordina a la denuncia o, en otros autores, a un mensaje de carácter ideológico. Lafourcade, por el contrario, en *Salvador Allende* reúne las dos caras de la moneda porque, si bien se explaya en los avatares biográficos del político chileno y en el golpe militar que terminó con su gobierno y su vida, lo que él está poniendo en juego es el problema del arte frente a la realidad 'real.' Y lo hace enfrentando, novelísticamente, en cada página, toda clase de documentos verídicos con el desesperado monólogo interior de Allende en las últimas horas de su vida. Frente al lenguaje de clisés de la prensa, el del angustiado y perplejo ser humano desata un contrapunto intertextual del que surge el drama, la falacia, los ideales, es decir, una visión objetiva a través de un texto que, en sus dos discursos, se hace a sí mismo, prescindiendo de toda voz narrativa, en un anulamiento total del narrador en aras de la verdad histórica.

La obra de Antonio Di Benedetto, cercana a la de Sábato aunque menos problemática que la de este autor, es de preocupación existencial y moral, como lo prueban las narraciones de su *Mundo Animal*,[15] fábulas con personajes animales que asumen personificaciones y en las que se convoca "con intermediaciones de crueldad y horror, a la meditación sobre la perfectibilidad del ser humano."[16]

A Di Benedetto le interesa "sugerir" y "estimular" a su lector con su escritura. Habiendo partido, en 1956, de unos cuentos 'objetivistas,' seguidos por una compleja *nouvelle -El pentágono-*,[17] compleja por su estructura narrativa, temática, y por un estrato lingüístico casi barroco, con *Zama*[18] Di Benedetto retomó aquella línea inicial de escritura para continuarla en forma cada vez más desnuda en sus dos novelas *El silenciero* y *Los suicidas*.[19] Ambas ponen al descubierto, indirectamente, el desamparo básico del ser humano, cuyo mundo, en un caso, es usurpado por los ruidos con que lo acosa la ciudad y que, en el otro, defiende su integridad por medio de la autodestrucción. Esta temática es desenvuelta por el autor mendocino en una escritura totalmente presentativa, buscando enmascarar lo literario a través de una vetusta sobriedad verbal a la que llega por un discurso que participa del monólogo interior indirecto y el diario íntimo en *El silenciero* y de la narración en primera persona de un narrador-protagonista, totalmente objetivo, que narra sólo lo que percibe, lo que está en la superficie de los hechos y los seres. Esta narración se matiza con diálogos acotados por el protagonista y con la interpolación de breves ensayos eruditos en pro o en contra del suicidio. Mientras en *El silenciero* el hombre es degradado por algo tan trivial, al parecer, como el ruido que hace imposible su descanso, su actividad mental, sus goces de toda índole, en *Los suicidas* la degradación estriba en que una indagación existencial y hasta metafísica -la de la muerte- es reducida a la trivialidad de un reportaje periodístico, a su tratamiento como mercancía de consumo masivo. En ambas novelas, a pesar de los desplazamientos espaciales de los personajes, la narración fluye pero *in situ*, con lo que se crea, desde el principio, una atmósfera agobiante que hace posible que la muerte llegue casi sin sentirse y como un accidente más del diario vivir, o que el protagonista -en *El silenciero*- se declare impotente en su lucha contra el ruido.

Manuel Puig es un 'caso' literario en el sentido de que él ha hecho su obra sin cuidarse de antecedentes literarios argentinos o hispano-americanos. El suyo es un intento de construcción de una novela popular, paródica, que es, en realidad, literatura culta hecha en base a elementos de la cultura de masas -letras de tango, de boleros, guiones de radioteatro, de películas, de telenovela, informes deportivos, textos periodísticos, etc. Sus personajes están totalmente absorbidos por el cine, la T.V. y la radio. Viven no una vida real sino una vida estereotipada de acuerdo a emociones y esquemas de pensamiento que Hollywood -o el equivalente nacional- les proporciona y que los despoja de sus propias personalidades individuales.

Lo más característico de su obra[20] y lo que la singulariza es lo que siempre se ha considerado materia paraliteraria. El no ironiza la cursilería de sus personajes porque, como narrador, no existe en sus novelas, las que, por lo general, avanzan por medio de diálogos, diarios íntimos, cartas, composiciones escolares, conversaciones telefónicas, grabaciones, transcripciones de documentos, etc. Esta desaparición del narrador deja, violentamente, en primer plano a los personajes y su mundo. Y en tanto que los expone crudamente, las novelas de Puig, a pesar de manejar situaciones y seres con los que un lectorado masivo puede identificarse, no obstante, conllevan el rechazo de ese mismo mundo al que los lectores pertenecen.

Tal como están estructuradas estas novelas de Puig admiten, por lo menos, dos tipos de lecturas: una literal de novela rosa y otra analógica que goza con los *pastiches* y con las oposiciones intertextuales que revelan el enajenamiento a que lleva una cultura de mitos.

El modo expresivo de Puig va de una elocución coloquial ciudadana -para la que su autor demuestra un extraordinario oído y una rara capacidad en su reproducción sostenida- a la imitación de estilos de la paraliteratura. Con respecto a esto cabe observar que si bien *Boquitas pintadas* y *The Buenos Aires Affair* llevan sendos subtítulos -*folletín* el primero y *novela policial* el segundo- ninguno de los dos libros observa ortodoxamente la factura de esas formas de literatura 'de consumo' ya que sólo intentan ser, *Boquitas*, una *remozada versión* del folletín, y la otra, una *parodia* del género policial.

Un antecedente de la escritura paródica de Manuel Puig puede hallarse en *Rosaura a las 10*, de un 'adelantado' de esta generación: Marco Denevi.[21] Aunque, en verdad, y aparte Roberto Arlt, el pionero del lenguaje coloquial y lunfardo, el parodista -en la década del 30- de los modos estereotipados de decir fue el cordobés Juan Filloy, quien, coincidentemente, fue editorialmente revivido en 1967, en plena vigencia de la generación del 57, junto con ese gran visionario que se llamó Macedonio Fernández. Cuando hoy nos volvemos (como él quería) "lectores salteados" de ciertos no-personajes, cobran una relevancia y actualidad extraordinarias aquellas *Belarte de la palabra* o la *Ilógica del arte* o la *Estética de la invención* macedonianas que quizá, en su época, sólo Borges tomó en serio.[22] Todo lo cual pone de relieve esas articulaciones transversales entre generaciones, mencionadas al principio, que demuestran la complejidad del proceso literario y la imposibilidad de abarcarlo en todos sus entrecruzamientos.

Junto a estos autores de la generación del 57,[23] parece absolutamente necesario mencionar a dos autores de la generación del 42 que han continuado publicando y sin los que es imposible comentar la literatura argentina actual. Por supuesto que me refiero a Ernesto Sábato y Julio Cortázar. No se trata aquí de discutir la obra de estos dos autores, sino de subrayar el hecho de la aparición de sus últimas novelas, *Abadón el Exterminador* y *Libro de Manuel*,[24] ya que ellas son un buen ejemplo de cambio en la posición del narrador, pero por distintas maneras. En *Libro de Manuel* un no-personaje, semejante a *mi paredro* de *62*, una suerte de *doble colectivo* -el que te dije- es el narrador y testigo omnisciente que ficha todo, que discute lo que es y no debe de ser la literatura, y que presencia la *Joda* en que están empeñados sus amigos. Pero el que te dije, hacia el final de la novela, desaparece, y su tarea queda al cuidado de Andrés. La diferencia entre ambos es que el que te dije no es personaje -no actúa- y su único conflicto es con las palabras, mientras que Andrés sí actúa en la ficción; los hechos lo afectan y llegan a cambiarlo. No se limita, como el otro, a observar y relatar. Pero hay todavía alguien más: Lonstein, el refutador dialéctico de la estética literaria de el que te dije, que propone una situación particular pues está dentro y fuera de lo propiamente anecdótico del libro -la *Joda*- como también dentro y fuera de la escritura en tanto que haciéndose. Actúa con los otros personajes -un poco en escorzo, eso símas igualmente los observa e interpreta y lo mismo con los acontecimientos. Es decir, que la novela se va haciendo a través de múltiples narradores (el que te dije, Andrés, un narrador omnisciente, confundido con o separado de el que te dije y/o Andrés, Lonstein, Oscar, Ludmilla, Francine) y a través de la discusión que sobre sus alcances se proponen Andrés, Lonstein y el no-personaje. En suma, una minuciosa metanovela.

Sábato, por su parte, sumido en similares cavilaciones acerca del quehacer literario, va sin embargo más lejos que Cortázar cuando, en *Abadón*, se desdobla en su yo-literario y su yo-real arrojando a ambos, en dialéctico contrapunto, a las páginas del mundo narrado para terminar destruyendo ¿a los dos? ¿al escritor? ¿al hombre? Preguntas para las que el libro no ofrece inequívoca respuesta y que, junto a los elementos demoníacos y a la absurdidad del mundo que el libro trata de explicitar, evidencian en Sábato un afán de búsqueda de nuevas dimensiones para la novela. Estas antenas tendidas hacia adelante, el éxito de público con que se lo lee desde 1948 -fecha de aparición de *El túnel*-, renovado y sobrepasado en 1962 con la publicación de *Sobre héroes y tumbas*, son comentarios elocuentes en sí mismos de la vitalidad de este creador. No obstante, no pueden señalarse 'discípulos' de Sábato, en la medida en que puede hacérselo con Cortázar, por ejemplo.[25] Esto no implica una comparación de ambos escritores que vaya en desmedro de Sábato. Este, a diferencia de Cortázar, no posee manerismos estilísticos de fácil imitación exterior -que es el caso también de Borges-. Como para Sábato lo que cuenta es la estructura de la obra literaria y su temática, aquella imitación de superficie no tendría razón de ser en quienes la intentaran. Por eso no creo que se pueda hablar de una 'corriente sabatiana' dentro de la generación del 57 aunque sí de 'elementos sabatianos' en muchos de los escritores que la pueblan.[26] Elementos que hacen, mayormente, a la temática y a la concepción y función de la literatura. *Abadón*, no obstante, como novela que se comenta a sí misma (y esto es también válido para *Libro de Manuel*), como novela en que la despersonalización del narrador llega al límite de que éste sea un personaje más dentro de la ficción, esto es, de que esté en convivencia con sus propios desdoblamientos ficcionales en un afán de explicarse, a la vez, el misterio de la creación literaria y el de la vida humana, que sea directamente cuestionado y satirizado por sus personajes, *Abadón*, que, en sus diferentes modos elocutivos, en sus repeticiones de las otras ficciones o ensayos de su autor parecería exterminarse a sí misma, puede llevar a dos interrogantes opuestos: ¿suicidio o nueva epifanía del texto literario?[27] Pregunta sobre la que se volverá al final de este trabajo ya que no es privativo de *Abadón* el proponerla.

Párrafo aparte debe de reservarse para Adolfo Bioy Casares, también de la generación del 42, cuyas obras se articulan, asimismo, con las de autores de la generación del 57 en cuanto ellas señalan pautas de ironía, de humor, pautas fantásticas recogidas, entre otros, por Marco Denevi, Pedro Orgambide, Juan José Hernández. Bioy Casares escribe tersas novelas en que un tiempo o un espacio o una circunstancia fantástica que altera amenazantemente la realidad cotidiana, son medios cognoscitivos de esa realidad y no meros juegos intelectuales. Tal *La invención de Morel, El sueño de los héroes, Diario de la guerra del cerdo* y *Dormir al sol.*[28]

Nombrar a Bioy trae la obvia asociación con Borges, con el apócrifo H. Bustos Domecq, B. Suárez Lynch y B. Lynch Davis que ambos autores pergeñaron y a través de los que escribieron notables relatos policiales de alto valor literario. Nombrarlo también es conjurar la literatura fantástica argentina, una de las vetas más fecundas y originales que la narrativa argentina presenta en comparación con la del resto del continente y, en general, de los países de habla hispánica. Sin embargo, ella no se yergue tan única como a primera vista parecería, aunque sí más rica y diversa que en otras latitudes del continente. María Luisa Bombal -en la misma generación del 42-, José Donoso, en Chile, y algunos de los narradores mexicanos de aquélla y subsiguientes generaciones, dan buena prueba de que hay otros focos de literatura fantástica en el continente.

Mario Benedetti domina por completo la escena literaria de Uruguay ya que entre sus compañeros de generación no hay nadie que pueda igualársele en calidad, diversidad y cantidad de obras que, por otra parte, y a despecho de sus búsquedas formales, configuran un *corpus* plenamente coherente. A partir de *Poemas de oficina* (1956), Benedetti va a hacer su prosa con las mismas palabras comunes del hombre medio uruguayo, siguiendo por la huella que había abierto una *nouvelle* de 1939: *El pozo,* de su compatriota Juan Carlos Onetti, huella de la que ya nunca se apartaría la narrativa uruguaya. Los temas de Benedetti reflejarán siempre experiencias por todos compartidas y sus recursos literarios serán los que tomará de un código que su público comparte ampliamente. Benedetti se volverá así el escritor "*comunicante*" por excelencia en el Urugray. Y su mundo será el de la mayoría, el de la mediocridad al que reflejará sumido, simbólicamente, en esa gran maquinaria burocrática que toda la Banda Oriental parece ser.

Benedetti experimentó, desde sus primeros cuentos, con la estructura del mundo narrado y con el estrato lingüístico de ese mundo, y ha habido siempre en él una preocupación con la liberación de la palabra, "esa nueva cartuja," como la llama, que lo llevó ya en *La tregua* (1960) a cuestionar la carga semántica dada a palabras como *falleció, muerte, Dios,* tan minimizadas por el uso. Pero su novela *El cumpleaños de Juan Angel,*[29] una *nouvelle*-en-verso, señala una de las formas extremas de la transformación que la narrativa parece estar experimentando en estos momentos en nuestro continente.

*El cumpleaños* es la historia de la transformación individual de un pequeño-burgués en un guerrillero; transformación desenvuelta a través de los distintos cumpleaños (de los 8 a los 33 años) de Osvaldo Puente, ahora el tupamaro Juan Angel. O sea, que lo que se enfatiza son las diversas etapas de su toma de conciencia política, ideológica. El núcleo estructural de la novela está dado por la naturaleza y carácter del narrador que es *dual*, ya que cuenta la historia de Osvaldo, pero desde la perspectiva de Juan Angel. Esto es, Osvaldo narra pero a la vez es narrado por Juan Angel. En otro plano, *El cumpleaños* viene a ser la síntesis artística e ideológica de Benedetti ya que aúna sus búsquedas literarias con las de índole política. Y esta búsqueda -que implica una posición crítica- se ha vuelto ahora materia narrativa misma a través de ese narrador dual con el que Benedetti trata de conseguir una literatura de función social y política, aunque sin forzar su naturaleza literaria.

Junto a este heredero y continuador de Onetti, dos palabras acerca de Jorge Onetti quien está un poco a horcajadas de los dos países rioplatenses. Dos libros -*Cualquiercosario* (Montevideo: Arca, 1967) y *Contramutis* (Barcelona: Seix Barral, 1969; Primer Premio de Cuentos, Casa de las Américas, 1965; finalista del Premio Biblioteca Breve de 1968)- lo muestran en una línea similar a la de Puig, ya que hay en él una escritura paródica e ironizante que distancia al lector y hace evidente el carácter literario de lo que lee. Jorge Onetti está preocupado con el texto como texto, con lo que robustece su literaturidad, su autonomía como texto literario. Lo hace desplegando ante el lector los artificios del relato, sub-rayando el carácter ficticio de su historia. Lo que también está acentuado por la utilización paródica de tiras cómicas, guiones cinematográficos o de ironizaciones de la ciencia-ficción y del informe policial. Pero es la posición del narrador lo que determina la total ficcionalidad del texto ya que Lupo—el protagonista de *Contramutis*—, narra la historia de una pareja que, a su vez, lo cuenta a él. Y él y la pareja son, por su parte, productos -personajes- de un narrador omnisciente que desaparece en el monólogo final y que da lugar a dos novelas: aquélla en que Lupo es narrador-personaje, en tercera persona, y la otra en que él inventa a la pareja para que lo narre. La novela concluye por mirarse a sí misma de una manera que recuerda *La vida breve*.[30]

Esta generación de 1957 está lejos de haber cerrado su etapa de vigencia. Su contribución a la narrativa hispanoamericana actual, en estos países como en los restantes del continente, es madura y fecunda. Son los consolidadores de las realizaciones innovativas de los del 27 y 42 y, para bien o para mal -no puede aún juzgarse-, es evidente que están señalando pautas que otros siguen.

Con la generación del 72 (los nacidos de 1935 en adelante) estamos frente a un grupo de escritores que asumen, con plena conciencia, el sistema literario con que sus coetáneos los confrontan pero lo hacen más lúdica, más innovadoramente, y de esa manera lo transforman, lo están transformando y recreando, mejor dicho.[31] Dado que esta generación se halla aún en plena etapa de gestación, sólo cabe describir sus obras ya que no es posible formular una prognosis.

Los autores elegidos son: Antonio Skármeta, para Chile; Eduardo Gudiño Kieffer, para la Argentina, y Cristina Peri Rossi y Eduardo Galeano, para el Uruguay.

Hay en Antonio Skármeta[32] un extraordinario narrador con rasgos muy particulares. En primer lugar, el carácter totalmente oral de su discurso, lo que lleva, casi sin excepción, a una voz que cuenta, desde dentro o desde fuera del personaje, en primera o tercera persona, en segunda en interpelación a un alguien que el lector no percibe, o en saltos subitáneos de una a otra de ellas, su visión de los seres, las cosas, las situaciones. No hay una estructura argumental, sino sólo un discurso en donde y por donde la narración vive. El erotismo de los protagonistas -casi sin excepción adolescentes, algo característico de esta generación- es el motor que, por lo general, los lleva a la madurez en verdaderos ritos de pasaje,[33] como en "Basketball."[34] Sin embargo, ni la oralidad ni el erotismo agotan el carácter peculiar de la prosa de Skármeta. La otra característica es la de ser una escritura rítmica, que se acopla a la frase musical para reproducir el ritmo de una determinada música. Muestra de esta "verdadera simbiosis de la escritura y la nota musical,"[35] es "Final de Tango,"[36] especie de canto al tango como cópula, como enlazamiento de la hembra y el macho fuera del tiempo y del mundo.

Como todos los de esta generación -y la anterior-, Skármeta está condicionado por el cine, lo que, en términos de su mundo narrado, se trasunta en el sistemático cotejo de sus personajes con la realidad -más real- del cine. "Pajarraco" (también de *Desnudo en el tejado*, su libro premiado por la Casa de las Américas en 1969), está significativamente dedicado a Alfred Hitchcock. El relato encarama, unos sobre otros, elementos diversos -una paráfrasis evangélica, una parodia de tiras cómicas y de guiones y acciones cinematográficas- que diluyen al narrador y arrojan el mundo narrado al campo de lo fantástico. Pero la frase final es sintomática: "este hombre (. . .), se entrega a la otra pantalla, recuerda su infancia, y se le borra la película, como quien dice."[37] Esto es, que todo es *biógrafo*, tanto la literatura como la vida.

Skármeta se vale de una elocución coloquial, excesivamente dialectal, por momentos, de *slang*, así como de un abundante muestreo escatológico pero, de pronto, su lengua se enciende en bellas metáforas de resonancia poética y el resultado de esta combinación es una prosa fuerte, machista y visceral que, aunque más para ser oída, dicha, que leída, resulta incantatoria y poemática.[38]

En la Argentina creo que no es temerario reputar a Eduardo Gudiño Kieffer como el más destacado de entre los escritores jóvenes y el que ya ofrece un *corpus* de obras sobre el que pueden elaborarse algunas observaciones.[39] Como en Skármeta, el modo expresivo de Gudiño es totalmente oral. Pero de una lengua oral, coloquial y hasta lunfarda, apegada a *slogans* publicitarios, a clisés lingüísticos, a juegos de palabras, predominante en su primera novela -*Para comerte mejor*-, Gudiño Kieffer ha ido deslizándose hacia un plano poético, ya entrevisto en el *leit motiv* temático de aquella novela y ahora desembozadamente presente en sus últimos libros. *Guía de pecadores*, al igual que *Será por eso que la quiero tanto*, tienen como preocupación central una misma: la ciudad de Buenos Aires. Pero mientras *Será* es desenvuelta por un narrador-testigo en un monólogo interior, alrededor de una fábula concreta -la historia de una familia provinciana que viene al soñado Buenos Aires-, con el contrapunto lírico de versos de Borges, la *Guía* está decididamente en el camino del poema (lo que hace ambigua su filiación genérica.) La *Guía* se estructura a partir de cinco poemas (uno en prosa, los demás en verso blanco) a Reyna = Buenos Aires, en los que se la invoca en sus diversos aspectos para rematar en un "credo" de resonancias claramente cortazarianas. Cada uno de esos poemas constituye una parte y en cada parte hay cinco bloques narrativos en cada uno de los cuales siempre se desarrolla la historia de un idéntico personaje. Es decir, que si se ve cada parte como una estrofa, cada bloque narrativo sería un verso que rimaría con el colocado en el mismo lugar en cada una de las otras estrofas: el primer bloque contiene la historia del muchacho que trabaja de sordo-mudo; el segundo, la del homosexual atado a su explotador; el tercero, la de la pareja de amantes; el cuarto, la de la adivina, y el quinto, la de la teleteátrica. La última parte, además del "credo" en Reyna, agrega un "estrambote" que une todos los hilos de las diversas fábulas. Un "*Happy end* en bicicleta" cierra el libro, con la irrealidad de la T.V. imponiéndose a la verdadera realidad. Como se ve, una especie de caleidoscopio de naturaleza picaresca y paródica en que un(os) narrador(es) anónimo(s) hurga(n) diversos niveles de la realidad porteña dramatizando así, lúdicamente -al volver lo trivial insólito-, la absurdidad e irrealidad de un medio social, de un mundo en que el narrador, a fin de deshacerse de una palabra vaciada de significado, debe de crear juegos, alegorías yuxtapuestas que entreguen, en su caricaturismo, en su imaginismo, la verdadera faz de ese mundo. A través de la exasperación del lenguaje "como espectáculo,"[40] el problema existencial de la soledad básica del ser humano resulta muy claramente mostrado. Es evidente, por lo demás, que Gudiño Kieffer tiene una gran "fascinación por las palabras," fascinación que ha experimentado desde su niñez; y es la escritura, más que la literatura en sí, "la que se me ha hecho carne."[41]

De entre la considerable legión de escritores que producen en la Argentina en esta generación, Mario Satz merece un comentario, aunque brevísimo por fuerza. Conocido como poeta (como lo atestiguan cuatro libros de poesía escritos entre 1964 y 1975), ahora Editorial Noguer ha lanzado su primera -y voluminosa- novela, *Sol*, que inicia una trilogía denominada *Planetarium*.[42] La novela es el "diálogo cerrado" (*Sol*, 21) de un hombre con la mujer que amó, "pretexto" para el texto escrito (Ibid.) que intenta recrear seres y acontecimientos vividos en tres años y que responde "a una estructura mitológica: aparición, creación, hierofanía, muerte, resurrección, fornicación en el fondo del mar, etc." (Ibid.) Un débil hilo anecdótico -ella quiere saber cómo ha muerto su hermano y qué es la Secta (¿influjo de los ciegos sabatianos? )- vertebra ese diálogo cerrado que es, en verdad, el viaje de un hombre a través del inicio de un amor hasta su paulatino agostamiento. En una prosa densa, mansa pero sobre todo líricamente bella, se van dando los personajes, las aventuras, las concepciones filosóficas, míticas, políticas, las situaciones reales y fantásticas en diversos lugares del globo -Israel, New York, París, Buenos Aires, Lima, Machu Pichu- todo envuelto en una atmósfera de misterio generada por la naturaleza enigmática del amor de la protagonista (una suerte de Nadja peruana), por la personalidad y actividades de su hermano y también desarrollada en una atmósfera cabalística en que todo está presidido por el número 3 y en la que hay un eterno retorno muy borgiano. La escritura es un exorcismo para el narrador que a ella se entrega buscando, por su intermedio, "la clave de sol de esta *solitaria cantata* que me excede y me traspasa, la *larga melopea* del rumiante." (85. El subrayado me pertenece.) Frente a tanta parodia y espíritu lúdico, esta novela de Satz (esta "solitaria cantata" y "larga melopea") sobre el amor,[43] ¿indicará acaso un nuevo giro, un nuevo "sistema de preferencias" en la narrativa argentina? Y si esto es así, ¿tendrá seguidores en los otros países? [44]

En la generación uruguaya del 72 Cristina Peri Rossi y Eduardo Galeano están empeñados en igual tarea de reelaboración del lenguaje y de ambigüedad en cuanto al género literario.

Cristina Peri Rossi, en los tres libros que de ella he leído -dos de relatos: *Viviendo* (Montevideo: Alfa, 1963) y *Los museos abandonados* (Montevideo: Arca, 1969) y una novela, si es que así puede llamársela, *El libro de mis primos*, (Montevideo: Marcha, 1969)-[45] ofrece lo que Angel Rama señala, muy exactamente, como uno de "los ejemplos más libres de imaginación que hayan conocido las letras uruguayas."[46] Añadiría que me parece comparable a la imaginación de García Márquez, con la diferencia de que mientras el colombiano hiperboliza la realidad para crear una realidad-otra, la escritora uruguaya la 'surrealiza,' la musicaliza, pero, sobre todo, le confiere una romántica y poética melancolía. Poema en prosa, diario, crónica, fábula, *El libro de mis primos* es suavemente erótico y conscientemente político, a la vez lúdico y grotesco, con notas a pie de página que indican los fragmentos tomados de trovadores provenzales y de poetas italianos del *Trecento* y de Alberti, Padilla, Vallejo, Huidobro, Cardenal, etc. El narrador es aquí un temple de ánimo que colorea el mundo narrado con su depresiva tristeza o su grotesco humor o su erotismo y lo configura en manifestaciones fragmentarias de intenso lirismo.

Eduardo Galeano ya había probado en su *nouvelle Los días siguientes* (1963), en los relatos de *Los fantasmas del día del león* (Montevideo: Arca, 1967) y en los de *Vagamundo* (Buenos Aires: Crisis, 1973) su talento. Su novela *La canción de nosotros*, Primer Premio de la Casa de las Américas de 1975, vino a confirmarlo con creces.[47] En Galeano, hombre profundamente comprometido ideológicamente, la palabra creadora se funde con la experiencia política -como en Benedetti- y como en él no se convierte en planfleto sino que esa fusión le sirve para mostrar la realidad humana y su faz política en un universo que es exclusivamente literario y que, en este libro, se estructura en tres planos: uno, el lírico, de canto a la ciudad que, por supuesto, es Montevideo; otro, el histórico-simbólico dado por la intercalación de las crónicas del Tribunal del Santo Oficio de la Inquisición, "sutil diálogo intertextual"[48] entre ellas y el tercer plano, el propiamente narrativo, distribuido en los capítulos rotulados "El regreso," "Andares de Ganapán" y "La Máquina." Se constituyen así cinco secuencias que espejean diversos niveles de la realidad a los que se accede desde distintos puntos de vista -narrador omnisciente indeterminado, narrador-personaje en tercera y primera personas-. El carácter presentativo de la prosa, los diversos modos expresivos -lírico, arcaico, coloquial-, las dimensiones histórica, grotesca, fantástica, poética y cotidiana del mundo narrado, enfrentan al lector con la materia narrada en forma directa y así su toma de conciencia política se produce activamente, que es, en definitiva, la finalidad buscada por Galeano con su ficción.[49]

Pasemos ahora a la narrativa paraguaya. Aquí fuerza es que me aparte del criterio seguido para referirme -muy sucintamente- a algunos problemas que la narrativa de aquel país propone y que le son peculiares. Ellos están determinados por hechos de naturaleza política los que, a su vez, han incidido profundamente en la organización de la sociedad y la cultura. Las incesantes dictaduras y dos de las guerras más cruentas del continente han determinado, en el campo cultural, una *asincronía*[50] de este país con respecto a los módulos literarios y artísticos del resto de Hispanoamérica. Como así también el que la literatura paraguaya se haya gestado -por lo menos en lo que de más valioso tiene- fuera de las fronteras nacionales, en un fenómeno de *perspectivismo*, como lo designa Josefina Plá.[51] De modo tal que hay que llegar a dos volúmenes -*La babosa* y *El trueno entre las hojas*- de dos insignes exiliados paraguayos -Gabriel Cassacia y Augusto

Roa Bastos- y a los años 1952-1953 para que la narrativa paraguaya comience a andar a la par de la hispanoamericana que ya para entonces ha dado, en el cono sur, productos tales como *Historia Universal de la Infamia, Los siete locos, Fiesta en Noviembre, La vida breve, Hijo de ladrón* y, fuera, una obra de la envergadura de *Al filo del agua* del mejicano Agustín Yáñez.

La producción paraguaya hay, pues, que estudiarla en una doble vertiente: *intrafronteras* (como la rotula Josefina Plá) y *extrafronteras*, ya que el exilio parece ser la "condición potencial de todo paraguayo," según Rubén Bareiro Saguier.[52]

Los dos representantes de mayor calidad -Gabriel Cassacia y Augusto Roa Bastos- cuya obra queda fuera de los límites de este trabajo pues por su año de nacimiento pertenecen a la generación del 42, siguen produciendo, en la Argentina, una novelística que, por su extraordinaria calidad, sofoca y apaga lo que otros escritores paraguayos están realizando. Esto es especialmente verdadero en lo que respecta a Roa Bastos quien, con su *Yo, el Supremo*[53] ha enriquecido de modo originalísimo la narrativa hispanoamericana.

Si tomamos la magra producción novelística del Paraguay y la cotejamos con la de los países del cono sur, el saldo es desalentador. Obras como *Crónicas de una familia* (1966) de Ana Iris Chávez de Ferreira; *La quema de Judas* (1965) de Mario Halley Mora; *Imágenes sin tierra* (1965) de José Luis Appleyard; *Mancuello y la perdiz* (1965) de Carlos Villagra Marsal, *Yvypóra, el fantasma de la tierra* (1965) de Juan Bautista Rivarola Matto y *Las musarañas* (1965) de Jesús Ruiz Nestosa, hablan de un buen grado de profesionalismo de los escritores paraguayos "intrafronteras,"[54] de una toma de conciencia de los problemas con que su sociedad los confronta, pero también son claras pruebas del "exilio interior" (Roa Bastos), de la autocensura que los inhibe y que disuelve, por lo tangencial que resulta, todo propósito denunciatorio o de protesta.[55] No hay duda de que la temática se ha ensanchado, pero lo que no parece superada es la calidad literaria de un Roa o un Cassacia, ni en el modo narrativo ni en la expresividad. El problema del hallazgo de una lengua artística de neto sabor paraguayo aún parece sin resolución a pesar de que los esfuerzos son constantes y de la clara comprensión de que este problema es esencial. En este terreno, pienso que *Yo, el Supremo* está en otro plano. Superada ya por Roa la adquisición de una lengua literaria, lo que ahora él cuestiona es la limitación del elemento lingüístico. Y lo golpea para volverlo más flexible a lo que él espera del lenguaje. Roa está en una plano más hispanoamericano que paraguayo. Es evidente, luego de la lectura de las obras de los autores antes mencionados, que ellos están enfrentando la literatura con una actitud diferente, con una visión de futuro, con una necesidad de comprensión pero para construir algo distinto.

Existen, no obstante lo limitado del número y la calidad, dos nombres que se alzan por encima de los restantes: uno de estos escritores produce 'extrafronteras' pues vive en París. Me refiero a Rubén Bareiro Saguier. El otro es Lincoln Silva.

Rubén Bareiro Saguier publicó en París, y en francés, en 1972 un primer libro, *Pact de sang* y, en Caracas, ese mismo año, *Ojo por diente* -Primer Premio de la Casa de las Américas, 1971-, colección de cuentos que abarca *Pacto de sangre*. Se trata de once relatos que denuncian y que explicitan una ideología. Lo que, en mi opinión, confiere al libro superioridad sobre el resto de la producción coetánea paraguaya, es una estructura unitaria perfecta en que la realidad 'real' del Paraguay se trasmuta en una realidad artística creada verbalmente como entidad estética suficiente. A través de un mundo poético se da una interpretación de la realidad en y por su unidad con la palabra que la funda. Y la palabra en Bareiro Saguier es una metaforización en base a la lengua indígena y el resultado es una lengua que suena auténtica, natural como las cosas que describe o los seres que la hablan.

Lincoln Silva tiene en su haber, a la fecha, dos *nouvelles: Rebelión después* y *General general*.[5][6] *Rebelión* es una narración en primera persona autobiográfica de un narrador-protagonista que, en la cárcel, pasa revista a su vida. Hay desplazamientos témporo-espaciales, torturas, sexo, magia, violencia, fantasía, verismo en las denuncias de la corrupción de la policía, el ejército, el gobierno; unión del hoy con el ayer mítico. Todo en una lenguaje poético, otra vez amalgama del español y el guaraní que, aunque no alcanza la jerarquía del oído en Bareiro Saguier, conforma un libro fuerte, adulto. *General general* es la historia de un caudillo contada sarcástica y humorísticamente, con un humor negro que denuncia un entrañable mal hispanoamericano. Lo valioso del libro reside en cómo se cuenta y en el sarcasmo que, caricaturizando, desnuda la horrorosa situación política del Paraguay.

Es indudable, pues, que en el Paraguay la literatura, particularmente la narrativa, está todavía tiranizada por la situación política y por un reducido lectorado producto de una economía pobre, como así también por una débil y no-competitiva industria editorial, todo lo cual contribuye a coartar la producción y a quitarle peso cultural. Pero también es claro que esa narrativa ha dejado de ser un "fenómeno fortuito"[5][7] y que el aporte de estos narradores últimos le asegura continuidad.

Como resumen de este careo de la narrativa de los países del cono sur puede decirse:

- que el género narrativo, bajo la forma de novela o cuento, sigue predominando aunque -dentro y fuera de él- el ensayo y la poesía conciten

80

cada día más atención -de público y editoriales- por razones literarias y extraliterarias (entiéndase políticas y/o económicas);

- que, observada en dimensión panorámica, la novela de los países australes de Hispanoamérica es tan promisoria y original como la del resto del continente y no difiere mayormente de ella, aunque un tono 'populista' pudiera oponerse a uno 'barroco' (hermético) del área del Caribe;

- que estos países -como los otros hispanoamericanos- continúan afilando una lengua narrativa poética e idiosincrática pero a la vez universal.

Ahora bien, enfocada la narrativa de las dos últimas generaciones con el criterio adoptado, esto es, mirada la obra literaria en su inmanencia y considerada la despersonalización del narrador como el elemento fundamental del período, la exasperación de esa indeterminación del narrador, como se ha observado en los escritores analizados, parecería acentuar de tal modo la destrucción de los límites del género narrativo que sería lícito replantearse aquel interrogante propuesto a propósito de *Abadón*: el de si no se estará frente a la gestación de un nuevo género no conceptualizado aún, dado el estado evolutivo del fenómeno y lo imperfecto de nuestra percepción actual por la cercanía desde la que lo atisbamos.

*City College and the Graduate School,*
*The City University of New York*

## NOTAS

[1] C. Goić, "La périodization dans l'histoire de la littérature hispanoaméricaine," *Etudes littéraires* (Univ. Laval, Canada), VII, 2-3 (août-déc. 1975), 269-84.

[2] C. Goić, "Sobre la estructura del narrador en la novela contemporánea." Consultado en copia manuscrita.

[3] Walter Mignolo, "Aspectos del cambio literario. (A propósito de la *Historia de la novela hispanoamericana* de Cedomil Goić)," *Revista Iberoamericana*, XLII, 94 (en.-mar., 1976), 31-50.

[4] "Las generaciones son concebidas aquí como estructuras o sistemas de preferencias de un grupo de edad. El grupo diferenciado corresponde a los nacidos en una zona de fechas de quince años. Su participación histórica lleva a distinguir en ellos 15 años de *gestación*, de los 30 a los 45 años y 15 años de *vigencia*, desde los 45 a los 60. La denominación de las generaciones (. . .) es la de la fecha central de la zona de 30 años de la generación." Y también: "En las generaciones hay estructuras o sistemas dominantes (. . .), tendencias secundarias (. . .), dimensiones latentes. Comprensión e incomprensión son factores decisivos del dinamismo de las generaciones. Continuidad y discontinuidad en la trabazón sistemática subrayan el carácter no ideográfico de la concepción de estas estructuras" (C. Goić, *Historia de la novela hispanoamericana,* [Santiago: Ediciones Universitarias de Valparaíso, 1972], p. 16).

[5] ". . . el superrealismo, definido por la violenta querella generacional de las literaturas de vanguardia, ha extendido su sistema a las generaciones siguientes y conseguido perfilar en la actualidad un primer período de sostenida vigencia, que muestra, a partir de aquel origen, un carácter supragneneracional" (C. Goić, *Historia*, p. 178).

"El Superrealismo [es el] modo de representación de la realidad en la época contemporánea (. . .). La visión del mundo en él está reñida con el sistema racional y causal y con todo determinismo material de los aspectos del mundo. Conlleva el mito, la poesía, lo extraordinario o fantástico (. . .), ilumina en la contradicción convencional el signo de una verdadera sobrerrealidad, descubre en la ambigüedad el resorte de una reveladora experiencia, de un conocimiento poético. En la desconexión, en la gratuidad de la motivación, en la irrisión de toda causalidad mecánica y racionalista, consolida la irrealidad del mundo por encima de toda fidelidad a la experiencia ordinaria de lo real. Presenta lo insólito e inhabitual, lo sorprendente y momentáneo. La esfera dominante de representación es la conciencia muy diversamente cualificada. Rapsódica o musicalmente estructurada, circular y dinámicamente dispuesta (. . .). No hay ya reclamo exigente de seriedad de la representación de la realidad. Es el humor el que domina la presentación de irrealidad reveladora. No se trata ya de mezcla de estilos, sino de la anulación de todo criterio o norma tradicional (. . .). Estilísticamente, por tanto, un expresionismo generalizado domina el nuevo modo de representación de la realidad. Los términos de realidad y fantasía, extrañeza o grotesco ponen el nuevo signo distintivo y la tensión configuradora del mundo representado" (C. Goić, *Historia*, pp. 14-15).

[6] ". . . es la primera generación superrealista y la definidora de un sistema nuevo como acontecimiento cuya institucionalización crece y se desarrolla como una nueva época en la historia literaria. En ella se dio antes que en ninguna otra la conciencia de la poesía y el creacionismo fundamental de la nueva novela. Sus figuras principales se cuentan entre las más originales e innovadoras y su significación no es ni siquiera discutida. Sus grandes poetas y narradores la convierten en la primera generación auténticamente contemporánea y universal que gravita además poderosamente en el mundo de las letras sobre América y Europa. Asturias, Borges, Carpentier, Mallea, Yáñez (. . .) son (. . .) los auténticos adelantados y fundadores de la nueva novela" (C. Goić, *Historia*, p. 181).

[7] ". . . sus características son (. . .) la proyección de mundos creados o revelados en construcciones notables, en las cuales se acentúa la indeterminación de lo real y la incoherencia del tipo de narrador (. . .), el Neorrealismo de esta generación debe verse en una doble dimensión contradictoria: nuevo realismo frente a nueva realidad. Es, además, el conflicto a que se enfrentó la generación y el origen de su crisis interna" (C. Goić, *Historia*, pp. 181-82).

[8] Pertenecen a ella los escritores nacidos entre 1920 y 1934.

[9] Resumimos conceptos de C. Goić en la primera parte de su *Historia de la novela hispanoamericana*.

[10] Una elección es siempre un acto subjetivo, por lo que los autores escogidos para este somero panorama contrastativo serán discutibles. Soy consciente, pues, de las reservas con que puede acogerse mi nómina. Empero, la disyuntiva entre el mero catálogo y el detenimiento en unas pocas figuras relevantes, hace preferible correr el riesgo. Agrego, a los nombres que considero más destacados, algún otro que merece notarse. Reservo para los notas, en cada caso, la mención de los nombres de otros integrantes de la generación.

[11] la. ed. (Barcelona: Seix Barral, 1970).

[12] Jorge Edwards, *El patio*, cuentos (1952); *Gente de la ciudad*, cuentos (1961); *Las máscaras*, cuentos (1967); *El peso de la noche* (1971); *Persona non grata* (1973).

Margarita Aguirre, *El huésped* (1958); *La culpa* (1964); *El residente* (1967); *La oveja roja* (1974).

Jorge Guzmán, *Job-Boj* (1968).

Enrique Lafourcade, *El libro de Kareen* (1950); *Pena de muerte* (1952); *Asedio. La muerte del poeta* (1956); *Para subir al cielo* (1958); *La fiesta del Rey Acab* (1959); *El príncipe y las ovejas* (1961); *Fábulas de Lafourcade* (1963); *Invención a dos voces* (1963); *Pronombres personales* (1967); *Frecuencia modulada* (1968); *Palomita Blanca* (1971); *En el fondo* (1973); *Salvador Allende* (1973); *Variaciones sobre el tema de Nastasia Filíppovna y el Príncipe Mishkin* (1975).

Hernán Valdés, *Cuerpo creciente* (1966); *Zoom* (1971).

[13] Hugo Correa, *Los Altísimos* (1959); *Alguien mora en el viento* (1959); *El que merodea en la lluvia* (1962); *Los títeres* (1969).

[14] A. Skármeta, "De la sangre al petróleo" en *Novios y solitarios*; E. Galeano, "Los fantasmas del día del león" en el libro de igual título.

[15] Buenos Aires: Fabril Editora, 1971.

[16] Ibid., "Borrador de un reportaje," p. 9.

[17] Ahora rehecha y publicada bajo el título *Annabella: novela en forma de cuentos: "El pentágono,"* pasado en limpio por el autor (Buenos Aires: Orión, 1974).

[18] Buenos Aires: Ediciones Doble P, 1956.

[19] *El silenciero* (Buenos Aires: Troquel, 1964). *Los suicidas* (Buenos Aires: Sudamericana, 1969).

[20] Manuel Puig, *La traición de Rita Hayworth* (Buenos Aires: J. Alvarez, 1968); *Boquitas pintadas* (Buenos Aires: Sudamericana, 1969); *The Buenos Aires Affair* (México: J. Mortiz, 1973); *El beso de la mujer araña* (Barcelona: Planeta, 1976).

[21] Marco Denevi, *Rosaura a las 10* (1955); *Ceremonia secreta*, cuentos (1965); *Falsificaciones* (1966); *Un pequeño café* (1966); *Parque de diversiones* (1970); *Los locos y los cuerdos* (1976).

Un ejemplo extremo del lenguaje como "la textura íntima de la narración" lo da la narrativa de Néstor Sánchez: *Escuchando a tu hijo* (1963); *Nosotros dos* (1966); *Siberia Blues* (1967); *El amhor, los orsinis y la muerte* (1969); *Cómico de la lengua* (1973).

[22] Macedonio Fernández pertenece a la generación de 1897 pero su obra sólo ha empezado a ejercer influjo 'directo' (y no a través de Borges) desde su exhumación editorial en 1967. Lo mismo sucede con Juan Filloy: nacido en 1894 pertenece, por lo tanto, a la generación del 27 pero su obra, realizada y publicada en pequeñas ediciones en los 30, no fue masivamente conocida hasta 1967.

[23] Otros nombres de esta generación: Haroldi Conti, *La causa* (1960); *Sudeste* (1962); *Todos los veranos* (1964); *Alrededor de la jaula* (1966); *Con otra gente*, cuentos (1967); *En vida* (1971).

Sara Gallardo, *Enero* (1958); *Pantalones azules* (1963); *Los Galgos, los galgos* (1968); *Eisejuaz* (1971).

María Granata, *Los viernes de la eternidad* (1971); *Los tumultos* (1974).

Beatriz Guido, *La casa del ángel* (1955); *La caída* (1956); *Fin de fiesta* (1958); *El incendio y las vísperas* (1964); *Escándalos y soledades* (1970). Cuentos: *La mano en la trampa* (1961); *Los insomnes* (1973).

Marta Lynch, *La alfombra roja* (1962); *Al vencedor* (1965); *La Sra. Ordóñez* (1968); *El cruce del río* (1972); *Un árbol lleno de manzanas* (1974). Cuentos: *Cuentos tristes* (1967); *Los dedos de la mano* (1976).

Daniel Moyano, *Una luz muy lejana* (1966); *El oscuro* (1968); *El trino del diablo* (1974). Cuentos: *Artistas de variedades* (1960); *El monstruo y otros cuentos* (1967); *Mi música es para esta gente* (1970).

H. A. Murena, *La fatalidad de los cuerpos* (1955); *Las leyes de la noche* (1958); *Los herederos de la promesa* (1965); *Epitalámica* (1969); *Polispuercón* (1970).

Cuentos: *El primer testamento* (1946); *El centro del infierno* (1956); *El Coronel de caballería y otros cuentos* (1971).

Elvira Orphée, *Dos veranos* (1956); *Uno* (1960); *Aire tan dulce* (1967); *En el fondo* (1969); *Su demonio preferido* (1973).

Pedro Orgambide, *Mitología de la adolescencia* (1948); *El encuentro* (1957); *Las hermanas* (1959); *Memorias de un hombre de bien* (1964); *El páramo* (1965); *Historias cotidianas y fantásticas* (1965); *Los inquisidores* (1967); *La buena gente* (1970).

David Viñas, *Cayó sobre su rostro* (1955); *Los dueños de la tierra* (1959); *Dar la cara* (1962); *En la semana trágica* (1966); *Los años despiadados* (1956); *Un dios cotidiano* (1958); *Los hombres de a caballo* (1967); *Cosas concretas* (1969). Cuentos: *Las malas costumbres* (1963).

²⁴*Abadón el Exterminador* (Buenos Aires: Sudamericana, 1974). *Libro de Manuel* (Buenos Aires: Sudamericana, 1973).

²⁵Influjo, el de Cortázar, debido casi exclusivamente a *Rayuela* y a sus libros de cuentos o a los misceláneos que contienen gran parte de su poética como *Vuelta al día* ... y *Ultimo Round* y no a las dos novelas publicadas con posterioridad a *Rayuela*, esto es, *62. Modelo para armar* y *Libro de Manuel* que fueron recibidas, por razones extraliterarias, en forma negativa, en general, en la Argentina.

²⁶Por ej., en José Donoso, Haroldi Conti, Syria Poletti, Abelardo Castillo, Antonio Di Benedetto, Abel Posse, Fernando Sánchez Sorondo, etc.

²⁷*Cfr.* Reseña por David W. Foster, *Revista Iberoamericana*, XLI, 90 (en.-mar. 1975), 148-50.

²⁸Adolfo Bioy Casares, *La invención de Morel* (1940); *Plan de evasión* (1945); *El sueño de los héroes* (1954); *Diario de la guerra del cerdo* (1969); *Dormir al sol* (1973). Cuentos: *El perjurio de la nieve* (1945); *La trama celeste* (1948); *Homenaje a Fco. Almeyra* (1954); *Historia prodigiosa* (1956); *Guirnalda con amores* (1959); *El lado de la sombra* (1962); *El gran serafín* (1967).

²⁹1a. ed. (México: Siglo XXI, 1971).

³⁰Otros nombres de autores uruguayos de esta generación:

Anderssen Banchero, *Mientras amanece* (1963); *El otro. Un breve verano* (1967).

Hiber Conteris, *Cono Sur* (1963); *Virginia en flashback* (1966).

José Pedro Díaz, *El habitante* (1949); *Tratados y ejercicios* (1954); *Los fuegos de San Telmo* (1965); *Partes de naufragios* (1969).

Sylvia Lago, *Trajano* (1962); *Tan solos en el balneario* (1962); *Detrás del rojo* (1967); *La última razón* 1968).

Carlos Maggi, *La trastienda* (1957); *La biblioteca* (1958); *El patio de la torcaza* (1967); *Cuentos de humoramor* (1967).

Jorge Musto, *Un largo silencio* (1965); *Noche de circo* (1966); *La decisión* (1967); *Aproximación al ángel* (1971). Cuentos: *Nosotros, otros* (1971).

Alberto Paganini, *Confesiones de un adolescente* (1965).

Juan Carlos Somma, *Clovis* (1961); *Forma de piel* (1967).

³¹"La opción creadora que ejercen al seleccionar las formas que constituyen ( . . .) la razón de ser genérica de la novela que escriben, es clara y definida y, por ello mismo, no rinden servilismo alguno a lo ajeno y tradido, sino que, muy por el contrario, con su aparición genuina despliegan su actitud creadora, innovadora, polémica, que modifica y destruye la herencia, para recrearla en otro estadio de la eterna metamorfosis.

Las asunciones concretas del acervo contemporáneo alcanzan a la concepción de la literatura y de la obra literaria, a los modos de representación de la realidad, a la retórica y al lenguaje del superrealismo, a su matización irrealista, actual y vigente.

Todo, sin embargo, resulta más enfático, más lúdico, más libre y desenvuelto, más desenfadado y cínico, fresco y, por momentos, descarado (. . .).

Algo de lo más original reside en la opción ejercida (. . .) sobre una esfera de la realidad y un modo de experiencia (. . .) bien definido: el mundo de la infancia y especialmente de la adolescencia. (. . .). Las consecuencias de la contemplación de lo real a la luz de la perspectiva adolescente son novedosas. En la novela joven se representa un mundo eminentemente inestable (. . .). De esta manera la representación se dinamiza en extremo (. . .). El mundo (. . .) no es nunca un cosmos acabado: es siempre una suerte de creación en estado naciente, imbuida de ludismo y de imaginación extremada.

Los personajes, como las situaciones y el espacio, resultan contradictorios, equívocos, mutantes.

La indeterminación temporal es igualmente una norma y se expresa en la inconexión apabullante del discurso narrativo: el flujo verbal lleno de recurrencias; una yuxtaposición de modos de decir, *bricolages*, oscilaciones y anacolutos (. . .). La disposición narrativa es más musical que nunca antes, pero es sincopada, disonante y da lugar a variadas y a veces extensas improvisaciones, en las cuales se tratan una y otra vez los mismos motivos y/o variaciones (. . .). La novela de los jóvenes novelistas se configura dentro de la conciencia de irrealidad del mundo narrado, de la esencial imaginariedad de la creación novelística" (C. Gioć, *Historia*, pp. 275-77).

[32] He incorporado a Antonio Skármeta -cuentista- a pesar de haberme limitado hasta aquí a la novela, porque su valor lo justifica. Mis observaciones se basan en la lectura de todos sus cuentos y del fragmento que de su novela -*Soñé que la nieve ardía*- apareció en *Hispamérika*, IV, 11-12 (1975), pp. 168-72. La novela ha sido ahora publicada: Barcelona: Planeta, 1976. Sus obra comprende: *El entusiasmo* (Santiago: Zig-Zag, 1967); *Desnudo en el tejado*, 1a. ed. (La Habana: Casa de las Américas, 1969); *Tiro libre*, 1a. ed. (Buenos Aires: Siglo XXI, 1973); *Novios y solitarios* (Buenos Aires: Losada, 1975).

[33] Cf. Nicolás Rosa, "La felicidad de la letra," *Los Libros*, I, 4 (oct. 1969), 12-13.

[34] En *Desnudo en el tejado*.

[35] N. Rosa, "La felicidad de la letra," p. 13.

[36] En *Desnudo en el tejado*.

[37] "Pajarraco" de *Desnudo en el tejado* en *Novios y solitarios*, p. 153.

[38] Otros escritores chilenos de esta generación:

Poli Délano, mayormente cuentista, con tres novelas: *Cuadrilátero* (1962); *Cero a la izquierda* (1966); *Cambalache* (1968).

Cristián Hunneus, *Las dos caras de Jano* (1962); *La casa del algarrobo* (1968); *Cuentos de cámara*, (1960).

Juan Agustín Palazuelos, (1936-1969), *Según el orden del tiempo* (1962); *Muy temprano para Santiago* (1965).

Rodrigo Quijada, *Bajo un silencio* (1963); *Graduación* (1970).

Claudio Trobo, *Sin horizonte* (1963); *Los amigos* (1963); *El invitado* (1965); *Dorsal 10* (1972); *Junto a lo anterior* (1968); *Ciudad al Sur* (1968).

Mauricio Wacquez, *Cinco y una ficciones* (1963); *Toda la luz del medio día* (1967); *Excesos* (1969).

[39] Esas obras son: *Caballos* (Buenos Aires: Paidós, 1968); *Para comerte mejor* (Buenos Aires: Losada, 1968); *Fabulario* (Buenos Aires: Losada, 1969); *Carta abierta a Buenos Aires violenta* (Buenos Aires: Emecé, 1970); *Guía de pecadores* (Buenos Aires: Losada, 1972); *La hora de María y el pájaro de oro*, relatos (Buenos Aires: Losada, 1975); *Será por eso que la quiero tanto* (Buenos Aires: Emecé, 1975).

[40] C. Goić, *Historia de la novela hispanoamericana*.

[41] Frases de una carta que Gudiño Kieffer me envió en marzo de 1974.

[42] Dice Satz en nota que precede a la novela: "*Sol*, el primer libro de una tríada que incluye las novelas *Luna* y *Tierra*, describe series de constelaciones donde los personajes tienen un movimiento doble: de rotación sobre sí mismos y de traslación con respecto a los demás. Las constelaciones son imaginarias y también los personajes. Sólo la poesía que desnuda el ojo del lector es real. Las palabras son estrellas fugaces: los hombres que las dicen, su verdadera luz" (Barcelona: Ed. Noguer, 1976), p. 13.

[43] "En mi ignorancia musical y religiosa, en mi torpeza y desesperación, en la causa cuya consecuencia es mi presente *aquí*, no estoy solo, ni triste, ni temo la distancia que me separa para siempre de ti, y todavía de Dios. Sé (. . .) que este acto se apoya en la *Kawanah* kabalística, en su intención más profunda, puente que el creyente traza entre su insignificancia y la grandeza divina. Sé que hay dos clases de encuentro con El: por temor o por amor, y que el mío es un encuentro de amor (. . .). Nada me apartará ahora de este amor que produce y continúa todo (. . .). En la Jerusalén Alta no se venden periódicos y, en realidad, nadie lee (. . .). *Aquí* no hay judíos, cristianos o musulmanes. *Aquí* hay solamente ángeles: hombres que han trascendido, por una muerte justa o un amor absoluto, los límites de las murallas" (Satz, p. 110). (El subrayado es del autor.)

[44] Otro poeta de cuerda mística que novela es Fernando Sánchez Sorondo: *Piedra libre para Flavia* (1968); *Por orden de azar* (s.a.); *Jardín de invierno* (1976).

Otros narradores argentinos de esta generación:

Marcos Aguinis, *Refugiados* (1969); *La cruz invertida* (1970).

Jorge Asís, *Don Abel Zalim* (1972); *Los reventados* (1975). Cuentos: *La manifestación* (1974).

Germán Leopoldo García, *Nanina* (1968); *Cancha Rayada* (1970).

Amelia Jamilis, *Detrás de las columnas* (1967).

Osvaldo Lamborghini, *El fiord* (1969); *Sebregondi retrocede* (1973).

Héctor Lastra, *La boca de la ballena* (1973). Cuentos: *Cuentos de mármol y hollín* (1965); *De tierra y escapularios* (1969).

Héctor Libertella, *El camino de los hiperbóreos* (1968); *Aventuras de los Miticistas* (1971); *Personas en pose de combate* (1975).

Ricardo Martín, *Los ojos y la boca* (1970).

Juan José Saer, *Responso* (1964); *La vuelta completa* (1967); *Cicatrices* (1969). Cuentos: *En la zona* (1960); *Palo y hueso* (1965); *Unidad de lugar* (1967).

Rubén Tizziani, *Las galerías* (1969); *Los borrachos en el cementerio* (1974).

Luisa Valenzuela, *Hay que sonreír* (1966); *El gato eficaz* (1972). Cuentos: *Los heréticos* (1967).

[45] Son de su autoría otros dos libros a los que no he tenido acceso: *Indicios pánicos* (Montevideo: Nuestra América, 1970); *Tarde de dinosaurios* (Barcelona: Planeta, 1976), con prólogo de Julio Cortázar.

[46] Angel Rama, *La generación crítica. 1939-1969* (Montevideo: Arca, 1972), p. 244.

[47] La novela fue publicada, simultáneamente, por la Casa de las Américas en La Habana, por Sudamericana en Buenos Aires, por Hermes en México y por Edhasa en Barcelona, en 1975. He manejado esta última edición.

[48] Hugo Verani, "Los restos del naufragio: *La canción de nosotros* de Eduardo Galeano," artículo aún inédito.

[49] Otros autores uruguayos de esta generación:

Fernando Aínsa, *El testigo* (1964); *En la orilla* (1966); *Con cierto asombro* (1968); *De papá en adelante* (1970).

Enrique Estrázulas, *Pepe Corvina* (1974); *Los viejísimos cielos*, cuentos (1975).
Mario Levrero, *La máquina de pensar en Gladys*, cuentos (1970); *La ciudad* (1970).

[50] Augusto Roa Bastos, "Pasión y expresión de la literatura paraguaya," *Universidad* (Sta. Fe, Argentina), 44 (abr.-jun. 1966), p. 167.

[51] "Situación de la cultura paraguaya en 1965," *Cuadernos*, 100 (sept. 1965), p. 151.

[52] "El tema del exilio en la narrativa paraguaya contemporánea," *Caravelle*, 14 (1970), pp. 79-96.

[53] Augusto Roa Bastos, *Yo, el Supremo* (Buenos Aires: Sudamericana, 1974).

[54] La fecha de publicación de todas estas novelas -excepto *Crónicas de una familia*- es 1965, año excepcionalmente fructífero, pero sus autores pertenecen a dos generaciones diferentes: la del 57 y la del 72 (sólo Ruiz Nestosa.) Sin embargo, debido a las especiales circunstancias político-económicas en que se ha desenvuelto la vida literaria intrafronteras -determinantes de la asincronía mencionada- he vacilado en incorporar a los novelistas paraguayos al esquema generacional de Goić. Este es problema que demanda un replanteo hecho con más tiempo y espacio. Remito, entonces, al único intento de ordenación generacional que de la literatura paraguaya se ha hecho, el de Rubén Bareiro Saguier, "El criterio generacional en la literatura paraguaya," *Revista Iberoamericana*, XXX, 58 (jul.-dic. 1964), 293-303. Su periodización difiere de la de Goić ya que él no parte de una concepción inmanente de la obra literaria sino de presupuestos sociológicos.

[55] Josefina Plá, *Literatura paraguaya del siglo XX* (Asunción: Ediciones Comuneros, 1972), p. 45.

[56] *Rebelión después* (Buenos Aires: Tiempo Contemporáneo, 1970); *General general* (Buenos Aires: Crisis, 1976).

[57] Juan Bautista Rivarola Matto, "Algunas ideas acerca de la literatura paraguaya," *Cuadernos Americanos*, XXXI, 1 (en.-feb. 1972), 234.

# Periodization and Typology of the Novel of the Cuban Revolution

Seymour Menton

ABSTRACT

One of the most consistent policies of the Cuban Revolution has been to make that country the cultural center of all Latin America. To this end, large editions of both Cuban and Latin American books have been published; annual prizes in the different literary genres have been periodically awarded by international selection committees to Cubans and non-Cubans: the editorial committee of the journal *Casa de las Américas* has included many outstanding non-Cubans and many issues of the journal have featured the works of young authors from Colombia, Venezuela, Chile, and other Latin American countries.

Within that policy, however, significant changes have occurred since the initial triumph of the Revolution in January 1959. These changes are intimately linked to Cuba's internal politics as well as to its international relations. The novel, because it reflects society more directly than the other literary genres, has been particularly susceptible to official changes in government policy. In fact, in spite of all the dangers of rigid classification, I maintain that the production of Cuban novels may be divided into four clearly discernible chronological periods: 1959-60, 1961-65, 1966-71, 1972-77. Although the degree of adherence to the regime varies from one chronological group of novels to the next, some individual variations make the establishment of a typology more complicated than the periodization.

In evaluating the individual novels as well as the total novelistic production, one must measure the Cuban Revolution against pre-revolutionary Cuba, other revolutionary regimes throughout the world, and other contemporary non-revolutionary regimes in Latin America. (SM)

It is both paradoxical and at the same time totally predictable that the current institutionalization of the Cuban Revolution should be accompanied by a most restrictive policy towards the arts. Since the failure to harvest ten million tons of sugar cane in 1970, greater emphasis has been placed on economic and political planning, Fidel Castro's charismatic role has been reduced, and the regime has been stabilized. During 1976 the first

87

national convention of the Cuban Communist Party was held and the first revolutionary constitution was written. Since the revolutionary government is perhaps more secure today than in any previous moment during the past eighteen years, it is indeed paradoxical that writers are not allowed greater freedom. The so-called friends of the Cuban Revolution are fond of quoting Fidel Castro's June 1961 words, "Dentro de la Revolución, todo; contra la Revolución, nada,"[1] in order to convince doubters that widespread freedom, provided that it is not counterrevolutionary, does exist in Cuba today. However, ingenious as the slogan may be, it no longer represents the official policy towards the arts. In fact, there is some question as to whether it ever did constitute the official government policy. The current ten-point policy was formulated at the First National Convention of Education and Culture held in Havana in April 1971 and reaffirmed at the 1976 Communist Party Convention[2] although, the general attitude towards the role of the writer was first expressed and officially adopted at the October 1968 meeting of the Union of Cuban Writers and Artists in Cienfuegos. Without a clear awareness of these ten points, it would be difficult to explain the absolute dearth of Cuban novels since 1971 in contrast to the abundance during the 1960's:

1. Art is an instrument of the Revolution.
2. Culture in a socialist society is not the exclusive property of an elite but rather the activity of the masses.
3. The Revolution frees art and literature from the bourgeois law of supply and demand and provides the means for expression based on ideological rigor and high technical standards.
4. The ideological formation of young writers and artists in Marxism-Leninism is an important task for the Revolution.
5. Works of art will be judged politically according to their usefulness to man and society. A work without human content can have no aesthetic value.
6. Art and literature are valuable means of training youth within the revolutionary morality, which excludes selfishness and the typical aberrations of bourgeois culture.
7. A cultural movement should be promoted among the teachers, emphasizing children's literature and educational and cultural radio and television programs for children.
8. An apolitical attitude toward culture is despicable and reactionary.
9. The rules governing national and international literary contests will have to be revised as well as the criteria for awarding prizes and the analysis of the revolutionary credentials of the judges.
10. Great care must be exercised in order to avoid inviting foreign writers and intellectuals whose works and ideologies are in conflict with the interests of the Revolution.[3]

As a result of the 1971 policy, no Cuban novel has been awarded the Premio Casa de las Américas since Manuel Cofiño López's socialist realist *La última mujer y el próximo combate* was so honored in 1971. As an example of how the prizes are being utilized for political purposes, the three novels chosen for prizes in the 1976 competition were: *Wages Paid* by the Jamaican James Carnegie; *Ikael Torass* by the Guayanan Noel D. Williams—both reflecting Cuba's recent attempts to increase its influence in Africa and the Caribbean—and *Klail City y sus alrededores* by Rolando Hinojosa, a Chicano writer from Texas. Since 1971, no Cuban volume of short stories has received the Casa de las Américas first prize. Since 1971, very few, if any at all, Cuban novels have been published in Cuba and none has attracted international attention since *La última mujer y el próximo combate.*

Although there is an apparent inconsistency in the almost total disappearance of Cuban prose fiction at a time when the revolutionary government is exuding self-confidence over its economic recovery, its increasing trade with Canada and several Latin American countries, and its military and political success in Angola, this inconsistency becomes perfectly understandable when the history of the revolutionary government in Cuba is compared to that of the other socialist nations of today and also to the revolutionary governments of France in the 1790's and of Mexico in the 1920's.

In France, changes of policy occurred much more quickly than in Cuba. The success of the Revolution in 1789 brought about the immediate demise of many of the Old Regime institutions including the highly prestigious Academy. It was not replaced, however, until 1793 when artist Jacques Louis David founded the *Commune des Arts*, a free and democratic artists' association. However, it was in turn replaced by the *Société populaire et républicaine des Arts*, and shortly thereafter by the *Club révolutionnaire des Arts*, as the Revolution became more radicalized under Danton and Robespierre. In a speech to the Convention, David stated that "the cultivation of art constituted an instrument of government. . . . Each one of us is responsible to the nation for the talents he has received from nature."[4]

Although writers were less constrained and regimented under the various presidents who held office following the Mexican Revolution of 1910, the importance of literature and the arts in general as a social and political tool was early recognized. In 1915, Carrancista Félix Palavicini called for the dedication of literature to the Revolution: "The vigorous impulse which has been stirring our country for five years cannot be understood nor will it ever be substantiated unless it is accorded literary consecration."[5]

It was, however, in the field of mural painting rather than literature that government policy bore fruit initially. Under Secretary of Education José Vasconcelos (1920-1924) and later, Diego Rivera, José Clemente Orozco, and David Alfaro Siqueiros were commissioned to cover the walls of many public buildings with panoramic murals that linked revolutionary heroes Madero, Carranza, and Zapata (Villa was purposely omitted) to their predecessors who fought for similar revolutionary ideals: Juárez, Morelos, Hidalgo, and Cuauhtémoc. This mythmaking process did not appear at first in the Mexican novel, probably because adequate techniques were not yet readily available. Vasconcelos' successor as secretary of education, José Manuel Puig Casauranc, promised to continue the former's policies and committed the government specifically to the promotion of realistic literature: "The Secretariat of Education will publish and will assist the divulgation of any Mexican work in which the mannered decoration of a false understanding of life is replaced by the other kind of decoration, rough and severe and often gloomy, but always truthful, taken from life itself."[6] This statement notwithstanding, Bernardo Ortiz de Montellano, the editor of the avant-garde journal *Contemporáneos*, commented in 1929 that "unlike the works written in the Soviet Union, Mexican literature of the Revolution does not reflect any particular social dogma." He argues that "the works of Mariano Azuela and Martín Luis Guzmán are masterpieces because they are not propagandistic."[7] Indeed, quite a number of the Mexican novels of the 1930's as well as Rodolfo Usigli's play *El gesticulador* were openly critical of the corruption of revolutionary ideals. If we leap into the 1970's, despite all the public criticism that the Mexican government has received for its authoritarianism, the publication of recent works by Octavio Paz, Carlos Fuentes, Rodolfo Usigli, René Avilés Fabila,[8] and many others bears witness to the degree of intellectual freedom prevalent in Mexico today in sharp contrast with the situation in Cuba—and I might add, in many of the military dictatorships of the right, namely Chile, Brazil, Paraguay, Guatemala, and others.

The circumstances surrounding the evolution of the arts in Cuba seem to be following the pattern established by the Soviet Union and China of a decade of relative freedom, followed by an absolute demand for the artist's positive incorporation into the Revolution. Between 1917 and 1929, tight Soviet censorship was employed "to prevent the appearance in print of openly 'counterrevolutionary' work,"[9] but Anatoli Lunacharsky, who was responsible for Party supervision of literary and artistic affairs during the 1920's, had written: "I have said dozens of times that the Commissariat of Enlightenment must be impartial in its attitude towards the various trends of artistic life. As regards questions of artistic form, the tastes of the People's Commissar and other persons in authority should not be taken into account. All individual artists and all groups of artists should be allowed to develop freely."[10] Whereas Cuban writers have tended to avoid writing about contemporary events, the "Soviet prose of the period was, on the whole, remarkably objective in portraying the realities of the

Revolution, the Civil War, and the period of N.E.P."[11] However, in 1929 came the final defeat of all political opposition to Stalin and the attack of the fanatical Association of Proletarian Writers (RAPP) on the All-Russian Union of Soviet Writers, which included most of the best authors with varying degrees of loyalty to the regime. The charges against Boris Pilnyak, chairman of the latter organization, and Evgeni Zamyatin, the author of *We* and chairman of the Leningrad branch of the Union, were "the first application to Soviet cultural life of the technique of the campaign against certain chosen scapegoats with the object of terrorizing a whole group into submission."[12] As in Cuba's Padilla case, the charges included contact with foreigners for the publication abroad of the author's works, as well as the anti-Soviet nature of the works. The new Soviet policy also provoked serious divisions among the Intellectual Left abroad, as did the Padilla case, particularly in Paris: "Around 1930, when the aesthetic doctrine of socialist realism is being organized in an increasingly totalitarian form, the surrealist group breaks in two. Those who follow Breton will refuse to subscribe to all the aesthetic postulates from Moscow; on the other hand, Desnos will subscribe to them repeatedly."[13]

Before they gained power in 1949, the Chinese Communists debated the role of literature and revolution for many years. In 1925, Guo Mo-ruo, the leader of the Creation group and, at the time, a recent convert to Marxism, stated that the only justification for literature was its use as a propaganda instrument.[14] During the war against Japan, Mao Tse-tung reaffirmed the functional value of art. At the May 1942 Yenan Forum on Literature and Art, he stated that art cannot be isolated from political reality, that it must help the Revolution and be destined for the masses. Good revolutionary art is better than bad revolutionary art, but art must be revolutionary.[15] At about the same time, Mao urged writers "to leave their desks and concentrate on the effort to gain a truly proletarian consciousness."[16] His words could well have been directed at the Cuban writers as they joined in the universal cutting of sugar cane: "Therefore I advise those of you who have only book knowledge and as yet no contact with reality, and those who have had few practical experiences, to realize their own shortcomings and make their attitudes a bit more humble."[17]

Since 1949, the role of literature and writers has fluctuated. In the "Hundred Flowers Movement" of 1956-1957, Mao invited criticism of the regime by calling on the "hundred scholars" to contend: "The literary monopoly of the socialist regime was abrogated."[18] However, about ten years later, as in the Soviet Union and Cuba, the period of relative freedom ended abruptly with the Great Proletarian Cultural Revolution of 1966: "After years of bitter conflict with the writers, Mao appears to have concluded that it is not only writers but literature itself that is subversive."[19]

The novel, the short story, and even poetry have given way to the "true revolutionary literature: . . . an ultimate synthesis of dance, music, lyrics, drawn from the folk songs and folk tales of traditional China, blended with the true streams of a proletarian consciousness, girding itself for the final triumphant confrontation with the world of imperialism."[20]

Since 1959, the Cuban Revolution has gone through four distinct policy periods, each one with its own basic characteristics and each one reflecting directly national and international events. Since those periods are extensively delineated in my book,[21] I shall summarize them as briefly as possible.

*1959-1960*: This is the romantic period characterized by enthusiasm and spontaneity and improvisation both in government and literature. There was no clear policy towards the arts although the Casa de las Américas was founded in 1960 with the goal of making Cuba the cultural center of Latin America. The five novels published in this period are action-packed accounts of the urban clandestine struggle to overthrow Batista.

*1961-1965*: The elimination of the very successful literary journal *Lunes de Revolución* in June 1961 shortly after the Bay of Pigs invasion and Fidel Castro's proclamation that the Revolution was socialist led to a self-imposed censorship by the writers in spite of Fidel's assurances embodied in the slogan "Dentro de la Revolución, todo; contra la Revolución, nada." Novelistic production increased but writers limited themselves to criticism of the pre-revolutionary society, or in other words, to exorcising the past.

*1966-1970*: The publication in 1966 of Lezama Lima's highly sensual *Paradiso* and Jesús Díaz's collection of stories *Los años duros* with their sprinkling of obscenities heralded the relaxation of official restraints on Cuban writers. Novelistic production skyrocketed in terms of quantity and quality as Cuba joined the mainstream of the Latin American literary boom. This period of relative freedom and stylistic exuberance reflects Cuba's short-lived independence from the Soviet Union and her attempts to become the leader of the Third World countries. This period ended in August 1968 with Fidel Castro's qualified approval of the Soviet intervention in Czechoslovakia. In spite of the ensuing bitter controversy involving poet Heberto Padilla, dramatist Antón Arrufat, novelist Cabrera Infante, and others, the flow of highly experimental novels did not actually stop until the end of 1970.

*1971-1977*: We are now in the sixth year of the longest of the four distinct policy periods. Its characteristics promulgated in 1971 still hold true today as indicated by the most recent issues of *Casa de las Américas*.

Although I think that the historical approach is the best way to understand the novel of the Cuban Revolution, an added dimension may be gained by classifying the works according to their degree of commitment to the Revolution. Viewed in this perspective, a broad spectrum appears ranging from dogmatic propaganda to rather thinly veiled criticism that to some extent cuts across the chronological lines.

The most notorious of the pro-revolutionary novels was *Maestra voluntaria* (1962) by Daura Olema García (b. 1937) which, in spite of its total absence of artistry, was awarded the 1962 Casa de las Américas prize for the best novel of the year, Alejo Carpentier's *El siglo de las luces* notwithstanding. The purpose of *Maestra voluntaria* was twofold: to capture the tremendous revolutionary enthusiasm generated by the 1961 campaign to eliminate illiteracy and to promote support for communism and the Soviet Union in the period between the April 1961 Bay of Pigs invasion and the October 1962 Missile Crisis. The novel focuses on the conversion to communism of a volunteer teacher who is willing to leave her child with her mother in order to participate in the vigorous physical training and Communist indoctrination program. Atheism and the political economy of the Soviet Union are stressed. Even the personality cult of Fidel Castro is reduced for the sake of achieving communism: "The Revolution is in all of us, in the people, and don't forget that although Fidel is very useful, he is not indispensable for the Revolution to forge ahead."[22]

Even though Cuban novels became much more sophisticated in the 1966-1970 period, the unequivocal adherence to the regime may be seen in *Los niños se despiden* (1968) by Pablo Armando Fernández, who ironically fell under attack the following year for some critical remarks about the Cuban cultural scene delivered over TV. The novel was awarded the 1968 Casa de las Américas prize, at least partially, for its emphasis on the Ten Years War of 1868-1878; the centennial was being officially celebrated with every effort made to establish the continuity of the revolutionary movement from 1868 to 1959. The novel itself is a highly imaginative Dos Passos-like, or Diego Rivera-like, panorama of the Cuban nation from 1498 to the present. At the end of the twenty-sixth (in deference to the July 26 movement) and final chapter, the novel closes with a section deifying Fidel Castro and thus forming a new revolutionary trinity: the Luz de Yara (1868), the martyr Martí (1895) and Fidel Castro (1959): "Here he is seated on a white horse and he is called Faithful and True and he judges justly and struggles onward."[23] Nonetheless, the propagandistic aspects of the novel are definitely outweighed by the serious, if not always successful, attempts at linguistic and structural experimentation characteristic of the mainstream Latin American novels of 1968.

As a result of the official government policy change towards the arts promulgated by the UNEAC in October 1968 and reinforced by Fidel in 1971, the 1970 and 1971 Casa de las Américas prizes were awarded to two official novels, which, although certainly more sophisticated artistically than *Maestra voluntaria*, were also far less hermetic than *Los niños de despiden*. They were *Sacchario* by Miguel Cossío Woodward and *La última mujer y el próximo combate* by Manuel Cofiño López.

Although *Sacchario*'s one day in the life of a volunteer cane cutter takes place in April 1965, the novel was undoubtedly inspired by the supreme but unsuccessful effort to harvest ten million tons of sugar cane by 1970. However, the sugar-cane harvest is only the structural framework for the real theme, namely, the making of a revolutionary correlated with an official revolutionary view of Cuban history from the 1930's to 1965. The sterotyped vision of the 1930's, 1940's and 1950's emphasizes the all-pervasive American influence. The protagonist Darío participates in the clandestine struggle against Batista and then goes to the Sierra Maestra where he joins the revolutionaries. Once the Revolution is successful, Darío starts on the long, difficult road to socialism. He realizes that sex and love are obstacles. His socialist conscience grows with the combined fear and faith produced by the 1962 Missile Crisis. In order to be a true revolutionary, Darío rebels "against the mediocre lie of home and family,"[24] and against his ivory-tower name in order to become a cane cutter. Besides Darío, the second most important character is his cane-cutting partner, the older illiterate Negro Papaíto, whose experiences on a prerevolutionary sugar plantation, on the docks, in a circus, and in the Tropicana Nightclub as well as his familiarity with Afro-Cuban super-stitions broaden the vision of Cuba's past.

Although the three novels just discussed represented the official point of view at the time that they were written, they are not representative of the majority of the novels which are not that blatantly propagandistic. In fact, the majority of the novels, especially in the second and third chrono-logical periods, cover a broad range of themes and styles, including science fiction, humorous *costumbrismo*, and esoteric linguistic experimentation. However, since this paper is focusing on revolutionary attitudes expressed in the novel, I should like to proceed from the clearly prorevolutionary or propagandistic novel to the somewhat ambiguous novel and then to a clearly anti-revolutionary novel.

One of the most popular Cuban novels of the Revolution was Edmundo Desnoes' 1965 *Memorias del subdesarrollo*, which was made into a film and then widely distributed. The novel's success was undoubtedly due to the great sincerity with which the bourgeois anti-hero of the Revolution is portrayed. Although the theme of exorcising the past was typical of many of the 1961-1965 novels, Desnoes was more successful because he concen-trated on the personal experiences of only one man. The narrator is the typical existentialist hero or anti-hero. His wife, relatives, and friends have left Cuba but he remains, lonely and alienated. Although he recognizes all the negative aspects of prerevolutionary bourgeois life and despises all its representatives, he cannot liberate himself from his past and clings to such bourgeois habits as maintaining a lower-class mistress and complaining about the shortage of consumer goods. In true existentialist style, the protagonist is so obsessed with his own inner world that outside reality is reduced to an apparently insignificant role. Nevertheless, the novel acquires historical significance by the narrator's relating his own problems to an analysis of the Cuban national character and its possible consequences for the Revolution: "All the Cuban's talent is spent in adapting to the circumstances of the moment. In appearances, people don't follow through, they don't maintain for long the same feelings, they don't follow things through to their ultimate consequences. The Cuban can't suffer very long without bursting out into laughter. The sun, the tropics, the irresponsibility . . . can Fidel be that way? I don't think so, but . . . I don't want to be disillusioned again. At best, I can be a witness, a spectator."[25]

Although these doubts about the Revolution and about Fidel come from a negative character, one who collects a monthly stipend from the Reforma Urbana even though he refuses to participate in the revolutionary process, the sincerity with which they are expressed raises real doubts about the author's unswerving loyalty to the regime. Desnoes' narrator seems to be in agreement with Vargas Llosa when he states that the role of the artist, whether it be in a capitalist or socialist society is to criticize. Desnoes puts it even more bluntly: "The artist, the true artist (you know it, Eddy), will always be an enemy of the state."[26]

In addition to this confessional-type novel, two other works published within the following two years may also be considered ambiguous in their revolutionary enthusiasm. *Vivir en Candonga* (1966), which received the UNEAC prize for 1965, deals somewhat ambiguously with the responsibility of the individual to society. The protagonist is the butterfly-collecting naturalist Waldo Utiello who is totally oblivious to the proximity of Fidel Castro and his revolutionary guerrillas in the nearby Sierra Maestra. Even though Fidel himself upbraids the "mad scientist" for not knowing in which world he's living, the suggested resemblance between Utiello and Don Quijote makes Utiello's commitment to his scientific research more commendable. The novel was apparently criticized by some of the cultural bureaucrats causing literary pundit José Antonio Portuondo to defend the UNEAC decision: "It's originality was in the way it utilized techniques and language from the novel of the absurd for an absolutely realistic theme. which boils down to a sharp satire of the intellectual surprised by the Revolution. This satirical and absurd manner of expressing a fundamental problem besetting our present Cuban reality was destined to cause and will continue to cause irritation among many people.

But, for some members of the jury, at least, this is precisely one of the cardinal virtues of the novel."[27]

Another novel with a somewhat ambiguous political stance is the equally unknown *Recuerdos del 36* (1967) by Leonel López Nussa. Its experimental approach to language and structure make it representative of the 1966 to 1970 Cuban novels, while its open ridicule of doctrinaire communism reflects the official government policy of the time—which was more concerned about wooing the emerging Third World nations than of cultivating the friendship of the Soviet Union. The farcical novel takes place in the mid-1930's and, through the various members of a hold-up gang, it creates a panoramic tableau of Cuban society. Although they all belong to the Communist Youth Group, which is called Jóvenes Martianos, the doctrinaire Communist Dámaso has no compunctions about deflating José Martí for his "ideological limitations . . . Martí could have embraced the cause of proletarian internationalism. The time was ripe for it. Instead, he settled for a modest apostleship. . . . He was obsessed by the independence of Cuba, as if liberating Cuba were such a big deal. Wouldn't it have been much more glorious to liberate all mankind?"[28] Dámaso also bombastically defends socialist realism before borrowing three pesos from another member of the group, prompting the narrator to comment sarcastically: "Sir Dámaso López! . . . His only defect is being poor. But from that condition, another definite defect has reared its head: when Dámaso doesn't have any money, he asks others for it. In short, he's a sponger."[29] The author's anti-communist attitude is also revealed in his open criticism of Communist short-story writer Félix Pita Rodríguez and his praise of Carlos Montenegro, who left Cuba shortly after the triumph of the Revolution and who is rarely mentioned in Cuba today. Perhaps in keeping with the official government policy at the time, Alejo Carpentier's style is parodied in a full-page enumerative and excessively erudite description of the typical Spanish-Cuban *bodega* or grocery store.

Probably the most antirevolutionary work to be published by a writer residing in Cuba is the well-known *El mundo alucinante* (1969) by Reinaldo Arenas. Although the subject of the novel is the amazing Mexican priest Fray Servando Teresa de Mier, active during the period of the War of Independence, the fact that this novel has not yet been published in Cuba is proof that this is not an escapist historical novel. In the prologue, Arenas identifies completely with the nonconformist Fray Servando: ". . . you and I are the same person."[30] He even alludes to the problems of censorship in Cuba: "You are, dear Servando, what you are: one of the most important . . . figures of the literary and political history of America. An outstanding man. And that's sufficient grounds for some people to think that this novel should be censored."[31] Arenas apparently condemns Fidel Castro for having betrayed the ideals for which the Revolution was fought. He does so by using Fray Servando's own words in criticism of Napoleon and Augustín Iturbide, both of whom had themselves crowned emperor after gaining power through a revolution. Arenas's attitude becomes even clearer in his portrayal of Mexico's first president Guadalupe Victoria—which is not based on Fray Servando's *Memorias* nor on any other historical account. Fray Servando, Cuban poet José María Heredia, and thinly disguised Alejo Carpentier and Lezama Lima live in the presidential palace almost as court jesters. Fray Servando's choice of words in protesting against this situation are clearly intended to refer to the Cuba of 1968:

> What are we in this palace but a bunch of useless objects, museum relics, rehabilitated prostitutes. What we have done counts for nothing if we don't dance to the sound of the latest tune. It counts for nothing. And if you try to correct mistakes, you're only a traitor, and if you try to tone down the bestiality, you're only a cynical revisionist, and, if you fight for real freedom, you're courting death itself.... This constant hypocrisy, this constant repeating that we're in Paradise and that everything is perfect? And, really and truly, are we in Paradise?[32]

This novel has been well received by many critics in the United States, Europe, and Latin America, but oddly enough, as in the case of Alejo Carpentier,[33] there seems to be a reluctance to comment on the anti-revolutionary elements in works written by authors living in Cuba.

Although the staunchest defenders of the Cuban Revolution might argue that those writers and artists who grew up in pre-revolutionary times have incorrigible bourgeois mentalities and therefore should not be encouraged to continue exercising their talents, it should be noted that Reinaldo Arenas was born in 1943, was only sixteen years old in 1959, and did not publish his first book until 1967. Furthermore, Arenas belongs to the so-called second revolutionary generation comprised of writers born in the late 1930's and early 1940's, most of whom did not make their literary debuts until 1966, and who reacted against the highly ornate, highly experimental works of their predecessors. Although Jesús Díaz Rodríguez (1941), Eduardo Heras León (1941), Norberto Fuentes (1943) and others were primarily concerned with communicating directly in an objective, dynamic, fragmentary, elliptical style their personal impressions of the most heroic moments of the Revolution, they too have apparently stopped writing since 1970. Desnoes' words of 1965 seem to have been prophetic and explain why the more totalitarian the government, whether it be of the Left or the Right, the fewer the possibilities for authentic artistic creativity because: "The artist, the true artist, will always be an enemy of the state."

*University of California, Irvine*

# NOTES

[1] Fidel Castro, *Palabras a los intelectuales* (Havana: Consejo Nacional de Cultura, 1961), pp. 11, 20-21.

[2] See "Documentos del Primer Congreso del Partido Comunista de Cuba," *Casa de las Américas*, 99 (November-December 1976), 5-25.

[3] "Declaración del Primer Congreso Nacional de Educación y Cultura" and Fidel Castro, "Discurso de Clausura del Primer Congreso Nacional de Educación y Cultura in Lourdes Casal," *El caso Padilla: Literatura y revolución en Cuba* (Miami: Universal, 1971), pp. 106-120.

[4] Quoted by Arnold Hauser, *The Social History of Art* (New York: Vintage Books, n.d.), III, 148.

[5] Quoted by John Rutherford, *Mexican Society during the Revolution: A Literary Approach* (Oxford: Clarendon Press, 1971), p. 53.

[6] Ibid., pp. 57-58.

[7] Edward J. Mullen, "The Mexican Revolution in *Contemporáneos*," *The American Hispanist* (April 1976), p. 5.

[8] *Posdata, Tiempo mexicano, ¡Buenos días, señor Presidente!* and *El gran solitario de palacio.*

[9] Max Hayward, "Introduction," *Dissonant Voices in Soviet Literature* (New York: Harper and Row, 1964), p. xiii.

[10] Quoted in Hayward, *Dissonant Voices in Soviet Literature*, pp. xiv-xv.

[11] Hayward, p. xiii.

[12] Ibid., p. xvi.

[13] Emir Rodríguez Monegal, "Lo real y lo maravilloso en *El reino de este mundo*," *Revista Iberoamericana*, 37, Nos. 76-77 (July-December 1971), 627.

[14] Lucien Blanco, *Los orígenes de la revolución china* (Caracas: Tiempo Nuevo, 1970), p. 69.

[15] Mao Tse-tung, *Speeches* (Peking: Foreign Language Press, 1967), pp. 72-114.

[16] Jonathan Spence, "On Chinese Revolutionary Literature," in Jacques Ehrmann, ed. *Literature and Revolution* (Boston: Beacon Press, 1970), p. 222.

[17] Ibid.

[18] *Encyclopedia Britannica*, 1968 ed., V, 596.

[19] Quoted by Spence, "On Chinese Revolutionary Literature," in Ehrmann, p. 223.

[20] Spence, in Ehrmann, p. 224.

[21] Seymour Menton, *Prose Fiction of the Cuban Revolution* (Austin: University of Texas Press, 1975), pp. 1-122.

[22] Daura Olema García, *Maestra voluntaria* (Havana: Casa de las Américas, 1962), p. 102. This translation and subsequent ones are mine.

[23] Pablo Armando Fernández, *Los niños se despiden* (Havana: Casa de las Américas, 1968), p. 541.

[24] Miguel Cossío Woodward, *Sacchario* (Havana: Casa de las Américas, 1970), p. 245.

[25] Edmundo Desnoes, *Memorias del subdesarrollo* (Havana: Unión, 1965), p. 39.

[26] Ibid., p. 44.

[27] Ezequiel Vieta, *Vivir en Candonga* (Havana: Unión, 1966), jacket flap.

[28] Leonel López-Nussa, *Recuerdos del 36* (Havana: Unión, 1967), pp. 36-37.

[29] Ibid., p. 35.

[30] Reinaldo Arenas, *El mundo alucinante* (Mexico City: Diógenes, 1969), p. 9.

[31] Ibid., p. 10.

[32] Ibid., p. 207.

[33] See my *Prose Fiction of the Cuban Revolution*, pp. 44-46, 134; Juan Arocha, *La bala perdida* (Barcelona: Plaza y Janés, 1973), p. 60; Roberto Gonzales Echeverría, "Carpentier's Chronos-Logic," *Review 76* (Fall 1976), 9-10.

# Isaacs' *María* and Its Neoplatonic Legacy

Robert J. Morris

ABSTRACT

For more than a century Isaacs' *María* has epitomized the best of the Romantic sentimental novel in Hispanic America. Nonetheless, while critics have consistently lauded Isaacs for his original contributions to these letters, they have also been quick to substantiate his inspirational and, in some instances, his factual indebtedness to Chateaubriand's *Atala* and Saint-Pierre's *Paul et Virginia*. After years of debate, however, there is still no agreement concerning the extent to which either of these works actually served the Colombian.

Despite the continued popularity of *María* and the hundreds of critical studies it has engendered, therefore, the question of Isaacs' literary heritage still has not been answered satisfactorily, because the majority of critics have merely acknowledged the probable French influence and have been reluctant to view *María* as anything other than the best compendium of the various tenets of the Hispanic American romantic novel. In doing so, they have only reiterated those *costumbrista*, sentimental, and poetic elements that distinguish *María* from its French and Hispanic American counterparts.

Until now no one has approached Isaacs' novel as a product of the humanistic environment in which his genius was nurtured and as a reflection of his personal interests, particularly his lifelong devotion to the classic and neoclassic literatures. In addition to the obvious parallels that exist between *María* and the works cited, for instance, Isaacs' indebtedness to the neoplatonic tradition is also apparent when his novel is compared with Spain's best known pastoral novel, *La Diana* by Jorge de Montemayor. (RJM)

The first edition of *María*, by Jorge Isaacs, consisted of one hundred copies and was published in Bogotá in 1867.[1] Since that time there have been more than forty editions, not counting repeat and unauthorized printings, and the novel has become the most popular sentimental novel of all nineteenth-century Hispanic literatures. Despite its preeminence, the work has been viewed by too many critics in a myopic fashion. After

101

citing its historical importance and its autobiographical nature, most liter-arians have dwelled on Isaacs' inspirational debt to Chateaubriand or Saint-Pierre. In too many studies the conclusion is that Isaacs did little more than adapt either *Atala* (1801) or *Paul et Virginie* (1887) to the Colombian natural scene. The question of Isaacs' recourse to the French models has existed since 1867. It was made by José María Vergara y Vergara, Isaacs' mentor, in his "Juicio crítico" that served as the prologue to the second edition of *María*.[2] But Vergara rejects the influence of *Atala*, stating that, at best, it is a remote possibility based merely on the mention of the Frenchman's works, *Genie du christianism* (1802), and on some vague similarities in the idealization of the natural environment and the tragic destiny of the lovers. Regarding *Paul et Virginie*, Vergara points out that it is considerably different from *María*:

> *Pablo y Virginia* es la historia de dos niños solitarios, donde con poco esfuerzo pudo el autor pintar un amor inocente, infantil. *María* es la narración de los amores de dos jovenes, rodeados de muchas personas, viviendo en una misma casa y profundamente enamorados. Por lo tanto la pintura de su amor es más fecunda . . . más delicada por más peligrosa. *Virginia* es la pintura de un hogar excepcional, en que lo excepcional mismo constituye su principal encanto. No todos lo días se ven dos madres viudas retiradas a una isla despoblada, teni-endo la una una hija y una negra; la otra un hijo y un negro. Aquella simetría podrá ser, como es, muy bella, pero tiene que ser, como es, muy rara. (pp. 51-52)

Vergara notes other differences, but the foregoing is sufficient to evince the extent to which Isaacs' most intimate critic rejected the influence of the French models so often espoused. We might add that both of Chateau-briand's works were a defense of Christianity and reflect his study of the Holy Scriptures. *Paul et Virginia*, on the other hand, was termed a pastoral by Saint-Pierre, who published it as the fourth volume of his *Etudes de la nature* (1784-1792), renown for its nature descriptions and back-to-nature philosophy derived, in part, from Rousseau. The point is that both works are just as much a product of the humanistic tradition of eighteenth-century France as of the early Romantic philosophy.[3]

After more than one hundred years and numerous studies, the question of Isaacs' indebtedness to the French is still unresolved. Perhaps the most judicious analysis of the polemic has been tendered by Anderson-Imbert who, after recalling Efraín's love of Chateaubriand, states that, as a critic, he can neither defend nor deny the influence of *Paul et Virginie*. To paraphrase Anderson-Imbert, *María* is not indebted to any single source; it is a product of the literary and historical airs Isaacs breathed at the time in Bogotá.[4] This point is well taken because, by extending it, we are led to the question of whether *María* is more than an imitation or adaptation of another work or, even, a philosophy. The problem, of course, is to determine just what kind of historical air Isaacs may have breathed in addition to that of Romanticism emanating from European and American societies.

My purpose, then, is twofold: to reevaluate *María* in the light of influences which, in addition to the French, may have weighed upon Isaacs; and to expand the traditional interpretation of the novel as more than the archetype of Hispanic American sentimental prose fiction cast in the French, even the Western Romantic mold. As we turn to these sources of inspiration we should reiterate a point made by each of Isaacs' principal biographers—that from his earliest years as a student, he was an impassioned student of the classics. And while a basic preparation as a humanist was the rule, rather than the exception, at the time, Isaacs nurtured a profound interest in Virgil, Caesar, and, particularly, Plutarch who, on several occasions he termed his "maestro último y preferido." Little else is known of Isaacs' formal education, however, and there was nothing more than his novels, poetry, letters, and legal documentation to suggest his personal literary interests until 1941. In the *Romantic Review* of that year J. Warshaw published an article entitled "Jorge Isaacs' Library: Light on Two *María* Problems." In his brief presentation, some ten pages, Warshaw discusses the significance of the books and authors included in the scrutiny of Efraín's library and, in the second instance, concludes that "no convincing parallel can be drawn between *María* and *Paul et Virginie*."[5] For our purpose the article would be of minor significance if it were not for the inclusion of what he terms the Catalogue of Isaacs' personal library provided him by Emilio Robledo, the distinguished Colombian scholar. This Catalogue is by far the most valuable indication of Isaacs' personal literary interests and his wide range of intellectual pursuits. As Warshaw notes, the Catalogue "supplements in an objective way the critical and biographical studies of Isaacs and offers a better picture of the real Isaacs, the stages in his mental life, and the multiplicity of his interests than the majority of sketches of a biographical character written on him" (pp. 394-95). Warshaw divides the Catalogue into six general categories: Literature, Natural Sciences, History and Biography, Moral, Social and Political Subjects, Legislation, and Miscellaneous. The most extensive holdings fall under the Literature category, then Natural Sciences and History and Biography.

In the first category the only French novel is a Spanish translation of Flaubert's *Salammbô* (1862), a story inspired by the wars in ancient Carthage. English writers include Jules Verne and the critics Blaire and Macaulay. One of Isaacs' more intriguing interests, and one not generally recognized, is early Portuguese poetry, as attested by *Os Lusíadas* and lyric poetry by Camões. The Catalogue also lists a translation of the complete works of Virgil and a number of Spanish items: *La de Bringas* by Galdos,

*Gil Blas* by Padre Isla, *Tesoro del teatro español desde su origen*, several collections of early Spanish poetry, and *Tesoro del parnaso español* by the neoclassic literato Manuel José Quintana. There is also a work by the Catalan writer Jacinto Verdaguer, *La Atlántida*. The rest of this listing includes basic studies on literary history, criticism, lexicology, and rhetoric. Under the category of Natural Sciences there are more than a dozen works on geography, half that many on geology, and five on natural history, one by Humboldt. Under History and Biography there are *Biographical Studies* and *Historical Studies* by the neoclassic scholar Macaulay, and *Parallel Lives* by Plutarch. Among the works listed under Moral, Social and Political subjects Isaacs' concern with ethical philosophy is amply substantiated with translations of such basic treatises as Jeremiah Bentham's *Deontología y ciencia de la moral*, *El genio del cristianismo*, Voltaire's *La ley natural*, Tocqueville's *La democracia en América*, and others. The basic reason for dwelling on these items is to emphasize that the vast majority are of classical or neoclassical preoccupations and that of the five French writers (Flaubert, Chateaubriand, Voltaire, Tocqueville, and Volney) and of the English and Irish writers (Swift, Granville, Vernes, Shakespeare, Blaire, Macaulay, Bentham), only one, properly speaking, is Romantic.

In addition to the Catalogue, it is worthwhile to note that the intellectual and cultural environment in which Isaacs lived, from his early years as a school boy, was one of the most productive strongholds of classical humanities in Hispanic America. During his middle years, even before the publication of *María*, Isaacs was befriended and advised by the likes of Rafael Pombo who, in addition to his own poetry, manifested his classical interests with translations of a number of Latin works. Other acquaintances, most of whom belonged to El Mosaico, the foremost intellectual group in Colombia at the time, were also celebrated humanists: Rufino Cuervo, Miguel Antonio Caro, who together and individually are still celebrated for their classical investigations, translations, and semantic studies; Ezquiel Uricoechea, a philologist of considerable repute at the time; Diego Fallon; Ricardo Carrasquilla; and Rafael Núñez.

As we review the foregoing, the question of Isaacs' reliance on the French sources seems just as intriguing as the theory that *María* may well be more a product of the neoclassical tradition than heretofore has been emphasized. To be specific, it is my contention that Isaacs' literary heritage and his novel are essentially neoplatonic and that *La Diana* (1559 ?), by Jorge Montemayor, may have served as the model for *María* as much or more than did either of the French works discussed. I should reiterate that neither this sixteenth-century pastoral novel nor the French novels are mentioned in the Catalogue, the scrutiny of Efraín's library, or in any of

Isaacs' autobiographical data. So, just as the question of Isaacs' debt to the French sources cannot be rejected merely on the ground that he left no proof that he was acquainted with *Atalá* or *Paul et Virginie*, the same thesis must also hold true for *La Diana*.

Before proceeding to a comparative analysis of *La Diana* and *María* and their neoplatonic legacy, I would like to conclude my remarks on the Catalogue by pointing out those works and authors to which Isaacs may have turned or to which he may have been subconsciously indebted in the elaboration of his concept of the neoplatonic tradition.

In addition to *Parallel Lives*, Plutarch wrote *Moralia*, an extended body of miscellaneous treatises in which he extols the Platonic virtues of reverence for womanhood, tenderness for children, sympathy for animals, love, the family, and what one may term the Good Life. The majority of these essays were written after Plutarch abandoned the metropoli to retire to an obscure rural village. It was there, in the solitude and beauty of the natural environment that he could best discern the divine perfection of creation. For Plutarch, "the world is a hold and divine temple into which man is introduced at birth, not to look at motionless images, but at those things which the mind of God has brought forth as the visible images of the invisible, sun, moon, stars, fresh-flowing rivers, earth, the sustainer of all."[6] It was in the rural setting, then, that this early Platonist came to believe firmly in the reality and eternity of things not seen and rose to an intellectual vision of the eternal, unchanging Idea of Beauty.

Among the Romans, Virgil, in his *Eclogues* and *The Georgics*, strongly echoed the principles of the early Platonic philosophy while he perpetuated the pastoral tradition as come from Theocritus. Despite Isaacs' knowledge of Virgil, there is no real proof that the poet inspired the novelist, although there are a number of similarities in their major works. In the *Eclogues* and *María*, for example, the shepherds are autobiographically inspired, they speak of the confiscation of their farms, there are nationalistic overtones, and there is a romantic personification of nature. There are other similarities, but they are commonplace in bucholic literature and fail to substantiate Virgil's influence on Isaacs. Both authors, for example, use an idyllic setting, imply their disdain of cities, love Beauty, and praise the simple farming life. Among the neoclassic writers represented in the Catalogue are Fenelon, who in his *Telemachus* extols quietism and the pastoral life, and who also writes platonic works in which he seeks proof of the existence of the Diety in the wonders of nature; and the aforementioned Camões, who was significantly influenced by Virgil in his masterpiece and his pastoral lyric poetry. One of the best indications of Isaacs' concern with language is the number of studies dedicated to grammar and rhetoric and literary criticism. The most important of these is *Lecciones sobre la retórica y las bellas artes*, a translation of the original work by Hugh Blair and published in four volumes between 1798 and 1801. This work would have been of special interest to Isaacs because, in addition to the study of rhetorical devices, the last two volumes deal primarily with the pastoral poem, lyric and epic poetry, Hebrew poetry, and the works of Homer, Virgil, Lucano, Tasso, Camões, Fenelon, and Spanish epic poetry in general. The point is that Blair's work is a neoclassical treatise of, among other matters, the same platonists and neoplatonists that appear in the Catalogue. Macaulay, one of the three preferred writers of Isaacs, the others being Plutarch and Caesar, is also one of Great Britain's outstanding neoclassical intellectuals and defenders of the ancient world. In his *Literary Studies*, which Isaacs possessed, appears the *Lais of Ancient Rome*, a collection of poems and comments on sundry aspects of the early civilization. In these and other works Macaulay praised the virtuous contributions of the early Platonists and, in doing so, may have influenced Isaacs to admit the neoplatonic principles in the basic formulation of his own writings. Finally, and without wanting to belabor the Catalogue, I would like to note the presence of Swift and Shakespeare. Even though *Gulliver's Travels* is the only work by Swift mentioned, this English neoclassicist actually established his early reputation on his other works, such as *The Battle of the Books* and discourses such as the one " . . . Between the Nobles and Commoners of Athens and Rome." Shakespeare is not properly speaking a neoplatonist. However, at least half a dozen of his dramas are inspired by this philosophy or specific writers of the same. Plutarch is the most significant as seen in *Anthony and Cleopatra*, *Julius Caesar*, *Coriolanus*, and *A Midsummer Night's Dream*. Two plays are known to be influenced by the pastoral novels—*King Lear* by Sidney's *Arcadia* and *Two Gentlemen of Verona* by *La Diana*.

In addition to these insights, the relatively late publication date of *María* also points to its being more than the artificial, less sophisticated expression typical of the early Hispanic American Romantics. A few critics, in fact, have approached this idea in their discussion of *María* as a representative expression of the spiritual and thematic changes that mark the differences between the first and second generations of Romanticism in Hispanic America. The most explicit of these is Anderson-Imbert who, in his appraisal of Isaacs' generation, notes:

> Se vio entonces que algunos escritores recurrían a las luces de una literatura humanística. Es que el romanticismo no tiene ya los brillos teóricos de antes. Ahora es más bien un calmoso ejercicio práctico. Se hace literatura romántica sin ostentar beligerantemente sus fórmulas estéticas. Hay que escribir con más disciplina, con más estudio. Se busca, pues, el trato de los clásicos y los filólogos.[7]

While these comments are a generalization with regard to the cultural climate in Hispanic America at the time, they are clearly relevant to our thesis that Isaacs and his writings were the product of a neoclassical, a humanistic environment that was a receptive and fertile ground for the neoplatonic legacy Isaacs had nurtured since his early years as a student and was to reach fruition in *María*.

The vast majority who have studied the novel from a comparative point of view have been reluctant to classify *María* merely as a Romantic sentimental novel. Some critics imply that, with its lovers who live in harmony with an idyllic nature, *María* can be viewed as a modern extension of the pastoral novel. Vergara, for instance, admits that it does belong to the sentimental genre, but thereupon develops his analysis of the work as what he terms a "sinfonía pastoral" (pp. 51-52). It has been called an eclogue and compared to those by Garcilaso;[8] for one it is a bucholic idyll,[9] for another it is an idyllic elegy.[10] And the elegiac qualities of this pastoral symphony prompt Germán Arciniegas to wonder if Isaacs, "el clásico del llanto, no se habrá contaminado de los solloszos portugueses. . . . Comenzaba así Bernardim Ribeiro, allá en el siglo XVI: 'Menina y moza, me llevaron de casa de mis padres.' Le hace eco . . . Isaacs al cominezo de su *María*: Era yo niño aún cuando me alejaron de la casa paterna" (p. 40).

The lingering influence of the pastoral tradition has been studied by several contemporary literary historians. Avalle-Arce, in *La novela pastoril española*, however, offers one of the most succinct commentaries on this phenomenon:

> El pastor como tipo efectivo y actuante desaparece, pues, a comienzos del siglo xix, pero las aspiraciones que encarnó permanecen vivas, a la espera del nuevo tipo, más adecuado a la sensibilidad moderna, que las revista y las concretice. Se produce, así, una de las tantas anomalías de la literatura de los dos últimos siglos: El libro de pastores sin pastores.[11]

Of course, one should not imply by Avalle-Arce's comments that *María* is merely an imitation of the pastoral novel. But his statement is relevant to important similarities between *María* and the pastoral novel of the sixteenth century: for example, character development and treatment, including that of the secondary characters, the subjective descriptions of the bucholic scene, the harmonious relation between character and ambiance, the constant preoccupation with different types of love and lovers, and even the praise of the rural scene and condemnation of the city. There are also many minor similarities to suggest Isaacs' acquaintance with the typical pastoral language: Efraín hears the "Tañido lejano del cuerno de algún pastor, repetido por los montes" (p. 18); he imitates countless shepherds of old when "dominado por una honda melancolía dejaba correr algunas horas oculto en los sitios más agrestes" (p. 48). Efraín even sees the need to console those who, like him, suffer from love. Isaacs plainly recalls such a pastoral encounter with the following:

> Hacia el otro lado de una de las quebradas que por entre las quingueadas cintas de bosque bajan ruidosos el declive, oí una voz sonora de hombre que cantaba:
>
> > Al tiempo le pido tiempo
> > Y el tiempo tiempo me da,
> > Y el mismo tiempo me dice
> > Que él me desengañó
>
> Salió del arboledo el cantor, y era Tiburcio, quien con una ruana colgada de un hombro y apoyado en el otro un bordón, de cuya punta pendía un pequeño lío, entretenía su camino cantando por instinto sus penas a la soledad. (p. 224)

These similarities, however, are at best circumstantial evidence of Isaacs' indebtedness to the pastoral novel in general. And to theorize the influence of a specific novel, such as *La Diana*, on *María* requires a more detailed comparison and comparative evaluation of the two. It is possible, for instance, that Isaacs' anglophilia may have turned him to Sidney's *Arcadia*. But considering a long list of parallels and similarities between the novels in question, even personal qualities common to Isaacs and Montemayor, I suggest that the latter's novel is the more logical source of inspiration for Isaacs' even more so than *Atalá* or *Paul et Virginie*.

The numerous personal and literary similarities between the authors are well known: both have been evaluated in the light of their Hebraic tradition; they were prolific yet mediocre poets; both were products of a humanistic education, including some common preparation in the classic and Portuguese literatures. With regards to their novels, the list of similarities is too extensive to entertain now; and since my interest here is limited to their common neoplatonic legacy, I will only tempt your own comparison with the more obvious: both works recall a long list of classical expressions from Virgil to Garcilaso de la Vega in that they are cast in the autobiographical mold that allows the characters to revel in the morass of their own memories; both are dependent on the three principal motifs of Time, Fortune, and Love, and imply the neoplatonic defense of the bucholic and the rejection of the metropoli. Structurally, both novels generally suggest a diary form in that the episodic arrangement, as in an animated *retablo*, constitutes, by way of numerous memories, one grand flashback. Within this general structure, based on a succession of natural descriptions, narrative, and love stories, we find parallel love stories, even chain linked or a circular series of relations between more than two lovers, and interpolated short stories: in *María* the story of Nay and Sinar; in *La Diana* the story of Abindarráez. We might even note the parallel between the story of Efraín and María and the episode between Silvano and Alcida, which appears in the second, the 1560, and most subsequent editions of *La Diana*. López Estrada gives the following resume of this episode:

Así, si en el Silvano de la *Historia de Alcida y Silvano* pretendemos ver a Montemayor, entonces resulta que de vuelta de Andalucía en un lugar cerca del Duero se enamoró de una dama [Alcida]. Acogido al servicio del padre de ella, entra en el palacio donde reside la dama. Pero Alcida se enferma, y al cabo muere y deja desconsolado a Silvano.[12]

Finally, I would note that both works have been maligned by critics for their artificiality and plastic extravagance. For this writer, Wardropper's study, "*The Diana* of Montemayor: Revaluation and Interpretation," in which he puts this shortsighted judgment of *La Diana* to rest, can also be directed towards those who condemn *María* on the same grounds. For those not acquainted with Wardropper's work, he departs from the assertion that

the Pastoral setting of *La Diana* [where a loving humanity is fused with a sympathetic nature] is not mere convention or artifice. It is part of a technique for studying artistically the world of lovers. . . . The two main complications—man's need to earn a living and society's laws and customs for protecting womanhood—were minimized in the pastoral life in which Montemayor set his lovers.[13]

The only social obligation which exists in a pastoral society, whether in *La Diana* or *María*, is that of filial duty. As a result, neither the duty to one's father nor the duty to one's lover can be denied.

During the recent years several studies have appeared clarifying the relation between the Renaissance Pastoral novel and sixteenth-century neoplatonic philosophy. The previously cited book by Avalle-Arce is one of the most significant. In addition to the innate value of Avalle-Arce's study, it has inspired other scholars to pursue their own investigations of the Spanish genre. The most extensive of these is *Los libros de pastores en la literatura española* by López Estrada.[14] Among the many articles spawned by an apparent renewal of interest in Spanish Golden Age prose is David Darst's "Renaissance Platonism and the Spanish Pastoral Novel."[15] The latter is one of the most useful because, in addition to synthesizing the essential aspects of this relationship, it specifies the logical, yet nevertheless implicit, conclusions of Avalle-Arce's study. As Darst says, his is an "appendum in that it proposes to show that the Spanish pastoral novelists attempted to depict an atmosphere, character development, and theory of love which were distinctly Platonic in their conception" (p. 384). As a way of restating the philosophical applications of Platonism to fiction, we must reiterate that this philosophy is founded in the relationship between the sensible and the intelligible. In fact, as John Herman Randall, Jr. says,

the fundamental note of Platonism is the contrast it sees between the things of the senses and the things of the mind, between the body and the spirit. The first are ever-changing, impermanent, transitory; the second immutable, everlasting, eternal. True knowledge is of these things of the mind, of the ideas as Plato called them. . . . All things of the senses possess meaning and value only as they shadow these ideas; human life itself achieves significance in the measure that the mind forsakes the sense realm and communes with the intelligible world. Thus can man make himself immortal, by rising to the realm of imperishable things and dwelling with them in eternity.[16]

For the Renaissance humanist imbued with the application of Platonic principles to Christian beliefs, the problem was to resolve this polar antithesis by forming a convergence of opposites, in which the intelligible could be understood in and through the sensible. And, as Darst also emphasizes, for the Renaissance artist

> it was the pastoral ambiance of simplicity and harmony [that] proves to be the logical scene for the Platonic description of nature as the visual representation of the invisible archetypes. This is true because, if what one sees in nature with his visual perception is in reality only the reflection of the preexisting and transcendent Idea of the object, then to perceive the Idea itself one must strip away the imperfections that disfigure nature by a process of depuration and abstraction. In this way the *locus amoenus* of the pastoral novelist, as Montemayor, becomes the true picture of the idealistic forms; and the result is a scene replete with Fountain, Tree, Stream, and Field. (p. 384)

As a consequence of this depuration, the artist's descriptions of the natural ambiance are, in the main, brief and, by virtue of their symbolic nature, subjective. Whereas numerous examples may be gleaned from any of the Spanish pastorals for illustrating the impact of these depurated descriptions, that is the manner in which they effect a convergence of the sensible and intelligible worlds, the following may be considered as typical. On the first page of *La Diana* Sireno, with the memory of Diana still haunting him, is depicted thus:

> ... pues llegando el pastor a los verdes y deleitosos prados que el caudaloso Rio Ezla con sus aguas va regando, le vino a la memoria el gran contentamiento de que en algun tiempo alli gozado avia. ... [C]onsiderava aquel dichoso tiempo que por aquellos prados y hermosa ribera apacentava su ganado, poniendo los ojos en solo el interesse que de traelle bien apacentado se le seguia y las horas que le sobravan, gastava el pastor el solo gozar del suave olor de las doradas flores, al tiempo que la primavera, con las alegres nuevas del verano, se esparze por el universo .... (p. 9)

The better example is found in the opening passages of the last of the seven books in which Felismena and her companions are about to enter what, for Montemayor, was his beloved Lusitania. The description of the natural scene is at once the longest and, for some, the most realistic in the novel. Even so, the impression is essentially subjective and depurated, as the following passage suggests:

> Pues yendo una mañana por el medio de un bosque, al salir de una assomada que por encima de una alta sierra parecía, vio delante de si un verde y ameníssimo campo de tanta grandeza que con la vista no se le podía alcançar el cabo; el qual doze millas adelante yva a fenecer en la falda de unas montañas, que casi no se parecían; por medio del deleytoso campo corría un caudaloso río, el

qual hazía una muy graciosa ribera, en muchas partes poblada de salzes y verdes aliosos y otros diversos árboles; y en otras dexava descubiertas las crystalinas aguas recogiéndose a una parte un grande y espacioso arenal que de lexos más adornava la hermosa ribera. (pp. 280-81)

Even the description of the entrance to the city demands that the reader exercise his imagination if he is to capture the essential reality of Monte-mayor's abstracted depiction:

Por encima d[el río] estava la más sumptuosa y admirable puente que en el universo se podía hallar. Las casas y edificios de aquella ciudad insigne eran tan altos, y con tan gran artificio labrados, que parecía aver la industria humana mostrado su poder. (p. 281)

As we turn to *María* it is worthwhile recalling that, for every reader, the natural scene is constantly emphasized and that it is the most important element beyond the love story. Despite what may be an overbearing presence and significance that the natural ambiance may assume, nonetheless, Isaacs' descriptions are also depurated with the intent of effecting the same convergence of the sensible and intelligible words. In fact, there is, in the beginning passages, a moment in which Efraín, in a manner reminiscent of Sireno, also views the natural scene while the thought of María is lurking in the back of his mind:

Hacia el sur flotaban las nieblas que durante la noche había embozado los montes lejanos. Cruzaba planicies alfombradas de verdes gramales, regados por riachuelos cuyo paso me obstruían hermosas vacadas, que abandonaban sus sesteadores para internarse en las lagunas o sendas abovedadas por florecidos pisamos e higuerones frondosos. . . . Si los perfumes que aspiraba eran tan gratos comparados con el de los vestidos lujosos de ella. . . . Así el cielo, los horizontes, las pampas y las cumbres del Cauca, hacen enmudecer a quien los contempla. Las grandes bellezas de la creación no pueden a un tiempo ser vistas y cantadas; es necesario que vuelvan al alma empalidecidas por la memoria infiel. (p. 12)

This is also the same depurated nature that, later on, prompts Efraín to note:

no era eso lo que veían mis ojos: era lo que ya no veré más; lo que mi espíritu quebrantado por tristes realidades no busca o admira únicamente en sus sueños: el mundo, como Adán pudo verlo en la primera mañana de su vida. (p. 121)

Even during Efraín's return from London, that portion in which Isaacs emphasizes the Edenic qualities of the Colombian nature, the descriptions are not entirely detailed or realistic. They are still the product of Isaacs' determination to depurate nature in order to bring about what, for Darst and Avalle-Arce, is the neoplatonic concern with understanding the intelligible in and through the sensible. In fact, Isaacs seems particularly aware of the importance of this depuration in the portion describing the return, because the descriptions of nature toward the end of the trip, as a complement to Efraín's heightened emotions, are notably more depurated than those which mark the first moments of Efraín's trek from the coastal area to the Cauca valley. During the initial stages the natural scene is depicted in somewhat lengthy, yet always poetic passages, as the following:

> De allí para adelante las selvas de las riberas fueron ganando en majestad y galanura: los grupos de palmeras se hicieron más frecuentes; veíase la pambil de recta columna manchada de púrpura; la milpesos frondosa, brindando en sus raíces el delicioso fruto; la chontadura y la gualte; distinguiéndose entre todas las chontas de flexible tallo e inquieto plumaje, por aquello de coqueto o virginal que recuerda talles seductores y esquivos . . . todas . . . parecían con sus rumores dar la bienvenida a un amigo no olvidado. (p. 252)

As Efraín approaches the midpoint of the journey from the coast to the Cauca, the descriptions are briefer and, in most instances, substantially more abstract:

> Veía ya en el fondo de la profunda vega la población de Juntas, con sus techumbres pajizas y cenicientas; El Dagua lujoso con la luz que entonces la bañaba, orlaba el islote del caserío y rodando precipitadamente hasta perderse en la revuelta del Credo, volvía a platear muy lejos en las playas del Sobrerillo. (p. 262)

Finally, in the last description of the natural scene before Efraín is to receive the devasting news of María's death, we find that the descriptive paragraphs are short, often one-sentence entities and, especially, that the natural panorama has been depurated to such an extent that only the essential elements are mentioned:

> La tarde se apagaba cuando doblé la última cuchilla de las Montañuelas. Un viento impetuso de occidente zumbaba en torno de mí en los peñascos y malezas. . . . En el confin del horizonte a mi izquierda, no blanqueaba ya la casa de mis padres sobre las faldas sombrías de la montaña. . . . La ciudad acaba de dormirse sobre su verde y acojinado lecho; como bandadas de aves enormes que se cernieran buscando sus nidos, divisábanse sobre ella, abrillantadas por la luna, los follajes de las palmeras. (p. 266)

Thus it is that in the same way, and to the same extent that Efraín's intelligible perception is progressively heightened and restricted to the Idea of María, the natural descriptions are also depurated; they are reduced until, as in the final descriptions, the remaining elements are archetypal symbols of the total, yet subjective and abstractively depicted natural panorama.

As Darst also points out in his study, "A second and related use of the depuration of nature in the pastoral novel is to describe the hero or the heroine as being the perfection of all possible human characteristics" (p. 385). These characters, therefore, are not merely human, but archetypes. In *La Diana* and in *María*, moreover, the heroines can be viewed as extensions of the perfection of the divinely wrought nature. In the initial passages of *La Diana*, Montemayor has Sireno recall his lost love thus:

> Arrimóse al pie de una haya; comenzó a tender sus ojos al lugar donde primero avía visto la hermosura, gracia, honestidad de la pastora Diana, aquella en quien naturaleza sumó todas las perficiones que por muchas partes avía repartida. (p. 10)

And on a second occasion Selvagia notes:

> Ninguna perfición ni hermosura puede dar la naturaleza que con Diana largamente no la aya repartido; porque su hermosura no creo yo que tiene par, su gracia, su discreción, con todas las otras partes que una pastora deve tener. (pp. 243-44)

As these passages suggest, and in keeping with the depurative technique by which the novelist sought to perfect nature through art, Montemayor also strips away the exterior ornaments that would hide or detract from what, in neoplatonic terms, is the primordial Idea innate in, for instance, the heroine, the archetype of human perfection.

Isaacs' heroine, as Diana, is also an archetype of human perfection. The more significant realization, however, is that the Colombian's portrayal, as Montemayor's, is essentially dependent on abstract, although not always subtle, comparisons with elements of an already depurated natural ambiance and, with Isaacs alone, comparison with archetypes of Christian perfection. With regards to the latter, for example, María is described as the Christian Virgin, she is compared with the Virgin on numerous occasions, she is interested in *Imitación de la Virgen*, her prayers are to the Virgin, and in one of the more explicit analogues, Efraín notes that "esa sonrisa hoyuelada era la de la niña de mis amores infantiles sorprendidas en el rostro de una Virgen de Rafael" (p. 15). Isaacs' descriptions of María in terms of the natural elements are commonplace in the novel. Perhaps the most prelevant metaphorical comparison is between María and flowers, the lily and the rose. Her skin is as white as the lily and her cheeks are identical to fresh roses. Such comparative devices are now viewed as one of the more trite expressions of the Romantics, however, and by themselves would fail to substantiate María as an archetype of perfection. Isaacs was aware of the necessity of defending the unique and personal qualities of his heroine and for this reason depicts her as the ideal nurse, as evinced during her adopted father's sickness; as the ideal mother, as seen in her relation with young children, particularly Juan Angel; and Isaacs even draws her as a haven and defender of wild animals, as when the young deer sought refuge with her in order to escape the certain death of the hunt. But as the neoplatonic Ideal of human perfection, María even transcends the beauty of the natural ideal. The concept of her transcendent beauty, the idea of perfecting nature through art, is present throughout the novel: "Nunca las auroras de julio en el Cauca fueron tan bellas como estaba María cuando se me presentó al día siguiente" (p. 33), or "Aquellos momentos de olvido de mi mismo, cuando un pensamiento se cernía sobre regiones que casi me eran desconocidas, momentos en que las palomas que estaban a la sombra de los naranjos agobiados de sus ramicos de oro se arrullaban amorosos; cuando la voz de María, arrullo más dulce aun, llegaba a mis oídos, tenía un encanto inefable" (pp. 120-21). This last passage is one of the most revealing examples of how, in neoplatonic terms, Efraín rises from the sensible to the intelligible perception of the natural ideal and, ultimately, to the ineffable beauty of María.

In any idyllic expression, and particularly the neoplatonic expression, the ideal realtion between man and nature is one of harmonious participation between the two. For the Renaissance Platonist, as Montemayor, and also for Isaacs, even if one views him as a Romantic, the presence of nature was of special importance because it was proof of God's immanence in the world and, for this reason, could only be treated as a vital participant in the universal system. In *La Diana* and *María*, as a consequence, nature plays a role in the execution of novelistic events just as the characters. In both novels nature is a sympathetic agent that acts and reacts with the different characters. Examples abound in both works. In Montemayor's *La Diana* the following are typical:

> . . . comenzó a tocar tan dulcemente que el valle, el monte, el río, las aves enamoradas y aun las fieras de aquel espesso bosque quedaron suspensas. (p. 24)

> Quando triste yo nací
> Luego naci desdichada . . .
> El sol escondió sus rayos
> la luna quedó eclipsada
> murió mi madre pariendo
> moça hermosa y mal lograda. (p. 241)

In *María* the active role is especially important, and even indispensable to the development of Efraín's character. For the hero, "La naturaleza es la más amorosa de las madres cuando el dolor se ha posesionado de nuestra alma; y si la felicidad nos acaricia, ella nos sonríe" (*María*, p. 77). Shortly before his departure to England, he addresses his final goodbye to his constant companion: "Descendía lentamente hasta el fondo de la cañada: sólo el canto lejano de las gurrias y el rumor del río turbaban el silencio de las selvas. Mi corazón iba dando un adiós a cada uno de estos sitios, a cada árbol del sendero, a cada arroyo que cruzaba" (*María*, p. 232). It makes little difference whether we term this technique personification, an apostrophe, or even follow Ruskin's suggestion of pathetic fallacy; the point is that, by depurating and presenting nature as a sympathetic agent, both authors were able to overcome the barrier between the sensible and intelligible worlds. By establishing a harmonious relation between an inanimate scene and the characters, Montemayor and Isaacs have effected a convergence of opposites.

The principle of this convergence is also basic to the structural and, to some extent, the physical development of the characters. In both novels, in fact, character development is dependent on the extent that they overcome the barrier. In both the characters are basically differentiated by the extent to which they rise beyond their attraction to the opposite sex and elevate themselves to the intellectual contemplation of the past sex object as an extension of the divine perfection of nature.

In *La Diana*, with Sireno for example, and in *María*, with Efraín, this ascension from the realm of the sensible to that of the intelligible is the result of a physiological, even a physical experience through which the characters mentioned are clearly changed. For Sireno the change is simply effected by the magic potion administered by Felicia. For Efraín the change begins to take place when he learns of María's death. Up to that moment, we may say, he is still existing in the sensible world—he is still intent on marriage and even is incensed by the death: "Era la muerte que me hería. . . . Ella tan cruel e implacable, ¿Por qué no supo herir! " (p. 267). Immediately thereafter Efraín is literally comatose and is not even told the details of María's death until he has recovered his health, some two months later. Thereafter, now returned to El Paraíso, Efraín completes the final step in his spiritual development. He now completes his ascension from *amor sensitivus* to the higher realm of *amor rationalis*, from the sensible to the intelligible perception of María. This change takes place during his dream, in which he is married and alone with his love. After the dream, in which he caresses her tresses, he awakes to the cold morning. But Efraín can now at least cope with her memory because he is no longer the victim of his sensible past. He realizes that the tress he actually holds is the "único despojo de su belleza, la única verdad de mi sueño" (p. 278). This is the moment in which we realize that Efraín no longer suffers the physical and physiological pains of his corporal existence with regard to María. He has now transcended to that level on which his love for María is eternal, unchanging, divinely beautiful.

In both novels there is an implied yet gentle admonition that the perception of ultimate beauty is restricted to those who exercise the proper kind of love, *amor bueno*—the love for God and all elements of his creation. In keeping with Montemayor's goal of placing the value of *amor bueno* in the proper perspective, therefore, the trajectory of *La Diana* may be viewed as one in which various types of lovers ascend from the realm of corporal love, with the concomitant suffering brought on by Time and Fortune, to the realm of good, spiritual love, as that provided by matrimony. In *María* the trajectory is basically the same. Efraín progresses from the perception of María on a sensible plane to the perception of his love on an intelligible plane, the last step being the coma and the dream of marriage. Efraín also suffers from Time and Fortune, and in lieu of a supernatural intervention, as represented by the magic potion in *La Diana*, his ultimate step is the result of his exercising *razón*—his rational response to third party intervention. We should note here that the fulfillment of filial duty and the resulting obstacles in the love relation is common in the pastoral novel of the Renaissance. Even in *La Diana* Sireno, as Efraín, was separated from his love when forced to go to England.

When viewed from a different perspective, then, *La Diana* and *María* represent a study of different types of loves and the effect of love upon man placed in a situation from which he has no escape. Critics have already pointed out that several types of lovers are present in *La Diana*: the faithful, the jealous, the adventurous. Montemayor also implies the differences between good and bad love, between the sensible and the intelligible. Isaacs does essentially the same. In addition to the principal protagonists, María and Efraín, Isaacs includes the faithful and good love of Braulio and Tránsito, the jealous love and lovers with Salomé and Tiburcio, and in Carlos we find the antithesis of the love and lover which Efraín represents. In both novels the message is the same—that despite what kind of lover one may be, only those who transcend to the intelligible level will find true love. Those who do not take the magic potion, as Diana, never attain the blissful state of pure, good love. They are relegated to remain on the sensible level where they are bound to suffer their own desires and frustrations. In *María*, Carlos is the best example of this latter type. As Diana and her forlorn husband, Delio, Isaacs' character is not in harmony with the natural scene and is unable to perceive the invisible reality, the beauty, the platonic Idea of nature. Montemayor's description of Delio may well have been Isaacs' formula for Carlos' characterization:

> Aunque es rico de los bienes de fortuna, no le es de naturaleza, que en esto de la disposición, ya ves quan mal le va, pues de otras cosas de que los pastores nos preciamos, como son tañer, cantar, luchar, jugar al cayado, baylar con las mozas el domingo, parece que Delio no a nacido para más que mirallo. (p. 30)

To conclude, there is no doubt that Hispanic America's outstanding sentimental novel is more than a product of the literary and social incentives of its time or an adaptation of the precursors of French Romantic prose fiction. In this effort to explain the enduring appeal of Isaacs' masterpiece, we have evaluated its philosophical implications and literary directives in the light of *La Diana*, a significant and renown expression of Renaissance humanism. The comparison of these two works suggests that, in the depiction of the atmosphere, character development, and the theory of love, Isaacs and *María* share a neoplatonic legacy that has influenced Hispanic letters for centuries.

*Texas Tech University*

# NOTES

[1] Jorge Isaacs, *María* (Buenos Aires: Editorial Losada, 1968). Further references are to this edition and will be cited parenthetically.

[2] José María Vergara y Vergara, "Juicio crítico," a photostatic reproduction in Germán Arciniegas, *Genio y figura de Jorge Isaacs* (Buenos Aires: Editorial Universitaria de Buenos Aires, 1967), pp. 50-53. Further references to this work by Vergara will be cited parenthetically.

[3] Louis François Cazamain, *A History of French Literature* (London: Univ. of Oxford Press, 1963), p. 293. While Saint-Pierre's humanistic preparation is well known, the influence of classical literatures on Chateaubriand is not. Cazamian makes this point succinctly in this work.

[4] Enrique Anderson-Imbert, "Estudio preliminar a *María*" (México: Fondo de Cultura Económica, 1951), reproduced in Germán Arciniegas, pp. 143-58. Further references to Arciniegas' work will be cited parenthetically.

[5] J. Warshaw, "Jorge Isaacs' Library: Light on Two María Problems," *Romantic Review*, 32 (1941), 394. Further references to this article will be cited parenthetically.

[6] Plutarch, *Selected Lives and Essays*, introd. Edith Hamilton (Roslyn, N.Y.: Walter J. Black, Inc., 1951), p. xxiii.

[7] Enrique Anderson-Imbert, *Historia de la literatura hispanoamericana*, I (Buenos Aires: Fondo de Cultura Economica, 1962), 266.

[8] Mario Carvajal, *Vida y pasión de Jorge Isaacs* (Manizales, Colombia: A. Zapata, 1937), p. 74.

[9] Luis Carlos Velasco Madriñán, *Jorge Isaacs, el caballero de las lágrimas* (Cali: Editorial América, 1942), passim.

[10] Arturo Torres-Ríoseco, *The Epic of Latin American Literature* (Berkeley: Univ. of California Press, 1953), p. 76.

[11] Juan Bautista Avalle-Arce, *La novela pastoril española* (Madrid: Revista de Occidente, 1959), p. 6.

[12] Jorge de Montemayor, *Los siete libros de La Diana*, prologue and ed. Francisco López Estrada (Madrid: Espasa-Calpe, 1967), p. xxii. Further references to this text will be cited parenthetically.

[13] Bruce Wardropper, "The *Diana* of Montemayor: Revaluation and Interpretation," *Studies in Philology*, 48 (1951), 127-28.

[14] Francisco López Estrada, *Los libros de pastores en la literatura española* (Madrid: Editorial Gredos, 1974).

[15] David Darst, "Renaissance Platonism and the Spanish Pastoral Novel," *Hispania*, 52, No. 3 (September 1969), 384-92. Further references to this article will be cited parenthetically.

[16] John Herman Randall, Jr., *The Making of the Modern Mind* (Boston: Houghton Mifflin, 1926), pp. 46-47.

# A Comparative Look at the Literatures of Spanish America and Brazil: The Dangers of Deception

Gregory Rabassa

ABSTRACT

There is a great superficial resemblance between the literatures of Spanish America and Brazil, but this similarity inevitably wanes under a close examination. For reasons that are most likely historical, Brazilian literature settled down into a more orderly pattern of development with the establishment of definable movements and schools which corresponded closely to the European scene, while Spanish America seemed to be afflicted with a chaotic kind of drumbling and wambling. In recent times, however, there has, indeed, been a marked similarity between literary works from the two areas, and the problem for interpretation is how this converging of directions came about.

Brazil had a head start, partially due to the national unity she enjoyed after independence and also doubtless due to the fact that Portugal had hewn closer to cosmopolitan currents than had Spain. Spanish America's earlier Modernist movement was a beginning; the Modernist movement in Brazil was a renovation, a keeping abreast of the times. Only in the middle of the twentieth century can Spanish America be said to have come "into the mainstream," as Luis Harss has defined the phenomenon. Figures of the past like Machado de Assis, Cruz e Sousa, and Lima Barreto are evidence that Brazil was already there.

Now, however, with the "new novel" triumphant in Spanish America, there has been a large amount of direct contact for the first time: Cortázar and García Márquez are read as avidly in Brazil as in other non-Spanish countries. The reverse has not been so true. Guimarães Rosa, Clarice Lispector, and Nélida Piñon are still mainly vague names in the other half of the continent, but this may be the age-old difficulty that the Portuguese language has had in receiving its due. What has really come about is the final realization (in both senses of the word) that Octavio Paz is right when he says that literature is one. In this sense, then, Brazilian and Spanish American literatures are not members of a continental subdivision, but, rather of the whole universal body of literature, remaining, at the same time, separate but equal. (GR)

As God divided regions of this world
Into their separate parts, then all the stars

119

> Long lost in ancient dark began to light
> Pale fires throughout the sky. And as each part
> Of Universal being came to life,
> Each filled with images of its own kind.
>
> (Ovid, *Metamorphoses*, Bk. I.,
> Horace Gregory, trans.)

Coming to the consideration of the literatures of Brazil and Spanish America from a comparative perspective, we are faced with the enduring problem of truth, the same essentially comparative thing that bedevilled Pilate and which is often sloughed off in regnant literary criticism as some sort of given constant or other. In this comparison we shall tread through the dangers revealed in the uncertainty principle in physics which holds that it is impossible to specify exactly both the momentum and the position of any object, because measuring one of those quantities automatically alters the other. What the principle means in a broader application is that the very act of observing or measuring a phenomenon alters the behavior being studied. In literature this principle has been illustrated by the effects of Aristotle's definitions upon subsequent writing. a more subtle warning concerning the definition of truth and one which those of us who deal with writing and thought might take to heart is supplied by Juan Carlos Onetti in his rather protoplastic novella *El pozo* (The Well), where he writes:

> Se dice que hay varias maneras de mentir; pero la más repugnante de todas es decir la verdad, toda la verdad, ocultando el alma de los hechos. Porque los hechos son siempre vacíos, son recipientes que tomarán la forma del sentimiento que los llene. [1]

Let us not seek the truths behind the differing stories of development for Brazil and Spanish America, but, rather, the facts and also the feelings that have filled them. In spite of so many coincidences, the paths of development of these two major components of Latin America are isoclinal rather than equal. A more or less common combination of geographical elements is the most obvious trait which clouds the clear differences. Brazil shares landscape, flora, and fauna with any number of Spanish American countries, as Portugal does with Spain. Another common background which Brazil shares with many Spanish American countries is its racial admixture of Iberian, African, and indigenous elements, seasoned in later years by immigration from Europe and Asia. If one is valiant enough to eschew pettifogging statistics, he might make so bold as to assert that certain characteristics held in common by Brazil and Cuba could be based upon a sizable population of Yoruban descent and the cultivation of sugar cane during their formative years.

The differences between the two halves of Latin America are too often hidden by the similarities. Foremost among the separative elements are the

Portuguese rather than the Spanish roots. We need not dwell too long here upon the divergences of the two peninsular countries, although, also, the outside observer here tends to colligate them too tightly as Oliveira Martins has done. Iberia can only be studied as such if the political entity called Spain is broken down into its parts; then the independent phenomenon of Portugal will be better understood. A few cursory looks can take care of the broad picture: Portugal's maintenance of independence from Spain except for the interregnum of the three Hapsburg Philips; Portugal's position as a maritime nation and its subsequent greater interest in Asia than in America; Portugal's long-standing alliance with England, Spain's great colonial rival and enemy; and, with the exception of the short period of Spanish domination mentioned above, the presence of a native Portuguese dynasty on the throne.

In literature the effects of these historical differences are manifest. National unity was older than in Spain and so the theater developed earlier, with Portugal's playwrights being true forerunners of Spain's great Golden Age drama. As Spain invents the novel with Cervantes, Camões writes the only modern national secondary epic, based on the discoveries of Vasco da Gama and Portugal's maritime preeminence.[2] With the discovery of the New World we begin to see these same divergences in the colonies, almost from the start. The literary colostrum of these events is, quite naturally, of a practical nature: Columbus's letters, those of Cortés, and Pero Vaz de Caminha's relation of things in the new land discovered (accidentally or otherwise) by Cabral. It is with Caminha that we sense a note that is to permeate much of Brazilian literature from then on: *ufanismo*,[3] the exaggerated celebration of things Brazilian as beyond and better than things in other lands. This hyperpatriotic attitude, of course, exists in other countries; we have the slogan *"Como México no hay dos"* (There's only one Mexico), which Carlos Fuentes cruelly shoots down by adding "ni Paraguay, ni Indonesia, ni Albania," or words to that effect.

The feeling of being different on the part of Portuguese born in the New World follows fast upon the advent of *ufanismo*. Bahia, which was the flourishing colonial capital, produced the poet Gregório de Matos, whose epithet was *Boca do Inferno* (Mouth of Hell). Although his tirades reached all comers (blacks, mulattoes, clergy, and the city itself as a whole), some special ire was reserved for the Portuguese, as colonial administrators, but also simply as having been peninsula-born. The Peruvian Caviedes is close to Matos, but without such a deep sense of nativeness. Bahia was also the home city of the remarkable Padre Antônio Vieira, who, although born in Lisbon, came to Brazil at the age of six and thus must be considered Brazilian. It is noteworthy that Vieira was one of the few contemporaries of the seventeenth century who was spared the lash of

Gregório de Matos' tongue, evidently because the latter held him in high esteem.

Vieira was educated by the Jesuits and joined the order at an early age over his parents' objections. It is strange that although the Society of Jesus was founded by a Spaniard (if the Basques will forgive me), the order was of much greater importance and influence in the Portuguese colonies than in the Spanish. The first great Brazilian missionary was the Spanish-born Anchieta, who wrote *autos* in four languages (Portuguese, Spanish, Latin, and Tupi) as he catechized the heathen and the fallen-away in São Paulo. This early and pervasive Jesuit influence could well have spelled certain differences between the two areas in the formative years. Vieira, among other things, was famed as an orator and preacher. In many of his sermons, particularly the *Sexagésima*, he turns Quevedan conceptism against the Gongoristic style so much in vogue with rather bizarre results. There are those who see a "school" of Bahian oratory that begins with Padre Vieira and continues on down through Rui Barbosa into this century.

Because of Vieira's efforts for the protection of the Indian in Maranhão, the king was prevailed upon to summon him to Lisbon, where he became the royal preacher. His work in favor of the Indians has led to a comparison between him and Bartolomé de las Casas. In like manner, he has also been accused of espousing the introduction of African slavery as a means of protecting the Indian. After a bout with the Inquisition in Lisbon, Vieira was banished to Rome. There he was absolved by papal decree of any charges brought by the Inquisition, past, present, or future. While in Rome he became an intimate of Queen Christina of Sweden and was a member of the original Arcadia. This poetical movement was brought back to Lisbon and thence to Brazil. In this way, and partly through the efforts of Vieira, the subsequent neoclassical influence and movement came almost directly from Rome to Brazil, where it would flourish much more vigorously than in the Spanish colonies. Vieira had also corresponded with Sor Juana Inés de la Cruz in a polemic on matters of style. This is one of the few literary contacts between the two colonies.

The advent of neoclassicism in Brazil drew strength from its dominance of the mood of the mother country. It is ironical, in more ways than one, that the baroque Jesuit Vieira should be so instrumental in introducing Arcadism and subsequently Academism into the Luso-Brazilian world, for the burgeoning of the Enlightenment in Portugal brought to the fore the Marquis of Pombal, who waged a strenuous campaign against the Jesuits, leading to their ultimate expulsion from Portuguese territory. The Jesuit influence in Brazil was over; it would gain strength in the Spanish colonies over the ensuing years. The former Jesuit partisan José Basílio da Gama would write the closest thing Brazil has had to a true epic in form as he toadied to Pombal and composed his *Uraguai* (a translation by Sir Richard Burton has recently come to light).

In the Spanish colonies, too, in imitation of the mother country, neoclassicism became the dominant mode. And, as in the mother country, no really strong movement emerged, all was imitative. As in the past, the divergent histories of the two peninsular nations had great and differing effects on their colonies. John VI of Portugal was able to escape Napoleon's invading forces and reach Rio de Janeiro, where he established the capital of the United Kingdom of Portugal, Brazil, and the Algarve. Brazil was no longer a colony; Rio de Janeiro was a court. But it was too late to halt the move towards independence which had been bred in Minas Gerais. The activists were a group of poets and a dentist. The outcome was failure, imprisonment, exile, and a cruel death for Tiradentes. The poets were neoclassical, the product of arcadias and academies; with certain exceptions the main content of their verse was pastoral love. The satirical *Cartas Chilenas* by Tomás Antônio Gonzaga, a broadside of a poem against the ruling Portuguese, may be the stylistic descendant of Montesquieu's letters, but the spirit is that of Gregório de Matos. Gonzaga himself, Portuguese-born, would end his days in exile in Mozambique to become a prosperous slave-owner. Such are the ironies of the struggle for freedom.

The presence of the court in Rio along with the new status of equality did not stanch the urge for independence, but, rather, exacerbated it. One cannot be sure what might have been the upshot had not the king's son declared, upon his father's return to Lisbon, that he was staying, and he proclaimed the independence of Brazil. Dom Pedro I became the first ruler of the Empire of Brazil. We must hearken back to Padre Vieira for this new designation. In addition to the many other facets of his life, Vieira was a visionary and saw Brazil as the seat of the Fifth Empire. This prophecy was maintained in the official designation of the newly independent country, but *ufanismo* could demand nothing less than such a grandiose title. The fact that Brazil had maintained its unity all through the colonial period in spite of various separatist movements led to a continuation of a national feeling after independence. From the presence of the court, Rio de Janeiro had become a national and dominant center. In the meantime, Spanish America had broken up into a gallimaufry of movements and campaigns in favor of independence; regionalism became nationalism, and the Bolivarian dream was not long in fading away in the wake of his drive.

In Brazil ties were still maintained with Portugal. The break with the mother country was peaceful and the royal blood-ties remained. Education was also a factor, and here we have another striking difference between Brazil and Spanish America. Universities were established quite early in

Spanish America; the best Brazil could do were professional faculties which took their stead but were limited in supplying needs. Even after independence Coimbra continued to be the educational center of Brazil well into the nineteenth century. In this sense Brazil had greater intellectual contact with the mother country. This fact, coupled with Portugal's closer ties to Europe, helped the movements which prevailed on the Continent to reach Brazil in a more coherent shape than they did Spanish America via Spain. The touch of Almeida Garrett was felt in Brazil rather quickly and led to Castro Alves; where was Larra when Spanish America needed him? It seems that Brazil had dipped its dewlap into the mainstream ahead of its neighbors.

The rather secure situation of the Empire of Brazil, along with a tradition of literary establishments, meant that Brazilian literature had already passed through its hebetic stage and was following norms, norms which would subsequently have to be altered, not without certain aesthetic upheavals. The Romantic Movement was admirably suited to the ideological needs of a new nation with problems of growth and development. Almeida launched the urban novel with his *Memórias de um Sargento de Milícias* (1854-1855), somewhere between *costumbrismo* and the picaresque genre, a work comparable in some ways to Villaverde's *Cecilia Valdés*[4] (again the similarities between Brazil and Cuba). The Indian had by now been eliminated to a large degree in effective Brazil through slaughter and miscegenation. Thus he became an exotic figure and the fit subject for romantic writers. José de Alencar has given us pictures of the noble savage in his novels *O Guarani* (1857) and *Iracema* (1865). Other Latin American countries were going through their *indianista* phase at this moment; some cases in point like Mera's *Cumandá* (1879) and Galván's *Enriquillo* (1878-1882) resemble that of Alencar, while others like Clorinda Matto de Turner's *Aves sin nido* (1889) deal with the plight of extant Indians.

Alencar was not as charitable with blacks. He was in favor of abolition, but because he saw the slave as a threat to the morality of the Brazilian family, as seen in his play *O Demônio Familiar* (1857). As slavery had been abolished in the independent Spanish American nations, this problem was no longer a political and social factor except in the remaining Spanish colonies of Cuba and Puerto Rico. It was among the *condoreiro* group of younger romantics that slavery became a heated theme in Brazil. Castro Alves's poems *O Navio Negreiro* (1868) and *Vozes da África* (1868) can find counterparts only in European and North American literature, although the tone of the second poem would be maintained at a much later date by the Puerto Rican Luis Palés Matos. More noteworthy in some ways is Castro Alves's *A Cachoeira de Paulo Afonso* (1870) in which black characters lose their stereotype for the first time in Brazilian literature and are treated as normal human beings. As reactive poetry, perhaps, the products of Brazilian romanticism seem less posed, less bombastic (if that is possible with civic poetry of the Hugo mold) than their Spanish American counterparts. The seeming orderliness of transition from movement to movement implies some sort of solid underpinning here.

Realism comes to Brazil in a like way, in the European mold. It is modeled along the binary lines that prevailed in Europe: the psychological novel out of Stendhal and Flaubert, exemplified to a degree by Raul Pompéia's *O Ateneu* (1888) and the naturalism of Zola with Aluísio de Azevedo and others. These writers were not so much picking and choosing as following certain canons already laid down and applying them to the Brazilian situation. As mentioned before, thought must be given to the Jesuit influence in colonial Brazil as a possible factor in distinguishing its ways from those of Spanish America. In more recent times there was another all-pervasive influence from outside: the Positivism of Auguste Comte. Introduced largely through the efforts of Benjamim Constant (the Brazilian one). For an extended time Positivism held the status of an alternate faith in Brazil and even today the Positivist Apostolate still functions in Rio. Its influence was particularly strong in the army as the Escola Politécnica, the military academy, was staffed by a large number of positivist mathematicians. The strong military establishment which emerged from the war with Paraguay was deeply Positivist in attitude and became the most powerful force in the overthrow of the Empire and the inception of the Republic. This scientific approach to matters military and governmental has survived in the armed forces down to the present time. The Escola Superior de Guerra is known to its detractors today as *A Sorbona*. All of this is in strong contrast to the *caudillo*, the man on horseback so common in Spanish America.

Positivism and realism as stylistic or ideological movements were joined by their poetical *confrère* Parnassianism. As a reaction to overblown romanticism and as a yearning for order, the French movement took hold and dominated the poetical scene well into the twentieth century. Parnassianism was an ingredient, an important one, in Spanish American Modernism, but in Brazil it was an orthodox movement and the arbiter of taste. Thus we can see a distinct difference between the two literatures at the turn of the century: Brazil was already into a pendulum-like rhythm of movement and counter-movement, akin to that of Europe, while Spanish America was initiating what would be a more and more coherent expression of its own, still groping, testing, and forming a native literature which would not culminate in a great poetical outreach as much as a new novel which was to put it into the van.

An unexplainable phenomenon in the otherwise orderly and predictable progress of Brazilian literature is the figure of Machado de Assis. It is hard to say where he came from. By all powers of prediction he should have been the proper Parnassian poet, which he had been, who also wrote standard realistic prose, keeping within his contemporary confines. It was Machado, however, who condemned realism in the name of reality. Instead of being a superb craftsman of the realistic-naturalistic novel as was Eça de Queiroz, he saw fit to condemn the Portuguese master for his efforts, writing a withering review of *O Primo Basílio*. As we try to analyze Machado and his novelistic art, we sink deeper and deeper into the bog of misunderstanding, for he is so much out of the Brazilian mainstream of the time in his efforts. And yet Brazil now has its paragon. Machado would be maligned by those who came after, but yet he could stand as a model: Brazil would be the first American country, north and south, to have its own Cervantes, its own Camões, its own Shakespeare. Nowadays, whenever I am called upon to teach a course in the "new" Latin American fiction, I always begin with the *Memórias Póstumas de Brás Cubas* (1881) by Machado de Assis.[5]

Parnassianism tarried too long in Brazil. It was predominant as the "accepted" taste long after its brief eminence in France had come to an end. As seems to have been its wont, Brazil was still plugged into the main currents of European style. Baudelaire came to Brazil as a "realist," divorced from symbolism and as an afterbreath of Parnassianism. The symbolist movement took root in Brazil, however, and, although stifled by the pervasive Parnassian tone, it did produce a group of hidden poets who would blend, quite naturally, into the Brazilian Modernist revolt. João da Cruz e Sousa (1861-1898), that strange and isolated and unlikely black poet, would eventually be put down as one of the three true Brazilian voices of the period along with Machado de Assis and Lima Barreto. Although race is a minor theme in the poetry of Cruz e Sousa, there is a hint of what the francophone African poets would later call *négritude*, along with the idea of "black is beautiful," hampered, albeit, by Parnassianism's accepted norm of alabaster.

All these movements were taking place while in Spanish America Rubén Darío and Modernism were breaking out in all directions in what must be one of the greatest eclectic movements of all literary times. Spanish American poetry, then, runs ahead of the Brazilian, which did not find itself in such an inviting inchoate situation rife for new creation. Spanish American Modernism headed off in different ways into what is called Post-Modernism, Vanguardism, or what have you, finally settling comfortably (or uncomfortably, as is more fitting) down into the stream of world poetry. In Brazil there were shackles, native-forged, which had to be broken. While Spanish America's Modernism was a beginning, Brazil's was a renovation. In 1922, under the guidance of Mário de Andrade, the

Pope, Brazilian poetry overthrew the stylistic monarchy of bourgeois Parnassianism. The remaining symbolist poets come to the fore; such new European movements as surrealism and futurism are brought to bear. These literary activities paralleled the political turmoil which would bring to an end the Old Republic and pave the way for the crypto-fascist Estado Nôvo of the first Getúlio Vargas.

As Spanish American and Brazilian poetry merged, then, the first making an entry, the second going through a process of elutriation, the prose in both halves began to come into resemblance with a kind of neo-realism. In Brazil this, too, was a product of the Modernist revolt, as in reaction against the artificial neoclassical refinements of Parnassianism the Modernists sought out the essence of Brazil that had been hidden so long. Much of the credit for this must go to Euclides da Cunha, who turned against his positivist military education and dug out the basis of Brazil in his classic work *Os Sertões* (1902),[6] a very American work in scope and intent, comparable only to Sarmiento's earlier *Facundo* (1845).

As had been the case with positivism, European ideologies began to show their strength in Brazil and literature began to reflect them. The novel, like Modernist poetry before it, began to become investigative and proponential. The neglected Northeast, the earliest and perhaps the most traditionally "Brazilian" of regions, sought the essence of the whole nation in an analysis of itself. What Gilberto Freyre did in his historical essays of interpretation, Lins do Rêgo would translate into his novels. Here again there is a Cuban counterpart in the ethnic studies of Fernando Ortiz, and we must always remember that Alejo Carpentier's first novel was his Afro-Cuban *Ecué-Yamba-O* (1931). But this self-analysis was also taking place elsewhere in Spanish America: Martínez Estrada in Argentina, Alfonso Reyes and Octavio Paz in Mexico, and others. At this point there is a great similarity between the fiction written in Brazil and that of Spanish America. The theme is most often protest and a consideration of national (in Brazil regional) problems; the locale is, more often than not, rural. Jorge Amado and Rachel de Queiroz deal with poverty in the Northeast as Rómulo Gallegos looks into the interior of Venezuela. This period before World War II sees the two areas coming closer together in fiction, but, with certain exceptions, in that genre they are both behind poetry in slipping into the mainstream.

At the end of this period, which Alceu Amoroso Lima has called Post-Modernism in Brazil, fiction becomes more inward-looking, more personal. Lima calls this third phase Neo-Modernism, a useful enough chronological term which can be considered valid today. The figure of João Guimarães Rosa looms large upon the scene and with the appearance of his great novel *Grande Sertão: Veredas* (1956),[7] Brazilian fiction indeed enters the

Panel members contemplate as Professor Robert J. Morris presents his lecture. From left to right: Professors Marion C. Michael (chairperson), Jim M. Baker, Sydney P. Cravens, and Bart L. Lewis. (Photographed by Sheldon C. Klock, Jr.)

Professor Carl Hammer, Jr. introduces Professor Gregory Rabassa (guest speaker) and Professors Fred P. Ellison, and Norwood H. Andrews, Jr. (panel members). (Photographed by Sheldon C. Klock, Jr.)

mainstream. The situation is not unique: banditry in the region of the São Francisco River, but his manner of presenting the problem and the myriad motifs that permeate the narration give one the impression of a combination of Homer and James Joyce. The protagonist-narrator, Riobaldo, a retired *cangaceiro* (a type of backlands freebooter), tells his tale to a listener who is present but unheard. We, the readers, are at third remove, and we must wonder whether we can trust Riobaldo's story any more than we can trust the veracity of Odysseus' recounting of his fantastic adventures to the Phaeacians. Most of the time Riobaldo himself is puzzled; has he sold his soul to the devil? Rosa has divested this regional tale of the metaplasm which too often obscured the great enduring themes in the novels we call realistic.

There were forerunners, of course: Graciliano Ramos tries to open up the feelings of the primitive mind in *Vidas Sêcas* (1938),[8] even giving us what appears to be the first exposure of the true psyche of the dog; Baleia is a far cry from the humanized creatures folk tradition has given us. Farther back, of course, we have Machado's enigmatic figure of Dom Casmurro, who, also, is to be trusted no more than Odysseus. This vagueness falls well within the scope of existentialism, which, quite naturally, became the vogue immediately upon the horrors of the war. Although mainly removed from those horrors, Brazil was close to the European world and would ask itself the same questions. Riobaldo's narration in *Grande Sertão: Veredas* is essentially one long question sandwiched in between the words *nonada* and *travessia*, meaning nonsense, a trifle, but holding within themselves as in a pregnancy the feeling of nothingness and a crossing, perhaps a passage over to the third bank of the river, an image implicit in this novel and more explicit in one of Rosa's short stories. Clarice Lispector, coming forward at the same time as Rosa and under the tutelage of Lúcio Cardoso (an important author woefully in need of more attention), explored this vein more openly. In her novel *A Maçã no Escuro* (1961),[9] we have the figure of Martim, who goes through rebirth, redevelopment, or some such, only to find that he is back to ground-zero again. It is a question of revelation without epiphany, the meaningless circle fraught with incidents that always raise the question of some kind of social frankpledge. This situation will be seen later in much of the fiction of Gabriel García Márquez. It is the chunk of life that holds whatever meaning we might think is contained in the whole, so aptly seen in Clarice Lispector's subsequent novel *A Paixão Segundo G. H.* (1964, The Passion According to G. H.), where the only imprinted facts are the initials on her luggage.

This trend was slower in reaching Spanish America in such explicit terms. One who was ahead of his time in this and really should be considered the true precursor of the "boom" is Juan Carlos Onetti. There is a striking resemblance between Linacero in *El pozo* and Martim in *A Maçã no Escuro*, both blind in the night and groping in a fruitless search. The hero/heroine of the novel was being returned to the very roots of the genre: the noble, hopeless, quixotic quest. *Das Ding an sich* becomes frighteningly finite and, as García Márquez will show in *Cien años de soledad* (1967),[10] so do hope, expectation, and yearning. These coincidences are less likely to be ascribed to a common background than to a common moment. It may be that Brazil had gathered in cosmopolitan effects earlier than had the Spanish countries. Such effects might be seen in the orderly development of Brazilian literature, including such seeming aberrations as the wild macaronic poetry of Sousândrade and Mário de Andrade's novel *Macunaíma* (1928), baffling to contemporaries but, like Joyce's *Ulysses*, well understood in our own time. There is a coming together of trends, then, with each side falling into normal balance. Regionalism has become the microcosm which reflects the macrocosm, as seen in Guimarães Rosa and Vargas Llosa.

Trends coincide also with a new quest after the depths and heights of hidden meaning. Two writers, José Lezama Lima of Cuba and Osman Lins of Brazil stand hip-deep like a hernshaw in the hypostasis as they seek the thing hidden from Linacero and Martim, *das [heimlich] Ding an sich.* Both have recourse to the unheard and unsolved mysteries of Rome (Etruria, if we consider Manuel Mujica Láinez and his *Bomarzo*, 1962). In *Avalovara* (1973) Lins has superimposed the perfect quadruple Latin palindrome upon the figure of the spiral (which is infinite, up and down) to build his novel. The structure is then by needs related to the geometric and papiroplexic outcome of the catastrophe principle in mathematics as well as to the "traveling saleman" labyrinth of sorts which could keep Borges going on into infinity. In *Paradiso* (1968), Lezama goes underneath the crust of Cuban history to write a novel which might well be the scab that caps the entry into the island's emunctory innards. Macondo has become a continent, even a world, but this construction of the Latin American mythos in visible form has also been done in Brazil by Dalton Trevisan in his re-creation of the moral catacombs of a real city, Curitiba.

The ultimate differentiation of the two Iberian sectors has, of course, been language. In spite of superficial similarities, most often seen in more technical writing, Spanish and Portuguese have been quite divergent in their development. It is not a matter of distinction of alphabet and religion as in the case with Serbian and Croatian. Portuguese has been both more traditional and more inventive than Spanish (Castilian, if you will). The *última flor do Lácio, inculta e bela*, as Olavo Bilac called it, preserves the useful future subjunctive as, like English, it makes better use of the phonically parallel infinitive. Spanish is more protected against solecisms;

you can't say "he don't" in Spanish; you can get close to it in Portuguese. One of the more striking aspects of recent writing in Spanish America has been, precisely, an attempt to break out of the restrictions placed upon expression in Spanish by its very nature. Julio Cortázar wonders why we cannot say "*nosotros vio*" or "*yo vieron*." One can almost go this far in Portuguese. In *Pantaleón y las visitadoras* (1973, Pantaleón and the Visitationists) Vargas Llosa has hit upon a formula for dialogue that is an attempt at reshaping syntax but which just might be a new form of rigidity. In Brazil, Nélida Piñon has reduced her basic expression down to the utterance, with a separation by periods. Her novel *Fundador* (1969) has been translated into Spanish and there might be some influence if her style is followed. In Spanish America Demetrio Aguilera-Malta, in the more recent works, particularly *Siete lunas y siete serpientes* (1970, Seven Serpents and Seven Moons), has opted for this technique with a great staccato, telegraphic effect.

As we come to the "boom" we must take another look at Luis Harss's eminently descriptive title: *Into the Mainstream*. As it stands in many cases, the type of novel being done in Latin America now *is* the mainstream; outsiders look to it for renovation. Yet, we must not be deceived by these new similiarities between Portuguese and Spanish America. The similarities are universal, another coincidence. We can go back and forth across the language barrier with ease, but the same can be done with works written in English, German, French, and any number of languages. The new universalism in fiction as it spreads over the two areas of South America might best be seen in the Ecuadorean novel *Mi tío Atahualpa* (1972), written in Spanish by the Brazilian Paulo de Carvalho Neto. The ambience is Ecuadorean, very much so, but there is a Brazilian *jeito*. This is a rare combination and we must not let it go to our heads. The cultures do remain separate, in spite of outward similarities; what they have in common is most often shared, also, with other areas of the world. Octavio Paz has wisely said that literature is one. Languages, however, are not, and as a translator I know this only too well. So Brazil and Spanish America will remain separate but equal, the works of each will only come across through the haze of translation. But if we grasp the message that Jorge Luis Borges means to put across in his story of Pierre Menard, every reading is essentially an act of translation, sometimes even when what is read is one's very own, as Aureliano Babilonia discovered to his distress in *One Hundred Years of Solitude*.

*Queens College and the Graduate School, The City University of New York*

132

## NOTES

[1] Juan Carlos Onetti, *El pozo* (Montevideo: Bolsilibros Arca, 1965), p. 29. "It is said that there are several ways of lying; but the most repugnant of all is telling the truth, the whole truth, hiding the soul of facts. Because facts are always empty, they are receptacles which take on the shape of the feeling which happens to fill them." Translation mine.

[2] Spain's real national epic (not the *Castilian* epic of the *Poema del Cid*) would, ironically, be written in Catalan by Mossén Jacint Verdaguer, *L'Atlántida* (1877).

[3] *Ufanar-se* - to boast; to be proud of; to extol.

[4] *Cecilia Valdés* was written in 1839 and published with revisions in 1882.

[5] Machado de Assis, *Epitaph of a Small Winner*, trans. William L. Grossman (New York: Noonday Press, 1956).

[6] Euclides da Cunha, *Rebellion in the Backlands*, trans. Samuel Putnam (Chicago: The Univ. of Chicago Press, 1964).

[7] Unfortunately translated into English as *The Devil to Pay in the Backlands*, tr. Harriet de Onís and James L. Taylor (New York: Alfred A. Knopf, 1963).

[8] *Barren Lives*, trans. Ralph Edward Dimmick (Austin: The Univ. of Texas Press, 1971).

[9] *The Apple in the Dark*, trans. Gregory Rabassa (New York: Alfred A. Knopf, 1967).

[10] *One Hundred Years of Solitude*, trans. Gregory Rabassa (New York: Harper and Row, 1970).

# The Hidden Goddess in Julio Cortázar's *Hopscotch*

Daniel R. Reedy

ABSTRACT

Aspects of the mythic infrastructure of Julio Cortázar's *Hopscotch* are seen primarily in the major episodes of the life of Horacio Oliveira, the novel's central character, who seeks to identify avenues leading to the ultimate goal of his existence—an immutable and eternal zone of absolute reality—described variously in the novel as the Center, the Kibbutz of Desire, and Millenary Reign, among other terms. Oliveira's contacts with women provide significant understanding of his search for a means of passage to the Other Side. While the importance of these relationships has been recognized, little attention has been paid to the figure of the *clocharde*, Emmanuèle, with whom the protagonist has a sexual encounter before his departure from Paris for Buenos Aires.

Oliveira's casual comparison of the *clocharde* to a Syrian goddess suggests that Cortázar's conception of this character was based on some undisclosed model from antiquity. In all likelihood his source for the goddess archetype was a tract entitled *De Dea Syria* in which Lucian of Samosata relates his visit to the temple of the goddess Atargatis (also known as Ishtar and Astarte) at Hierapolis between 148 and 149 A.D. Lucian's descriptions of sexual rituals in the worship of the Mother Goddess offer parallels which enhance our understanding of the Oliveira/*clocharde* episode, since the rites and festivities at Hierapolis represented a ceremonial marriage or hierogamy whose purpose was to symbolize spiritual rebirth or renewal.

Cortázar's use of mythic structures in several of his earlier works makes plausible our assumption that a similar technique has been employed in this incident which, because of the nature of the sexual act, most critics have either avoided or have interpreted as convincing proof of the absurd nature of the protagonist's existence. The ritualistic nature of the scene, when examined in light of Lucian's commentaries and our knowledge of the symbolic meaning of other religious rituals, strongly suggests that rather than being an unnecessary, absurd interruption, it is one of the pivotal occurrences in the novel and constitutes a significant aspect of its interior structure. (DRR)

For those of us who have followed developments in the so-called "boom" in Spanish American prose fiction during the past two decades, there is little need to preface this discussion of aspects of Julio Cortázar's *Hopscotch* with an introduction to him as a writer. In the view of most critics, he stands at the forefront of an impressive group whose works have won them international attention and acclaim.

Unlike the regionally oriented novelists of Spanish America who preceded him during the first half of this century, the non-traditional, experimental, and cosmopolitan nature of Cortázar's fiction is its dominant feature, and reflects, perhaps, his own varied intellectual background and range of personal experiences: he was born in Brussels, spent his youth in Argentina, and has lived during the past twenty-five years in France.

With the publication of his first novel, *The Winners* in 1960, and then *Hopscotch* in 1963, his rapidly growing reputation as a novelist elicited from Mexico's Carlos Fuentes the assessment that Julio Cortázar was at the vanguard of contemporary Spanish American fiction . . . and that *Hopscotch* represented to prose in Spanish what Joyce's *Ulysses* had been to prose in English.[1] *Hopscotch* has since been followed by other novelistic successes for Cortázar, with several books of essays on a myriad of topics, and a significant number of volumes of short stories.

Many critics have found in *Hopscotch* a revolutionary model whose imprint on Spanish American fiction will be enduring. A kind of anti-novel, it shattered many traditional concepts of generic structure by offering a book consisting of many books, but two books above all.[2] One version can be read in the normal fashion beginning with Chapter 1 and ending with Chapter 56, with a division between Chapters 36 and 37. An alternate reading begins with Chapter 73 and, following the sequence indicated by the author, includes the ninety-five "Expendable Chapters." In this fashion, the reader hopscotches through a total of 155 chapters. The traditional manner of reading the novel presents an Argentine expatriate, Horacio Oliveira, who lives in Paris during the first part ("From the Other Side"), while in the second portion ("From This Side") he returns to Buenos Aires, where the work ends with Chapter 56 when the protagonist appears to be at the point of committing suicide. The alternate reading offers not only the work which we have just described but also includes the Expendable Chapters which contain a kaleidoscopic collage of notes, sources, newspaper clippings, bits of poetry, additional information about the characters, and observations on novelistic theory provided through the writings of Cortázar's *alter ego* Morelli. This version creates a kind of inconclusive open-ended structure to the novel, since Chapter 131, the final chapter, always returns the reader to Chapter 58 which in turn sends him back again to 131. Thus, the reader becomes an accomplice with the author and must decide for himself when the work will come to an end. As Fuentes has said, the novel is a kind of Pandora's box which, once opened, assails the reader with such a profusion of objects and possibilities that the effect is virtually overwhelming.[3]

The reader finds it particularly difficult to attempt to define *Hopscotch* in the traditional generic sense as novel or romance, as defined, for example, by Northrop Frye in his *Anatomy of Criticism*,[4] for Cortázar's masterpiece represents a different form of prose fiction which might well be termed mythic narrative. As Evelyn J. Hinz states in a recent article which examines in brief some aspects of the concept of mythic narrative, "the mythic artist is not simply a 'novelist' who sees things on a higher level than does the novelist; he sees things in a different way, from different perspectives." She goes on to add that " . . . the mythic artist, like archaic man, regards history as illusion, and the activities, institutions, and values associated with it as profane or symptomatic of man's fallen condition. Like archaic man, the mythic artist conceives of reality as that which is imbued with the divine, that which is eternally recurrent, that which is transmitted in sacred history and myth."[5]

Cortázar employs three interrelated symbols—the hopscotch, the labyrinth and the mandala—both structurally and thematically to serve as graphic representations of the nature of the protagonist's mythic quest in the work. The hopscotch relates to sacred rite and suggests the search for Heaven; the mandala offers at its center the door to nirvana; and the labyrinth, an image which has been present in Cortázar's works since *The Kings* in 1949, is analogous to the other two in that it presents a structure which defends the sanctity of the Center.[6] Critics have pointed out the correspondence of the composite hopscotch/mandala/labyrinth to various aspects of the work: the elective intercalation of chapters into its external structure; the maze of ideas presented through various characters, the numerous graphic images, the labyrinthine nature of the language, and the psychological dimensions of Horacio Oliveira's mind which contains its own inner labyrinth. In the internal structure of the work, Oliveira's experiences correspond symbolically to repeated efforts at advancement through the squares of the hopscotch, the zones of the mandala, or the corridors of the labyrinth with each major episode representing a new attempt to find a pathway which will lead him nearer to his goal.

In the initial chapter of the novel, Oliveira ponders the significance of many of his experiences in Paris, especially those connected with his companion, La Maga, who has since disappeared, and the members of the Club. He remembers it as a time when he first came to realize the nature of his being; he says, "It was about that time I realized that searching was my symbol, the emblem of those who go out at night with nothing in

mind . . . . " Oliveira's recognition of the search as a symbol of his existence is particularly revealing, since Cortázar has created a kind of mythic
infrastructure for his novel from the major episodes of the protagonist's
life.[7] Oliveira is not concerned ostensibly about the "what" of his search
(he seems to know what he is looking for), but about the "how" of
discovering it. The object of his quest is stated with sufficient frequence to
become a motif which provides a rhythmic cadence to the central concept
of the novel: axis, center, *raison d'être*, Omphalos, kibbutz of desire, the
last square of the hopscotch, center of the mandala, Yggdrasil, millenary
kingdom, Arcadia, Heaven, Yonder. Each configuration expresses the
essence of Horacio Oliveira's thrust toward the ultimate goal of his
existence—the immutable and eternal zone of absolute reality.[8]

Oliveira's experiences both in Paris and Buenos Aires are related to his
search for avenues which will lead to the attainment of his goal. He clearly
articulates this search in a conversation with La Maga when he says, "To
find out what's behind something . . . . Yes, that's one of the things I don't
know how to do" (p. 86). Obvious frustration is evident in the realization
that his objective must be sought through or behind ("a través de") some
avenue which he seems incapable of defining with precision. These are the
avenues which he must seek obsessively. The genetic archetype of these
avenues or interstices is described by Morelli in one of the Expendable
Chapters; he says, "I will never be able to escape the feeling that there,
clinging to my face, intertwined among my fingers, there is something like
a dazzling explosion towards the light, an invasion of me in the direction
of the other thing or of the other thing towards me, something infinitely
crystalline that could coalesce and become total light outside time and
space. Like a door of opal and diamond out of which one starts to be the
thing one truly is and does not want and does not know and is not able to
be" (p. 359).

At times Cortázar surprises the unsuspecting reader with somewhat
commonplace images which seem to reveal to Horacio Oliveira a glimpse of
the other side: a puff of smoke from a cigarette, a gourd of freshly brewed
*mate*, a particular piece of jazz, a kaleidoscope, an open window, or the
hole at the top of a circus tent. While all of these images provide fleeting
objectifications of the goal of Oliveira's search, they are not as intrinsically
a part of the work's inner structure, except in a thematic sense, as are
Oliveira's personal relationships with women. In the first half of the narrative, his search for avenues is clearly revealed in his sexual contacts with
two lovers, La Maga and Pola, and in the second half with his interest in
Talita, the wife of his friend and *doppelgänger*, Traveler. In fact, we are
reminded that Oliveira spends much of the novel searching for La Maga,
but his purpose is not motivated so much by a desire to have her personal

companionship again as it is to reestablish a contact which may afford him entry into metaphysical rivers which will lead him to the Center.

The other female involved in Oliveira's search for passage to the Other Side is Emmanuèle, a *clocharde*, with whom the protagonist has a sexual encounter in Chapter 36 at the close of the first half of the work. On the one hand she is a vagabond, a part of the lowest strata of Parisian society, but she is also likened to a Syrian goddess, the Great Mother incarnate, whose true identity is concealed, but whose symbolic function makes her relationship with Oliveira one of the important pivotal occurrences in the internal structure of the work.

Sexual relationships with both La Maga and Pola seems to have mystic significance for Oliveira, who senses that in these two women he may find the pathway leading to the Other Side. For him such relationships are a means of attaining a more perfect state of being, a kind of paradisical state, allowing him to transcend his present condition and enter into another. This idea is underscored, for example, in his revised paraphrase of the first verses of *Genesis*: "In the beginning was the copulative, to rape is to explain, but not always the other way around. To discover the anti-explanatory method, so that this I-love-you, I-love-you would be the hub of the wheel. And Time? Everything begins again, there is no absolute" (p. 36). Women seem to exemplify the quality of primal being for Oliveira, and they offer him a tempting view of the state of being which he wishes to attain.

Although La Maga seems at times to be awkward and intellectually simple (she prefers novels by Galdós for example to philosophy), her role in sexual interplay with Oliveira is both sacred and profane. Even in the grossly physical aspects of their relationship, Oliveira senses that he loves La Maga not so much because she belongs to him, but because she belongs to the other side from which she invites him to jump to make contact. However, he is unable to commit himself to the leap which must be made; as he puts it, "I'm tormented by your love because a bridge can't be supported by just one side" (p. 425).

La Maga seems to have qualities which transcend temporal and spatial boundaries. At one point the mirror reflection of her nude body reminds Oliveira of a small Syrian statue, a fertility goddess perhaps, and he finds a kind of eternity in her body (p. 11). One critic has observed that "the figure of La Maga evokes that of a Black Virgin—an exotic imbrication of Mary and Isis, of woman and deity, of virgin and mother, of paganism and orthodoxy."[9] Yet when the rite of loving La Maga no longer provides the illumination which Oliveira has come to expect, he turns to Pola in hopes of finding that same experience in her. Following La Maga's disappearance, she becomes one of the symbols in the novel which motivates Oliveira's quest. Perhaps in finding her, he can find himself.

In Pola, as with La Maga, Oliveira seems on the verge of breaking through to the other dimension for which he yearns. Pola represents for him a kind of microcosm, a mysterious center which is near, yet so remote (p. 457). This concept is emphasized during one period of sexual activity with her when Oliveira says, "Yes, in that instance of the most crouching animality, closest to excretion and its unspeakable apparatus, there the initial and final figures are sketched, there in the viscous cavern of your daily relaxation stands the trembling Aldebaran, genes and constellations jump, everything becomes alpha and omega, *coquille*, cunt, *concha*, *con*, *coño*, millennium, Armageddon ... " (p. 542). Yet in these visionary moments of mystic revelation, Oliveira cannot reach his goal of perfection, and these sexual encounters do not become as he wishes, "a passport-love, a mountain pass-love, a key-love, a revolver-love, a love that will give him the thousand eyes of Argos ... " (p. 425).

At the close of the first part of the work, "From the Other Side," Oliveira finds himself totally alone as a result of La Maga's disappearance and possible suicide, Pola's seeming fatal illness, and his own alienation from the members of the Club. He wanders aimlessly through the streets of Paris, making his way ultimately to the banks of the Seine, returning to the vicinity of the place where he had first met La Maga, as though his actions are a response to a pre-established cycle. Realizing that suicide in the river is not an alternative for him, he searches for a bridge under which he can take refuge and do some serious thinking about the idea of a kibbutz of desire—another of the terms which he employs as a configuration of the image of the Center. Beneath the bridge, Oliveira finds himself in the company of several *clochards* who snore under piles of papers and burlap bags, but he is only casually aware of them as he concentrates on the idea of a kibbutz of desire and ponders how to find it. He reflects that he might have been more successful had he been searching according to the pattern of a tribal rite (p. 204). His thoughts offer, perhaps, an unconscious clue to the nature and significance of the symbolic acts which occur between him and the *clocharde* Emmanuèle, later in the chapter.

Horacio's descent to the river bank follows closely the pattern of action typical of the trek of the mythic hero archetype, as described by Joseph Campbell in his *Hero With a Thousand Faces*.[10] It is a descent in search of adventure and encounter, motivated by an overwhelming desire to find some experience which will bring about psychological rebirth or transcendence into a new state of spiritual being. In a recent article Margery A. Safir points out that his movements in this scene "recall an entire Western tradition of ultimately redemptive descents: Odysseus and Aeneas, who descend to the underworld and emerge closer to the end of their journeys; Christ, who after descending into Hell, later arises resurrected; Dante, who also descends to the Inferno, emerging afterward closer to his final destination, Paradise. In other words, when Oliveira, in a critical moment of his life, descends to the banks of the Seine within a symbolic context which echoes this Western mythological and religious tradition, he is exemplifying Mircea Eliade's observation that in moments of crisis man imitates the acts of his gods or of his ancestors."[11]

As Horacio Oliveira meditates on the kibbutz of desire, he is approached by one of the *clochardes*, Emmanuèle, who asks for a cigarette. Described in terms which seem to conceal her identity, she is clothed in four or five dresses, topcoats and overcoats, has pink-powdered cheeks, blackened fingers and matted hair wrapped in a wool scarf which is distinguished by its red and green stripes (pp. 206, 208). In what seems a most unlikely liaison of an Argentine intellectual and a Parisian hobo, the two of them make their way, at the urging of the *clocharde* to a local shop where they buy two quarts of red wine before taking refuge in an arcade where they engage in what can best be described as a Dionysian orgy. At first Oliveira is repulsed by the filth and by the odors which emanate from the body of the *clocharde*, but little by little, he overcomes his nausea as they suck at the bottles of wine by turns. At this point in the narrative, Oliveira seems to experience a kind of epiphany, a revelation of the *clocharde*'s true identity, as he sees the face of Emmanuèle light up in the glow of her cigarette:

> and Oliveira saw the spots of dirt on her forehead, her thick lips stained with wine, the triumphal scarf of the Syrian goddess that had been trampled on by some enemy army, a chryselephantine head rolling around in the dust, with spots of blood and gore but keeping all the while the diadem of red and green stripes, the Great Mother stretched out in the dust and trampled on by drunken soldiers who amused themselves by pissing on her mutilated breasts, until the greatest clown among them knelt down to the accolade of all the others, his penis standing out erect above the fallen goddess, masturbating onto the marble and letting the sperm trickle into the eye-holes from which officers' hands had already plucked the precious stones, into the half-open mouth which accepted the humiliation as a final offering before rolling off into oblivion. (pp. 209-10)

We could dismiss the implications of this surrealistic vision of the *clocharde* as being nothing more than the result of the stuporific effects of the wine which the protagonist has consumed, but the tell-tale images of the Syrian goddess and the allusion to the Great Mother strongly imbue the scene with an aura of religious mystic ritual, suggesting that the *clocharde* is a primal being, and implying that this epiphany transcends both time and space.

The orgiastic nature of the ritual in which Oliveira and the *clocharde* are engaged is significant in light of what Cirlot tells us about practices involving drunkenness and sexual license. He suggests that orgies "correspond to a 'fall to chaos' as a result of a weakening of the will to accept the norm in the ordinary way. Hence . . . the orgy is a cosmogonic equivalent of Chaos and of supreme, ultimate fulfilment, as well as of the eternal moment and of timelessness . . . . In these uninhibited festivities the tendency is to 'confuse forms' by means of the inversion of the social pattern, the juxtaposition of opposites and the unleashing of the passions . . . . "[12] This idea is all the more cogent when we observe that through his vision of Emmanuèle as the Great Mother goddess, Oliveira senses the proximity of his kibbutz lurking somewhere in the background: "something told him that there was a kibbutz there, that in back of it all, always in back, there was hope for a kibbutz. Not a methodical certainty, oh no, dear fellow, never that, much as you might want it that way, nor an *in vino veritas* nor a Fichte-like dialectic or other Spinozan precious stones, only an acceptance in nausea . . . " (p. 210). His mental vagaries prompt a continuing psychic descent as he recalls the example of Heraclitus who, according to tradition, buried himself in dung as a means of curing himself of dropsy. For Oliveira, the association with the *clocharde* and the ensuing alcoholic orgy emulate Heraclitus' act of self-humiliation, and he envisions that he, too, by figuratively burying himself in dung, is somehow getting closer to that moment of encounter which he likens in his imagination to the wringing of the neck of the swan, that moment of exquisite beauty and ecstasy when the swan sings its last song or when the kibbutz is reached (an allusion to González Martínez' "tuércele el cuello al cisne . . . ").

As their revelries continue, Emmanuéle sings lines from *Les Amants du Havre*, presaging as it were the sexual activities which follow between the two. In a state of detached amusement and still thinking about his kibbutz of desire, Oliveira watches as the *clocharde* unbuttons his trousers and begins to perform fellatio on him:

> . . . for hygienic reasons he would have condemned the fact that Emmanuèle was little by little leaning more heavily on her drunken friend and with a tongue stained with tannin was humbly licking his deal, helping to maintain its understandable abandon with her fingers and murmuring things in the language one uses when holding kittens or nursing babies, completely oblivious of the meditation that was going on up above, bent on a duty that would afford her little profit . . . . (p. 212)

The moment of ritual illumination which appears imminent for Oliveira is abruptly terminated by a policeman who drags Emmanuèle to her feet. Even though reality has injected itself into the scene, Oliveira continues to see the *clocharde* as a Syrian goddess while the figure of the conquering soldier is replaced by that of the gendarme.

It would be easy enough to deal with this scene as many critics have done, that is, avoid commenting on it altogether, or we could state as some have observed that Cortázar included this explicit material as a kind of shock treatment for the reader who might be expected to recoil in disgust and disbelief at Oliveira's participation in such sexual activity with a nauseating hobo. Or we may suggest that it represents the ultimate extreme of absurdity to which Oliveira's life has come.[13] Others have found in this scene evidence of Cortázar's desire to interject social commentary into the novel by suggesting that Oliveira's is a symbolic act representing the desire to purge himself of alienation, deceit, and bourgeois egoism.[14]

My own contention is that this scene dramatically emphasizes, perhaps better than any other, the internal pattern of the protagonist's mythic search for self realization within the work through the act of love—not in the usual sense of intercourse between two individuals as with La Maga or Pola—but an act which signifies acceptance of total human reality, as one critic has put it, *in nausea*.[15] By entering into a relationship with the *clocharde*, even passively, Oliveira symbolically emulates the model of an archaic or mythic archetype. He abandons the world with which he has previously been associated and enters into a ritual relationship with the *clocharde*, thus reactualizing a kind of primordial mythic time and sacred event.[16] In his book, *The Sacred and the Profane*, in which he examines the nature and origins of religion, Mircea Eliade notes that for archaic man physiological acts often received religious meaning as imitations of divine models (p. 168), becoming a kind of mystical rite (p. 171) in a union which repeats the primordial *hieros gamos*, the union of Heaven and Earth (p. 170). The cosmic structure of such rituals or of ritual orgies, involving sexual practices, signifies a hierogamy of a Fecundating God and an Earth Mother (p. 146) out of which regeneration is anticipated as man is born anew and begins life over again (p. 80). In Jungian terminology, this hierogamous union signifies the "spiritual conjunction that takes place when the process of individuation is complete, with the harmonious union of the unconscious and conscious."[17] It is also important to note that the name of the *clocharde*, Emmanuèle, symbolically alludes to the idea of salvation, that is, through its implied promise of spiritual rebirth.

We cannot assert unequivocally that Cortázar had in mind a particular model in Oliveira's vision of a "Syrian goddess," but we are reminded that a number of Cortázar's earlier works contain structures based on classical and religious myths. Such is the case of his poetic dialogue on the theme of the Cretan Minotaur, *The Kings*, published in 1949. Roberto González Echevarría's recent article on this work provides convincing evidence of Cortázar's reliance on mythic or primal materials not only in *The Kings*, but in several short stories.[18] We can also add to this group, to name just a few, Cortázar's short story "Circe," the Bacchus myth in "The Menades," and the Dionysian rituals in "The Idol of the Cyclades."

In all likelihood, Cortázar's source for the goddess archetype, as revealed in the masquerading figure of the *clocharde*, was a tract entitled *De Dea Syria* by Lucian of Samosata.[19] Lucian visited the temple of the Syrian goddess Atargatis (also known as Ishtar, Astarte and Hera) at Hierapolis between 148 and 149 A.D. His descriptions of the cult and worship of this goddess of Northern Syria at her sacred city, now known as Munbij, have long been of interest to students and historians of religions of the ancient Near East, for he appears to be the only writer who dwells on the fundamental character of the cult and his firsthand observations enhance greatly our knowledge of early religious practices. Atargatis, the female deity who inhabited the temple at Hierapolis, is identified by Lucian as Hera, having been mated with a god, whom Lucian calls "Zeus." Lucian also recognizes in her traces of Aphrodite and aspects of the Mother Goddess or Great Mother, a term which Cortázar also employs in his description of the vision of the *clocharde* goddess.[20] The characteristic which most typified the cult of the Syrian goddess was the immorality of the females who inhabited the temple and who served as sacred prostitutes.[21] This, too, seems related to the characterization of the *clocharde* who, we are informed in one of the Expendable Chapters, was a whore in the provinces before going to Paris to join *clocharde* society (p. 465).

Lucian's own descriptions underscore the sexual nature of the sacred rites at Hierapolis; he says,

> There are in the temple many tokens that Dionysus was its actual founder; for instance, barbaric raiment, Indian precious stones, and elephants' tusks brought by Dionysus from the Aethiopians. Further, a pair of phalli of great size are seen standing in the vestibule, bearing the inscription, "I, Dionysus, dedicated these phalli to Hera my stepmother." This proof satisfies me. And I will describe another curiosity to be found in this temple, a sacred symbol of Dionysus. The Greeks erect phalli in honour of Dionysus, and on these they carry, singular to say, mannikins made of wood, with enormous pudenda; they call these puppets. There is this further curiosity in the temple: as you enter, on the right hand, a small brazen statue meets your eye of a man in a sitting posture with parts of enormous size.[22]

While it may be only sheer coincidence, we are also reminded by this description of the image of Oliveira slouched in the arcade with his erect member exposed, like the statue of Dionysus, and we are led to ponder whether or not the resemblance between Lucian's description of the statue and the image of Oliveira by Cortázar is only casual.

In his comments on the legends concerning the founders of the temple, Lucian relates that it was originally the work of Statonice, the wife of the king of the Assyrians (p. 58), who fell in love with her stepson and was exhorted in a vision of Hera to build a temple to this goddess at Hierapolis

(p. 60). During her work on the temple, Statonice fell in love with another young man who her husband, the king, had sent to accompany her in her work. While at first she could find no way to consummate her amorous desire, she finally hit upon a plan of drinking too much wine which would give her courage to overcome her own reluctance and seduce the young man (p. 62). Here, as with the scene between Horacio and the *clocharde*, the drinking of wine becomes an important part of the preliminary ceremonies leading to their involvement in the sexual act. As a way of showing his adoration for the goddess Hera and to win her favor, as well as being motivated by his desire not to dishonor himself and the king by giving into Statonice's desires, the young man castrated himself. Lucian notes that when he visited the temple, it was still common for many persons to castrate themselves each year as an act of adoration and complete submission to the goddess. We are left to wonder if, in fact, there is not some parallel to be drawn between the castrated men in Lucian's myth and the fact that two pederasts are in the police wagon as Horacio and Emmanuèle are carted away at the close of the chapter.

As a part of the ceremonies and customs which took place in the temple, women usually dedicated their bodies to the service of the goddess and they celebrated at regular seasons of the year with revelries which tended to become, with the passage of time, more and more orgiastic.[23] These ceremonies reflected the belief that such unions represented the ritual ending of the world and its re-creation, and that through them man, himself, would be regenerated or reborn. While orgiastic in their external appearance, they represented a union of *cosmic* and *sacred* dimensions. The act of love, in all its various forms, took on the significance of a marriage of heaven and earth, a hierogamy, whose object was cosmogony, i.e. the regeneration or rebirth of the cosmos.

As presented by Cortázar, Oliveira's sexual union with the *clocharde* symbolically represents holy union with the Syrian goddess, who in turn is equated with the concept of the Great Mother. The archetype of the Great Mother is often related to such feminine dieties as Ishtar of Babylonia or Astarte in Phoenicia, or Hera (Atargatis) in Lucian's essay, and usually embodies the attributes of the nature-goddess. As explained by Jung, the "Magna Mater represents the objective truth of Nature, masquerading, or incarnate, in the figure of a maternal woman . . . a goddess or a priestess . . . ."[24] And the red and green stripes of the scarf worn by the *clocharde* denote her qualities of passion and fecundity. We may be reluctant at first to ascribe the provocative qualities of a seductive goddess to Emmanuèle, but it seems clear that this is, indeed, her symbolic role in the work. In his vain attempt to reach a kibbutz, a kibbutz of desire, Oliveira feels its existence somewhere just outside his reach and through the *clocharde* he seems to glimpse the pathway which will lead him to that destination. When the ritual between him and the *clocharde*/goddess is interrupted, he does not reach his goal and is left to begin his quest anew, not in Paris but in Buenos Aires, the place where his origins began and where he will continue his search. As he notes at one point "Everything can be killed except nostalgia for the kingdom, we carry it in the color of our eyes, in every love affair, in everything that deeply torments and unties and tricks. *Wishful thinking*, perhaps; but that is just another possible definition of the featherless biped" (pp. 380-81). The relationships with La Maga, with Pola, and with the *clocharde* all represent attempts at using the avenue of love to reach Heaven, the top of the Hopscotch, but all fail to lift him to that point of mystic perfection.

There is no apparent lessening in the intensity with which Oliveira presses toward his goal in the second portion of the work, labeled "From This Side." His wanderings in search of La Maga have taken him without success to Montevideo prior to arriving in Buenos Aires where he meets with his *doppelgänger*, Traveler, and with Talita, whom Oliveira seems to identify as La Maga. However, Oliveira has still not found that passageway to the other side, or, as he puts it, "there was still no bridge as yet" (p. 266). And when asked about some of his experiences in Paris, he finds only two things worth mentioning, that the weather was very changeable and that he once dropped a lump of sugar beneath a table in a restaurant (p. 225).

In Buenos Aires, Oliveira also rejoins a former companion, Gekrepten, who has awaited his return from Paris like a patient Penelope. But it is Talita, the complement of La Maga, and not Gekrepten, who becomes the new avenue which attracts Oliveira. As was the case with both Pola and La Maga, Talita appears to Oliveira as a woman "with a lighted candle in her hand, showing a path" (pp. 292-93). On one occasion, he tells her, " 'You're Egeria, our nymph, our bridge, our medium' "(p. 265), in an obvious reference to his belief that she functions as a transmitter of hidden secrets and undisclosed pathways.

One of the most commented upon exploits in the novel involves Oliveira's desire to build a bridge of planks between his apartment and the building across the way where Traveler and Talita live. The scene is dramatically absurd as the two men tie planks together and extend them from one window to the other. And it is noteworthy that Talita is the one who straddles the planks and attempts to make her way to Oliveira's apartment, carrying with her some nails and *yerba* for *mate*, which Oliveira has requested. This scene offers a physical manifestation of Oliveira's symbolic attempt to erect a bridge between himself and others, particularly with Talita and with Traveler, who represents Oliveira's other complementary self. Both Talita and Traveler are serious participants in Oliveira's bridge-building ritual, but the game ends when Talita is forced to throw the nails and *yerba* to Oliverira for fear that the planks will give way and spill her into the street below. His inability to make a meaningful contact with Talita and Traveler is lamented by Oliveira, who senses the failure acutely and comments afterwards, "We let reality slip through our fingers like an ordinary trickle of water. We had it right there, almost perfect, like a rainbow between our thumb and our little finger" (p. 257). Had the bridge worked like a rainbow, as Oliveira describes it figuratively, perhaps he would have reached the golden treasure at its end.

The bridge-building attempt serves as the prelude to another scene involving Talita which closely parallels in significance that of Oliveira and the *clocharde*. In Chapter 54 we find Traveler and Oliveira employed in a mental hospital, although we are left to wonder whether in reality Oliveira is an employee or a patient. With greater frequency he confuses the identity of Talita with La Maga, and in a scene reminiscent of Orpheus' descent into hell in search of Eurydice, he succeeds in getting Talita to accompany him to the morgue in the basement of the asylum, to a kind of refrigerated Hades. It becomes his last major attempt to make contact with Talita—his Eurydice—and to effect "re-entry into the human family" (p. 319), as he had endeavored to achieve a lasting contact through La Maga, Pola, and the *clocharde*. When Oliveira attempts to kiss Talita, he says, "It was as if they were coming together from somewhere else, with some other part of themselves, and it wasn't a question of themselves, as if they were paying or collecting something for others ... " (p. 320). His thoughts suggest again a kind of re-enactment of an action which had occurred before. Although Talita tries to understand what it is he wishes for her, fear and uneasiness force her to retreat from the coldness of the morgue, because she seems to perceive some hidden meaning in the ritual nature of this encounter. For a moment Oliveira has seemed close to the last square of the hopscotch, through Talita, but its ultimate attainment eludes him once again.

In the final scenes of Chapter 56, the end of the novel-novel, Oliveira reaches the point of commiting himself to the most decisive act of his life. In his second-floor room of the asylum, he attempts to isolate himself from the rest of the world from which he feels completely alienated. Using spools of thread to make a barrier to protect against intrusions, he resembles a spider spinning its web, graphically suggesting a mandala barrier, in which he creates for himself a consecrated spot where his final ritual and liturgical performance will take place. He perches in the window in his self-created center, "telling himself that there was some meeting after all, even though it might only last just for that terribly sweet instant in which the best thing without any doubt at all would be to lean over just a little bit farther out and let himself go, paff the end" (pp. 348-49). As is well known, there is no conclusive answer to the question of whether or not Oliveira commits suicide by jumping from the window or whether he has gone insane, as the Expendable Chapters suggest. What is important is that for the first time in his life Oliveira commits a decisive act, whether in a physical or psychic sense, by making a leap which he hopes will land him in the heaven of the hopscotch, in nirvana, or the center of the labyrinth. It is suggested, however, that he has achieved an ultimate state of awareness through a kind of psychic transformation in which there is a mystical loss of consciousness in ecstasy. The eight Expendable Chapters which follow suggest that Oliveira was not killed by his leap, but is suffering from a severe state of neurosis, which is diagnosed by the doctor as *hysteria matinensis yugulata*. The most significant part of this diagnosis is the term *hysteria* which has its origins in the Greek work, *hystera*, meaning "uterus." In a sense the dissociated state of hysteria for Oliveira could be construed in a mythic context as a return to the womb and is outwardly depicted as a withdrawal from consciousness. Whatever the case, the possibilities of rebirth are symbolically present in the various endings offered by the open structure of the narrative's conclusion.

In summary, we can reiterate that Cortázar's inclusion of the *clocharde*, as a kind of hidden goddess in the work, reveals an important aspect of the mythic infrastructure of *Hopscotch*. Examined in the light of Lucian's commentaries and our knowledge of the symbolic nature of early religious rituals, the *clocharde* episode represents one of the work's pivotal occurrences because of the parallels to be noted in the protagonist's relationships with other women through whom he seeks the sacred Center. Above all, this episode offers a meaningful indication of the recurring mythic process in *Hopscotch*—a process which contributes significantly to the work's inner dynamics, while demonstrating, as well, Cortázar's ability as a writer to transcend temporal and spatial constraints in his search for comprehension of the nature of man and his universe.

*University of Kentucky*

## NOTES

[1] Carlos Fuentes, "*Rayuela*: la novela como caja de Pandora," *Mundo Nuevo*, 9 (March 1967), 68.

[2] Julio Cortázar, *Hopscotch*, trans. Gregory Rabassa (New York: New American Library, 1969). See "Table of Instructions," (n.p.). Subsequent textual citations from *Hopscotch* are to this edition and are cited parenthetically in the text.

[3] Fuentes, p. 67.

[4] Northrop Frye, *Anatomy of Criticism* (New York: Atheneum, 1969). See the essays entitled "The Mythos of Summer: Romance" and "Specific Continuous Forms (Prose Fiction)."

[5] Evelyn J. Hinz, "Hierogamy versus Wedlock: Types of Marriage Plots and Their Relationship to Genres of Prose Fiction," *PMLA*, 91, No. 5 (1976), 904-05.

[6] Ana María Pucciarelli, "Notas sobre la búsqueda en la obra de Cortázar," *Homenaje a Julio Cortázar*, ed. Helmy Giacomán (New York: Las Americas Publishing Company, 1972), pp. 181-93.

[7] Frye, *Anatomy of Criticism*, points out that the quest myth is one of the fundamental myths in literature. See in particular his essay, "Archetypal Criticism: Theory of Myths," pp. 131-239.

[8] Mircea Eliade, *The Myth of the Eternal Return*, trans. William R. Trask (New York: Pantheon Books, 1954). See the chapter "Archetypes and Repetition," especially the sections entitled "The Symbolism of Center," and "Repetition of the Cosmology," pp. 12-21.

[9] Lida Aronne Amestoy, *Cortázar: La novela mandala* (Buenos Aires: Fernando García Cambeiro, 1972), p. 69. Translation mine.

[10] Joseph Campbell, *The Hero With a Thousand Faces*, 2nd ed. (Princeton: Princeton Univ. Press, 1968), p. 30.

[11] Margery A. Safir, "An Erotics of Liberation: Notes on Transgressive Behavior in *Rayuela* and *Libro de Manuel*," *Books Abroad*, 50, No. 3 (1976), 559.

[12] J. E. Cirlot, *Dictionary of Symbols*, trans. Jack Sage (New York: Philosophical Library, 1962), pp. 232-33.

[13] Kathleen Genover, *Claves de una novelística existencial (en Rayuela de Cortázar)* (Madrid: Playor, 1973), pp. 114-15.

[14] Amestoy, p. 74.

[15] Graciela de Sola, *Julio Cortázar y el hombre nuevo* (Buenos Aires: Ed. Sudamericana, 1968), p. 95.

[16] Mircea Eliade, *The Sacred and the Profane. The Nature of Religion*, trans. W. R. Trask (New York: Harcourt, Brace and World, 1957), pp. 68-69.

[17] Cirlot, p. 160.

[18] Roberto González Echevarría, "*Los reyes:* Cortázar's Mythology of Writing," *Books Abroad*, 50, No. 3 (1976), 548-57.

[19] Lucian, *The Syrian Goddess*, trans. Herbert A. Strong, ed. John Garstang (London: Constable and Co., 1913).

[20] Ibid., "Editor's Preface," pp. vii-ix.

[21] Franz Valery Marie Cumont, *The Oriental Religions in Roman Paganism* (Chicago: Open Court Publishing Co., 1911), p. 118.

[22] Lucian, p. 57.

[23] John Garstand, "Introduction," *The Syrian Goddess*, p. 19.

[24] Cirlot, p. 127.

# Mexican Literature and Chicano Literature: A Comparison

Sabine R. Ulibarrí
Dick Gerdes (not pictured)

## ABSTRACT

Few attempts have been made until now to compare Mexican and Chicano literature. Is Chicano literature a branch, extension, or manifestation of Mexican literature? Is it one of the minority literatures that form a part of the main body of American literature? Or is it part of a larger realm, Latin American literature? Regardless of the answers, and reasons for the answers, one might give to these questions, it is undeniable that the Chicano still relates strongly to Mexican history and art. Even the contemporary "Renaissance" period (since 1945) shows the Chicano experience in literature, as in other ways, closely tied to "Mexicanness." This Mexican connection consists particularly of cultural and traditional materials—family, religion, moral concepts, youth and old age, death, time, and a sense of community—whose presence in Chicano literature derives from the pre-Columbian indigenous period, Hispanic values and the Mexican Revolution of 1910. Paradoxically or not, the very Mexicanness of Chicano literature has done much to create a feeling of "cultural nationalism" that we see in Chicano writing.

The Mexican heritage of Chicano literature also includes Hispanic influences which—since the Conquest, through the Colonial period, and up to the present century—had all but been lost in Chicano history, art and literature. But in the same way that the Mexican Revolution created a new spirit in art for the Mexican then, rediscovered Hispanic and Mexican values have influenced the Chicano Renaissance of today.

In a wider view, opinions regarding the relationship between Chicano and Mexican literature are varied and mostly general. Moreover, such opinions tend to reflect personal or political biases and spiritual concerns rather than an objective interest in the literature as literature. For this reason, an important truth has gone largely unstated: a certain narrative and stylistic sophistication in Chicano fiction and poetry confirms the participation of the Chicano artist, like the Mexican artist, in the major trends of contemporary literature. (SRU, DG)

Attempting to compare Chicano literature and Mexican literature invariably leads to an open-ended debate regarding the relationships the two might have in common. The American Southwest—now designated Aztlán—has been under the social, political, economic and even cultural domination of Anglo-America since 1848, the year when the Treaty of Guadalupe Hidalgo called for Mexico to turn over to the United States a land area corresponding to the states of California, Nevada, Utah, Arizona, Colorado, New Mexico and Texas for the sum of 15 million dollars. The Chicano poet, Nephtalí de León, says of the event that "Mexico's land was thus divided, but Mexico's soul was not. No Chicano respects any boundary set up by the United States today. Nor will Chicanos or Mexicans be hemmed in spiritually by any physical boundary imposed by force and aggression."[1] It is our intent here to search out the significance of this relationship between Chicanos and Mexicans, hopefully from a literary point of view.[2]

Some initial questions would be, then, is Chicano literature a branch, an extension, or a manifestation of Mexican literature? Is it one of the minority literatures that form a part of the main body of American literature? Or is it perhaps a part of a larger realm we know as Latin American literature? Some Chicano writers and essayists feel that Chicano art of the 1970's is seeking to establish a more substantial literary identity within the mainstream of American literature, and others see the last ten years of Chicano literature as a reflection of a distinct Hispanic-American culture. Rolando Hinojosa, noted scholar and prose fiction writer at Texas A&I University, says that "Mexican-American literature may be considered a part of American literature; however," he adds, "because it is written in Spanish, some may wish to categorize it as Mexican literature. The bilingual aspect that makes Chicano literature unique also makes it difficult to fit into this or that slot of the curriculum."[3] Whatever the case, it is certainly true that the reality of the Chicano experience in history, art and perhaps literature, and the Chicano's cultural values and aspirations, still depend on Mexican history and art.

For the artist Manuel J. Martínez, the Chicano creative experience is like a baby, whose mother is ancient Indian art, whose father is Spanish Colonial art and whose midwife is modern Mexican art.[4] It may be, then, that the historical perspective on Mexican-American literature devised by Professor Luis Leal is valid. His "Hispanic Period" (to 1821) confirms the importance Martínez gives to the Spanish Colonial period. Interestingly enough, Leal goes on to define four other periods since then, all of which essentially relate to Mexico, including the last and present period which, as most agree, is the "Chicano Period," or "Renaissance" (since 1945);[5] hence the Chicano experience is closely tied to—as one Chicano critic calls it—"Mexicanness."[6] For Octavio Paz, the Mexican poet and essayist, in an interview conducted by José Armas. editor of the journal *De Colores*, this means Mexican traditions and culture—family, religion, moral concepts, youth and old age, death, time and a sense of community.[7] The Mexican presence in Chicano history, art and literature is intensified by the pre-Columbian era on one end of the time scale and the Mexican Revolution of 1910 on the other.

For the Chicano scholar, Mildred Monteverde, the full range of Mexican heritage is the main contributor to the later Chicano art of Aztlán. Architectural style in Aztlán provides a good illustration of how this Mexican heritage is undeniable and yet is difficult to trace directly. From the time of the Conquest and through the Spanish and Mexican Colonial period, the Spanish "mission" style of architecture, spread throughout Aztlán. Although later influenced by the Indian *pueblo* style of low massive adobe constructions and adorned with the Mexican Churrigue-resque style of colorful stone inlay and carvings in Texas and California missions, the first mission appeared in New Mexico in the seventeenth century. However, not until after World War I do we find a conscientious effort to revive not only the Mexican Colonial style of architecture in the Southwest but also a concern for pre-Columbian forms and a sincere interest in Native American traditions. In the minds of some Chicanos the unfortunate outcome of this revival has been the superficial expropriation of these styles and traditions by middle-class Anglo-Americans. It is true that this colonial architecture is not concentrated in the *barrio* but has served as a popular style for mansions located in the wealthy Anglo residential areas. The fact is that much of the Chicano past has been either ignored by the dominant sector of society or expropriated when it was felt to reflect a faddishly popular grass-roots tradition.[8]

It seems only natural, then, as Professor Juan Bruce-Novoa of Yale University points out, that the presence of Mexico in the Chicano experience stems not only from heritage but also from a strong negative reaction to the Anglo-American presence in Aztlán.[9] This has tended to drive Chicano writers and artists to Mexico's past. The conclusions to Alba Irene Moesser's doctoral disseration on Mexican-American literature indicate that the Mexican-American has sought protection from the hostile Anglo society by finding refuge in the culture of his forefathers.[10] If we stop to look at this past and then direct our gaze up to the present century and finally consider the recent "renaissance" period, we see that Chicano literature—that which has mainly been written in or about the Hispanic Southwest by Mexican-Americans since 1848—has its roots and, consequently, logical and valid imitative aspects in Spanish and Mexican Colonial art and literature. The situation is similiar perhaps to the relationship between American Colonial literature and English literature, where older chronicles, diaries, travelogues, sermons and later the popularization of oral traditions found in the folk tale, drama and song are shared forms and sources.

Literary antecedents to Chicano literature that show the Hispanic influence are found in the historical-literary documents of the seventeenth and eighteenth centuries: Gaspar Pérez de Villagrás epic poem, *History of New Mexico*, recorded in 1610; the religious and secular dramas, such as *The Shepherds* and the *Three Wise Men*; other compositions such as the ballad and popular songs, known as the *romance, copla* and *corrido*; and, finally, folklore in the form of tales and legends.[11] Important scholarly findings about this period have been contributed through the research of Aurelio M. Espinosa, Arthur Campa, Américo Paredes, Rubén Cobos and Aurora White Lucero. Espinosa, born in Colorado in 1880, wrote a doctoral dissertation on the linguistic aspects of the Southwest.[12] Espinosa also found relationships between American Southwest folklore and Hispanic popular literature from before and during the Golden Age of Spanish Peninsular literature. This research has been documented in the *Journal of American Folklore* and other journals since 1910.[13]

In addition to his son, another disciple of Espinosa's is Arthur Campa, who has studied religious and secular drama and collected folk tales and legends in his book, *Treasures of The Sangre de Cristos*.[14] Américo Paredes has studied a South Texas *corrido* about the life of Gregorio Cortez in his book, *With a Pistol in His Hand*.[15] Rubén Cobos of the University of New Mexico is just finishing a multi-volume collection of Southwest folklore.[16] These studies not only show how the Hispanic and Mexican heritage in the Southwest is strong but also how New World conditions produced changes and new interpretations of certain universalized literary forms which are found in Mexico, as far away as Chile and, of course, in Spain.

We find some close ties between Mexican and Chicano literature, then, up to the nineteenth century. But, from this point on, establishing a Chicano literary tradition is difficult because too much has been lost and too much is at present virtually unknown.[17] However, a 1974 issue of *De Colores* presents the recently-discovered constitution and poetry of a New Mexican literary society, *La Sociedad Social, Literaria y de Devates de Agua Negra, Nuevo Mexico, 1898*, an organization whose possible sources of inspiration came from its Mexican counterparts, *La Academia de Letrán* and *El Liceo Hidalgo*, literary groups which spanned the Romantic Period of Mexican literature. Philip Ortego feels that this unknown element has occurred because from mid-nineteenth century onward the Mexican-American has been a marginal person living in the Anglo-dominated society which, for the Chicano caught between polarizing forces, is a no-man's land.[18] Francisco Lomelí and Donaldo Urioste, who have just published their highly-acclaimed critical and annotated bibliography, *Chicano Perspectives in Literature*, say in their introduction that "as a consequence, literary expression remained an amorphous body written by a few. Describing historical reality as it was became a dangerous matter, assuming that the conquered were supposed to resign themselves to their new position. These circumstances, then, tend to produce lyrical-escapist, unpublished-protest, nostalgic-filled prose and poetry which too often disintegrated in old family chests. In accordance with the spirit," they add, "literature was viewed as part of a social ritual and not as an instrument for understanding society."[19]

Even though frustration and alienation have resulted, such feelings exist because of these "sins of omission" that the Chicano "renaissance" began. Ortego says that even though Chicanos may know about Mexican poetry, "we don't know the extent to which the Hispanic poetic tradition influenced the North Mexican area."[20] With the aforementioned studies of oral traditions, liturgical plays and musical forms in mind, most students of Chicano literature assume the Chicano tradition is similiar to the Mexican. The lost portion of the Chicano literary tradition, however, has prevented or misdirected scholars from evaluating the relationships of Hispanic and Mexican culture and literature to Chicano literature with any confidence. Aside, then, from seeking refuge in the excuse of a hostile society and/or searching for a past in pre-nineteenth century Mexican heritage, we can make some strong claims about the influence of the Mexican Revolution of 1910 on Chicano art in general. From the Mexican Artist's Syndicate formed in 1922 came a new spirit of enthusiasm in art which recognized human values and their expression in a creative form. Instead of promoting "Art for Art's sake," this group—best exemplified through the muralist painters—contributed a socially-conscious art. Due to the importance given to the muralists in the arts, the new revolutionary art and its accompanying spirit of renewal, as generated by José Clemente Orozco, Diego Rivera, David Siqueiros and others, is felt to be the spearhead of the Chicano counterpart today; Chicano art also has social protest as its departure point.[21]

Concurrent with this new artistic spirit we find three literary tendencies in Mexico: the Novel of the Mexican Revolution; the vanguard writers; and the *Contemporáneos* group which strove to deal, respectively, with the Revolution as theme, innovation and experimentation, and the conflict between national and universal aspects of literature. The thematic concerns of the novel of the Revolution indicate three stages of development. These states can be seen through the works of Mariano Azuela, Martín Luis Guzmán and Gregorio López y Fuentes. While Azuela treats the active stage of the Revolution and Guzmán concerns himself with the post-revolutionary days, López y Fuentes exemplifies the social protest stage of development.[22] José Juan Tablada, whose vanguard poetry is innovative but usually not profound, invented new imagery and toyed with the haiku. With the appearance of the *Contemporáneos* magazine in 1928, a polemic between the loosely-defined group of the same name and the nationalists arose concerning how to conciliate nationalism and universalism. Whereas the *Contemporáneos* tended to follow vanguard ideas of a European nature, they were criticized for being too hermetic, lacking social commitment and concerning themselves too exclusively with aesthetics. Their opponents wanted to emphasize Mexican nationalism by making social commitment in their literature easily understood, which ultimately ended in the recreation of customs and regionalisms and, finally, propaganda. The *Contemporáneos* group includes such fine poets as Carlos Pellicer, José Gorostiza, Xavier Villaurrutia, Jaime Torres Bodet, and Salvador Novo; the use of imagination, imagery, symbolism, plays on sound and themes dealing with time, death, identity and the insignificance of everyday life were common to most of these poets.[2 3]

Unfortunately, unless separate interviews were made today with each of the contemporary Chicano writers, it does not seem possible to document and assess the influence of the revolutionary period of Mexican literary and art history on the Chicano. Parallels, however, do arise: In the same way that the Mexican Revolution of 1910 with the accompanying stimulation from universal literary tendencies in vogue at the time created a new spirit in art for the Mexican then, rediscovered Hispanic and Mexican values have influenced the Chicano renaissance of today. Paradoxically or not, the very Mexicanness of Chicano art and literature has done much to create the feeling of "cultural nationalism" that we see in Chicano writing today. For many Chicano writers and critics, the polemic of the 1920's between national and universal literature in Mexico is just beginning to see its parallel in the Chicano Movement today. The implications suggested by the term "parallels," as opposed to "influences," will ultimately produce unsatisfactory conclusions for some persons, inconclusive ones for others, yet perhaps meaningful ones for still others. Nevertheless, it is much wiser to speak of parallels.

Obviously, the Chicano writers today who maintain close ties to Mexico and those who consciously feel the presence of the Mexican heritage will reflect this more in their work than others who have mainly a neo-Mexican background. The majority of the New Mexican writers—for example, Rudolfo A. Anaya, Orlando Romero and now Sergio Elizondo, include as part of their reality a long heritage of special cultural traditions. Most recently did Anaya suggest to us that the best way to find out about the influence of Mexican literature on Chicano literature would be to conduct an individual survey which would pinpoint a writer's background and preferred reading material. Anaya, himself, indicates that he has never considered comparing these two literatures.

In a recent interview with José Antonio Villarreal, whose novel *Pocho*, published in 1959,[24] signals for some the beginning of the renaissance period of Chicano fiction, Juan Bruce-Novoa learns that the relationship of Chicano literature to Mexican literature is stronger than the ties to American literature. While many Chicano writers read in Spanish, all have easy access to Mexican and Latin American literature through translation. Villarreal states that frankly only the idiom separates Mexican literature from American literature; hence, they are quite similiar in many ways because Spain in the past has contributed to the development of the English novel. Nevertheless, he concludes—again as others have done—without specifying any definite relationship: "We cannot deny that Mexican literature is a strong influence on what we create."[25]

On the other hand, Villarreal feels that what is called Chicano literature today is really a part of American literature. It falls into the same categorization as Southern writers, New England writers, or Western writers. Villarreal adds that since most Chicano writers use English, most were educated in English and since experimentation in bi-lingual writing is not new, their style, form and technique is traditionally American.[26] Still, a closer comparison of these two literatures reveals the ever-popular Mexican qualities and traditions in Chicano literature. This "looking backwards' has been touched on in an intelligent way by Bruce-Novoa. He concerns himself with five topics of influence: the pre-Columbian period, the *mestizo*, the Revolution, the lost paradise, and disillusionment from searching for roots in both cultures.[27]

In addition to the thematic aspects that Bruce-Novoa mentions which—like a magnet—will attract writers to the Mexican heritage of times past, we might look to the benefit the new professional and university-educated Chicano writers have possibly derived from not only Mexican but other literary traditions available to them in their research and reading. For example, one might speculate about the influence of modern Mexican fiction and—more likely than not—contemporary Latin American literature on Chicano literature. As is the case with many Latin American writers, reality and fantasy, structural experimentation with space and time, linguistic innovations, symbolism and the use of new metaphor are concerns of the Mexican writers Agustín Yáñez, Juan Rulfo, Carlos Fuentes, Rosario Castellanos and José Agustín. One other factor common to all of these writers is that they depart from a purely Mexican environment to establish mythic and universal concepts of man. Yáñez novel, *The Edge of the Storm*, published in 1947,[28] is generally considered to be the beginning of the new novel in Mexico. If we look closely at this novel we can see how language and structure create an environment—especially in the opening sections—of inhibition and restraint in a small Mexican town on the brink of the Revolution. It has been shown how unity in the novel is created through spiritual, anecdotal, artistic and interior movement, all of which puts the reader in the environment.[29]

In *Pedro Páramo*, a novel by Juan Rulfo published in 1955, we see regional traits centering around the *cacique* (local boss) take on universal aspects when these are manifested in themes of ambition, greed, self-preservation and love. But this plausible reality transcends to a mythic level in which time is negated and a constant change in the narrative point of view becomes a dynamic factor. The style is varied but vital to the meaning of the novel; there are poetic aspects, rural speech, dialogue and simple imagery which give sensorial impact to the narration. Time negated by death becomes a major theme.[30]

Although the important Mexican author, Carlos Fuentes, would certainly occupy a position of importance in this scheme, we could jump beyond the confines of Mexican literature and consider the possible parallels to Latin American literature.[31] Because of the impact of the "boom" novel of the 1960's on international literature—and especially of the propulsion of the contemporary Latin American novel onto the international scene in 1967 with *One Hundred Years of Solitude* by the Colombian novelist Gabriel García Márquez—a certain interest by Chicano writers in Latin American literature has been generated.[32] Not long ago Orlando Romero from northern New Mexico and author of *Nambé-Year One*, published only four months ago,[33] stated in a discussion on The University of New Mexico campus that the community of Chicano writers belongs to this larger realm, Latin American literature. In the first issue of *Revista Chicano-Riqueña*, Tomás Rivera shows his interest in the Argentine writer, Jorge Luis Borges. Romero, however, cited the works of García Márquez while at the same time mentioning the works of William Faulkner. It seems, then, that certain aspects of *One Hundred Years of Solitude*—apart from magnetic cultural relationships—might be perking the professional and technical interest of some Chicano writers. Thematic considerations like solitude—a universal concept common to all mankind—or incest—a taboo with certain underlying psychological implications—can be seen to have a structural value, functioning as centrifugal and centripedal forces of fear and desire, rejection and attraction. More important, however, is the invention of a new reality in the novel; through elements such as exaggeration and, consequently, fantasy, a larger than life quality is created.

Professor John Brushwood in his recent book, *The Spanish American Novel*, says that the major innovation to come from writers such as Carlos Fuentes, Gabriel García Márquez, Julio Cortázar, Mario Vargas Llosa and others, has been their ability to communicate "man's dissatisfaction with the signs, symbols and forms of culture he has created. This mood has produced the fiction of dissident youth, and an apparent anarchy in the making of fiction."[34] When considering the age-old polemic between regionalism and universalism, he has also said that from the turn of the century to the 1930's most writers held to the idea that when reality is described in a work of fiction, it is to be imitated; hence, a novel was evaluated in terms of how "real" it was. Then from the 1940's through contemporary times, a kind of universalized regionalism has been operating which probes the regional character more deeply; thus, the experience of the novel is one of having known the regional character more deeply. The contemporary writer's concern has been, therefore, one of creating the experience rather than portraying a region. The novel of the 1970's in Latin America, Professor Brushwood asserts, is the voice of Spanish America, not its portrait.[35]

In the last few pages we have established that the presence of Mexico in Chicano literature and, hence, its possible influence on Chicano literature, has been mainly through culture, traditions and themes inherited from the Mexican of past times. In terms of literary concepts and tendencies, we have transformed the word "influences" to "parallels" which has permitted us to see in a larger context not only Chicano and Mexican literature but others as well. The result would be the confirmation of a new perspective toward Chicano and Mexican literature and, hopefully, a new basis for the evaluation of Chicano literature.

When we look at the trajectory of Chicano literature and the presence of Mexican history, values and traditions in it—as one of my students of Chicano literature has pointed out to me—most Chicano fiction can be seen to follow one of two vectors: It either uses the Mexican Revolution of 1910 as its take-off point and then describes aspects of the Chicano living in the Southwest, or it rejects any direct reference to Mexico and narrates situations as they form a part of contemporary Chicano reality. *Pocho, Chicano* by Richard Vásquez, *The Plum Plum Pickers* by Raymond Barrios, *Macho* by Edmund Villaseñor and *Peregrinos de Aztlán* by Miguel Méndez are examples of the works that are closely related to this Mexican experience, whereas Tomás Rivera's "*. . . And The Earth Did Not Part*," Oscar Zeta Acosta's *The Revolt of The Cockroach People*, Ron Arias' *The Road to Tamazunchale*, Orlando Romero's *Nambé-Year One*, Rudolfo Anaya's *Bless Me, Ultima*, Alejandro Morales' *Caras viejas y vino nuevo*, Joseph V. Torres-Metzgar's *Below the Summit*, and only recently Rudolfo Anaya's *Heart of Aztlán*—despite neo-Mexican references to culture and tradition which all form a part of that larger Hispanic or Latin American realm, not to mention the universal sphere of human values—deal with contemporary Chicano reality of the Southwest.[36] This classification and its implications would go far in establishing criteria for a comparison between Chicano literature and Mexican literature.

Having mentioned at one point or another the spiritual impact of the Mexican Revolution of 1910 on the Chicano and his art, I should mention here what Guillermo Rojas of the University of California at Davis tries to do in comparing Rivera's "... *And The Earth Did Not Part*," Rolando Hinojosa's *Estampas del valle* and Méndez' *Peregrinos de Aztlán* to the works of Azuela, Guzmán and López y Fuentes, which fall under the category of the novel of the Mexican Revolution. Calling the Chicano novels successors to their Mexican counterparts, Rojas finds that anonymous characters in Rivera's novel correspond to those characters without a name in the Mexican novels which, Rojas says, leads to the creation of a collective protagonist, or society itself. Other influences Rojas finds include a simple style, a concern for social problems, a mixture of linguistic styles and a lack of unifying themes and plots. The vagueness and generality of this list show us something important: If outright influences of Mexican literature on Chicano literature exist, they seem coincidental.[37]

If, however, we were to look at this Chicano fiction in terms of parallels, we could speak more specifically. We might, for instance, seek out the unique relationship of the *estampa* (sketch) between Hinojosa's work and that of the Mexican writer, Julio Torri. The narrative style of Méndez' novel—because of its personification of Nature and its dehumanization of the characters—might coincide with that of Mariano Azuela. Méndez, however, effectively employs narrative techniques of the most contemporary vein: flashbacks, stream of consciousness, cinematographic montage of multiple time levels and narrative points of view. The incorporation of myth into the narration certainly places this novel alongside the novels written by the contemporary "boom" writers. We should not forget that *The Underdogs*, first published by Mariano Azuela in 1916 in El Paso, Texas, was very innovative for its era, and has since become a classic work of literature.[38]

There are other possible parallels, those that arise from the polemic between regional and universal literature. In the development of Chicano fiction during the last decade or so, we can see parallels of the polemic that developed earlier in Mexico. Looking back to 1959 and the publication of *Pocho* by Villarreal—a novel written in English as are the majority—we encounter a work of fiction by a writer whose commitment to authentic reality, like that of a historian, overrides any artistic ambition. The work attempts to reflect the life of the Chicano during the late 1940's and 1950's when assimilationism was the prevailing attitude as a response to a search for identity and a place in the dominant society. The departure point for *Pocho* is Juan Rubio's participation in the Mexican Revolution and his consequent trip northward to the United States where he raises his family. The narration then follows Rubio's son and his assimilation into North American society. The feeling of strong ties to Mexican values is an important part of the novel. The woman's traditional role of maintaining family cohesion disintegrates in the face of the demands placed on her by assimilation. The imitation of reality here aims to create a believable work of art and is communicated through a traditional structure, a third person omniscient narrator and a linear story line. The autobiographical elements of the novel also help to create the feeling that the work is a historical document based on and reflecting reality, hence, a portrait. In fact, the thematic presentation of the pre-Movement era—the *pocho* who assimilates into society—is so strong in the novel that many younger committed Movement people refuse to accept the novel as a part of Chicano reality.

Without tracing in a step-by-step fashion the development of this polemic between the regional and the universal, let us say that *Pocho* is a timebound portrait of Chicano experience during a particular historical period. We must ask ourselves where, then, is the voice of the universal Chicano experience? In order to answer this question, we may consider Rudolfo Anaya's 1971 Quinto Sol National Literary Award Winner, *Bless Me, Ultima*, although another novel, *The Road to Tamazunchale*, written by Ron Arias and published in 1975, is an excellent example of the direction recent works of Chicano literature are taking. For many Chicano critics, the young protagonist of *Bless Me, Ultima*, Antonio Márez Luna, is the epitome of the Chicano experience in Aztlán. Others feel, in contrast, that Anaya's novel is a cop-out to the problems facing the Chicano of the 1970's and was written with only the commerical market in mind.[39]

Herein lies the polemic because some feel Chicano literature should be socially-committed, easy to understand, and carry a social message to its readers. *Bless Me, Ultima* is possibly all of these things, but the nationalists seem to opppose the writer who transforms reality to communicate universal values that go beyond the limits of the regionalists' concepts of fiction. True, there is no direct social conflict between the *gabachos* (Anglos) and the *batos locos* (*barrio* dudes) in the novel. But, through the *rite de passage* which serves to give a universal structure to the novel, certain magical qualities and, hence, legendary and mythical aspects soaked in cultural elements of Antonio's past—best exemplified by the *curandera* (witch doctor), Ultima—give a new perspective to at once old and new concepts of a collective vision toward life and Nature.

Lomelí and Urioste state that Anaya's novel, rich in myth and legend, represents oral history in print. They see a magical quality about the novel that converts "wizardry and dreams into dimensions of reality, a process which foretells happenings and reveals otherwise unknown happenings."[40] These two critics are right in saying that *Bless Me, Ultima* implies a need for formulating a new way of life through an "eclectic syncretism of experience."[41] The relationship between fiction and reality, or imagination and actual existence, respectively, has been seen by Tomás Rivera as a labyrinth in which search and tension are alternated.[42] For the Chicano the labyrinth is life in search of form and, in literature, the Chicano invents himself and thereby complements his will, a process which is well-defined in *Bless Me, Ultima*.

As we turn our thoughts to *The Road to Tamazunchale* we see a deepening division of the polemic between different attitudes toward Chicano literature. Why? The novel narrates a fragmented look at the life of an old book dealer on the verge of death. The thrust of the novel comes in his quijotesque trip through reality—his *barrio*—and fantasy—his imagination—while the theme of death remains a constant in the novel. Tomás Rivera says that with this novel, "Chicano literature gains a most creative dimension.'[43] The vitality of the novel and, hence, the transformation of regional aspects of the Chicano experience reveals, Rivera adds, "the main character not in contemplation of Death as some social anthropologists would have Chicanos do as part of their cultural traditions but rather in the creation of Death. *The Road to Tamazunchale* is then a creation of death, a most accurate, at times humorous approach to the unapproachable."[44]

The polemic, ultimately, is in the minds of the nationalists or regionalists. The problem does not exist for their supposed opponents—the artists who tend to be free of commitment to the political dictates of the Movement. To the contrary, they present a different perspective on life that intensifies human values—hopes, emotions and imagination. As a final note on this polemic which, as we have suggested, parallels earlier conflicts in Mexico, Luis Dávila, editor of the *Revista Chicano-Riqueña*, searches out the concept of fantasy—a childlike suspension of disbelief which plays an important role even in the immortal work *Don Quijote de la Mancha* and says that through fantasy Chicano writers have been able to delve deeply into Chicano reality. The use of imagination in this sense by Chicano writers, which ultimately gives greater insight into the ironies of life, has been openly denounced as a luxury in Chicano literature by the social activists. Citing the propagandists' thinking, Dávila states that they believe if Chicano literature "does not preach explicitly about chicano ideals and virtues, it is considered frivolous."[45] Frank Pino, who has studied reality and fantasy in Rivera's novel, shows that by juxtaposing reality and fantasy in a work of fiction, a whole set of complex paradoxical symbols communicate—through Hispanic folklore and Anglo ideology—universal themes common to all. The effect is the intensification of human values.[46]

Having created a labyrinth of parallels, polemics and paradoxes here, it is important to briefly consider the relationship of poetry and, if space permitted, theatre, to what we have put forth to this point. Chicano poetry, as opposed to Chicano fiction, has served on the whole to carry the banner of social commitment and to portray the social condition of Chicanos in the Southwest. Poetry has been the spearhead to maintain the cultural front, reflect the past, clarify desires and rights, preserve culture and create unity. With some few exceptions, the message communicated via Chicano poetry calls for change in the social system, and from this a new poetics—according to Philip Ortego—has developed which "embraces the politics and sociology of poetry as well as new linguistic parameters."[47] Although Villarreal has said that an attempt at innovation through code-switching is not new, this phenomenon has at least crystalized from a unique cultural situation in the Southwest. Some attention has been given to this interesting phenomenon. Still, the problem of language has not been solved. New or not, code-switching is the language of many poets, and it more than adequately reflects a way of life. The best example is Alurista's poetry—*Floricanto en Aztlán, Nationchild Plumaraja* and, recently, *Timespace Huracán*—which has been studied extensively.[48] The carefully planned mixture of Spanish, English and *caló* (*barrio* slang) produces many effects: a sense of polarization between two cultures, a historical past and a view of contemporary life. These effects evoke a whole emotional, cultural and philosophical reality.[49]

Some Chicano literary critics continue to see Chicano literature as necessary propaganda whose goal is not to explore the inner depths of Chicano reality nor find universal planes of truth within but rather to maintain a cultural front, even create culture and recruit young people into the ranks of the socially conscious and politically motivated.[50] No one should be denied the right to pursue those ends—it is a necessary task—but I am also interested in what one Chicano critic is doing to relate poetry to more transcendental levels. Sylvia Alicia Gonzales sees similarities among all poets in as much as they share a spirit that marks an era rather than individual aspects of a national character. A writer's reaction to an experience, Gonzales feels, can only be effectively communicated through a singular style which at the same time has to be universal in essence.[51] This effect is what the poets Alurista and Sergio Elizondo, author of the profound book of poetry, *Perros y antiperros*, achieve.[52] In the process of defining culture, reflecting the past and then preserving culture which had been lost due to the Anglo "sins of omission,' other poets have attempted in the so-called initial phase of Chicano literature to portray culture and traditions. Abelardo, Ricardo Sánchez, Juan Felipe Herrera and other poets have written poetry embued with culture.[53] Mexico, consequently, became the focal point; essayists like Octavio Paz and José Vasconcelos, and mural painters like Rivera and Orozco, became objects of endless study.[54] But what many Chicano writers have since discovered is that these Mexican roots had been uprooted and obscured hopelessly. Indeed, for some poets the paradox of seeking refuge and finding only rejection at every turn stimulated them to go further back to pre-Columbian times to find important values in the philosophy of the indigenous gods Huitzilopochtli and Quetzalcóatl.[55]

Then, too, the popularity and importance of code-switching in poetry is testimony to the fact that exclusive identification with either Mexican or Anglo-American values and culture is misleading. If Herminio Ríos has shown the importance of syntactical elements in this poetry, Jesús Maldonado finds the phonetic position of the mixture and the consequent progression to be of utmost importance. However, Maldonado himself raises a question about the universality of this poetry since he maintains that the mixture of languages and dialects can only be appreciated by Chicanos who have lived these experiences.[56]

This question of universality seems to be paradoxical. Can we consider influences? Guillermo Rojas, in studying Alurista's poetry, finds the influence of Octavio Paz' poetry, *Libertad bajo palabra*, because both use symbolism; he sees influence of the Mexican Marco Montes de Oca's poetry because both use the first verse of many poems as titles; he discovers the influence of E. E. Cummings' poetry because Alurista favors grammatical displacement, structural ambiguities and typographical elements.[57] Unless Alurista confirms these influences, we are not convinced. Alurista has experimented with the poetic form, haiku. Are we to assume, then, that he was influenced by the 1920's Mexican vanguard poet, José Juan Tablada?

If talk about influences is on shaky ground, what about parallels? One that comes to mind is the strong anti-imperialist/anti-authoritarian movement supported by young Mexicans in the 1960's. A vanguard magazine of poetry, short fiction and essays that came from that tumultous period, *El corno emplumado*—and which had the active participation of poets from many different countries—was politically committed; the January 1968 issue was dedicated to Che Guevara. The magazine sought to create an *art nouveau* that encompassed "life." During its seventh year, the editor wrote that the magazine had seen life through the eyes and ears and hands of poets living and interpreting their years. In that particular issue, William Carlos Williams was translated into Spanish and Ernesto Cardenal into English.[58]

It is within this same spirit of an era that Chicano poetry made its debut as the genre in literature that initiated a renaissance in all the Chicano arts. Chicano poetry has been—and to a large extent continues to be—revolutionary with a heavy emotional thrust, whereas Mexican poetry since 1968 and until recently has been imbued with intellectualism. While attempting to relate the chaotic times of the present to cosmic forces beyond the logical, some recent Mexican poets have stripped themselves of intellectual clothing to become much simpler in their lyrics. Notwithstanding different underlying causes, a parallel between Chicano poetry and Mexican poetry does seem to be the search through myth in order to find universal planes of meaning of life.

The aforementioned polemics, paradoxes and parallels point to a largely unanswered question. Over a year ago the Modern Language Association's Commission on Minority Groups and the Study of Language and Literature asked itself "how much should works by minority-group writers be assimilated into the American literary tradition, and how much should they be treated as a part of a 'discrete' literature separate from the Anglo-European tradition? "[59] With this problem still facing the critic of Chicano literature but not necessarily the Chicano writer, I would like to conclude by referring to Gustavo Segade's statement on the Chicano experience in literature. For him the experience has been one of synthesis which has evolved from a dialectical process of opposing forces—Mexico and the United States; hence, he states that

> in the 1960's, the reality called Chicano was recognized and asserted. It was created by and out of historical fact, and was as inevitable as any of the essential assertions of the great human entities. Chicano is a synthesized reality that had to be recognized and affirmed by those who were aware of living it. Furthermore, it is a synthesis which, because it was created, brought forth as a new entity, in the unidentified zone between two world powers, it was itself powerless. Chicano reality cannot, by itself, destroy the antithetical elements which created it. Chicano reality must continue to relate to that of Mexico and the United States, while affirming its own, unique existence.[60]

Bruce-Novoa says that there is still confusion among Chicano writers because many still seek refuge in a Mexican past and others flatly reject the Anglo present. However, in spite of the fact that Chicanos have begun to create their own art, Bruce-Novoa feels the predominance of both Mexican and American influences on Chicano literature cannot be denied. The Chicano writer is not Mexican nor American, nor Mexican-American, but the space—and not the hyphen—between the two, a special area which allows for new visions and concepts of reality.[61]

By concluding that Mexican history, Mexican art—and to a much lesser degree up until recently—Mexican literature are represented in Chicano literature as a source of heritage, culture, traditions, art and philosophy, we are back to where we started: Luis Leal says that Chicano literature derives both its erudite and popular forms—not to mention its spirit of rebellion—from Mexican literature. Tomás Rivera sees the Chicano in fiction and poetry as a life in search of form, and Rolando Hinojosa believes that "there is no immediate nor—what is less likely—definite answer to where this literature properly belongs."[62] We believe a search whose principal goal is to find an identity explains the thrust of recent Chicano literature to capture and transform a multiform reality into meaningful experience. We should reaffirm, finally, three recurrent aspects of this paper: (1) the importance of the regional-universal polemic; (2) the presence of paradoxes such as the problem about which of the two principal languages is the language of Chicano literature because one language dominates in some cases and the other language in other cases; and (3) the persistence of existing parallels which strengthen the fabric of a literature, showing it to be one—like Mexican literature, American literature and beyond, Latin American literature—that participates in the major trends of contemporary literature.

*University of New Mexico*

## NOTES

[1] Nephtalí de León, *Chicanos: Our Background and Our Pride* (Lubbock, Texas: Trucha Press, 1972), p. 33.

[2] See also Charles M. Tatum, "Contemporary Chicano Prose Fiction: Its Ties to Mexican Literature," *Books Abroad*, 49, No. 3 (1975), 432-38. Although some of our observations seem to point in the same direction, Tatum chooses to underscore linguistic, thematic and technical "similarities" between the two literatures. I will herewith concern myself with comparative implications of a wider nature.

[3] Rolando Hinojosa, "Mexican-American Literature: Toward an Identification," *Books Abroad*, 49, No. 3 (1975), 422-23.

[4] Manuel J. Martínez, "The Art of the Chicano Movement and the Movement of Chicano Art," *Speaking for Ourselves*, eds. Lillian Faderman and Barbara Bradshaw (Glenview, Illinois: Scott, Foresman and Company, 1975), p. 314.

[5] Luis Leal, "Mexican-American Literature: A Historical Perspective," *Revista Chicano-Riqueña*, 1, No. 1 (1973), 32-44.

[6] Philip D. Ortego, "Backgrounds of Mexican American Literature," Diss. University of New Mexico 1971, p. 239.

[7] José Armas, "Entrevista con Octavio Paz," *De Colores*, 2, No. 2 (1975), 12.

[8] Mildred Monteverde, "Contemporary Chicano Art," *Aztlán*, 1, No. 2 (1971), 51-61.

[9] John D. Bruce-Novoa, "México en la literatura chicana," *Revista de la Universidad de México*, 29, No. 5 (1975), 13.

[10] Alba Irene Moesser, "La literatura mejicoamericana del suroeste de los Estados Unidos," Diss. University of California, Los Angeles 1974, p. 342.

[11] In addition to Moesser's dissertation, refer to Ortego's dissertation. "Backgrounds of Mexican American Literature," the Luis Valdez and Stan Steiner anthology, *Aztlán: An Anthology of Mexican American Literature* (New York: Vintage Press, 1972), and Francisco Jiménez, "Chicano Literature: Sources and Themes," *The Bilingual Review*, 1, No. 1 (1974), 4-15.

[12] Aurelio M. Espinosa, *Estudios sobre el español de Nuevo México*. 2 Vols. (Buenos Aires: Falcultad de Filosofía y Letras de la Universidad de Buenos Aires, 1930).

[13] See, for example, his articles in the *Journal of American Folklore*: "New Mexican Spanish Folklore, Parts I and II: Myths, Superstitions, and Beliefs," 23

(1910), 395-418; "New Mexican Spanish Folklore, Part III: Folktales," 24 (1911), 397-444; and "New Mexican Spanish Folklore, Part IV: Proverbs," 26 (1913), 97-122.

[14] Arthur Campa, *Treasures of the Sangre de Cristos*, (Norman, Oklahoma: Univ. of Oklahoma Press, 1962).

[15] Américo Paredes, *With a Pistol In His Hand* (Austin, Texas: Univ. of Texas Press, 1958).

[16] See, for example, Cobos' *Refranes españoles del sudoeste/Spanish Proverbs of the Southwest* (Cerrillos, New Mexico: San Marcos Press, 1973).

[17] Tatum, in "Contemporary Chicano Prose Fiction: Its Ties to Mexican Literature," mentions the importance of the traditional *cuento* and *cuadro de costumbres* to this period (p. 432).

[18] Philip D. Ortego, "Chicano Poetry: Roots and Writers," *New Voices in Literature: The Mexican American* (Edinburg, Texas: Pan American Univ., n.d.), p. 3.

[19] Francisco Lomelí and Donaldo Urioste, *Chicano Perspectives in Literature: A Critical and Annotated Bibliography* (Albuquerque: Pajarito Publications, 1976), p. 10.

[20] Ortego, "Chicano Poetry: Roots and Writers," p. 3.

[21] Arthur Campa traces the element of protest to folk poetry in "Protest folk poetry in the Spanish Southwest," *The Colorado Quarterly*, 20, No. 3 (1972), 355-63.

[22] For a closer look at this period, consult John S. Brushwood, *Mexico in Its Novel* (Austin, Texas: Univ. of Texas Press, 1966).

[23] For criticism, see Frank Dauster, *Ensayos sobre poesía mexicana. Asedio a los "Contemporáneos"* (Mexico: Ediciones de Andrea, 1963).

[24] José Antonio Villarreal, *Pocho* (New York: Doubleday, 1959).

[25] Juan Bruce-Novoa, "Interview with José Antonio Villarreal," *Revista Chicano-Riqueña*, 4, No. 2 (1976), 44.

[26] Bruce-Novoa, "Interview," p. 43.

[27] See note 9.

[28] Agustín Yáñez, *The Edge of The Storm*, trans. Ethel Brinton (Austin, Texas: Univ. of Texas Press, 1963).

[29] John S. Brushwood, "La arquitectura de las novelas de Agustín Yáñez, *Revista Iberoamericana*, 36, No. 72 (1970), 437-51. See also Raymond D. Souza, 'Two early novels of Agustín Yáñez,' *Romance Notes*, 11, No. 3 (1970), 522-25, and Michael J. Doudoroff, "Tensions and Triangles in *Al filo del agua*," *Hispania*, 57, No. 1 (1974), 1-12.

[30] Brushwood, *Mexico in Its Novel*, pp. 30-34. See also Luis Harss and Barbara Dohman, "Juan Rulfo, or the Souls of the Departed," in their *Into the Mainstream* (New York: Harper and Row, 1966). Linguistic, thematic and characterization similarities between Rulfo's prose fiction and Hinojosa's *Estampas del valle* and Rivera's *". . . And The Earth Did Not Part"* is the thrust of Charles M. Tatum's article, "Contemporary Chicano Prose Fiction," 436-38.

[31] For a closer look at the prose fiction written by Carlos Fuentes, Agustín Yáñez and Juan Rulfo, see also Joseph Sommers, *After the Storm* (Albuquerque: Univ. of New Mexico Press, 1968).

[32] Besides *One Hundred Years of Solitude*, trans. Gregory Rabassa (New York: Harper and Row, 1970), see also *Leaf Storm and Other Stories*, trans. Gregory Rabassa (New York: Harper and Row, 1972), and *No One Writes to the Colonel, and Other Stories*, trans. J. S. Bernstein (New York: Harper and Row, 1968).

166

[33] Orlando Romero, *Nambé-Year One* (Berkeley, California: Tonatiuh International, 1976).

[34] John S. Brushwood, *The Spanish American Novel: A Twentieth Century Survey* (Austin: Univ. of Texas Press, 1975), p. 334.

[35] Brushwood, *The Spanish American Novel*, p. 335.

[36] José Antonio Villarreal, *Pocho* (New York: Doubleday, 1959), Richard Vasquez, *Chicano* (New York: Doubleday, 1970), Raymond Barrios, *The Plum Plum Pickers* (Sunnyvale, California: Ventura Press, 1969), Edmund Villaseñor, *Macho* (New York: Bantam, 1973), Miguel Méndez, *Peregrinos de Aztlán* (Tucson, Arizona: Editorial Peregrinos, 1974), Tomás Rivera, "*. . . y no se lo tragó la tierra"/"And the earth did not part"* (Berkeley, California: Quinto Sol Publications, 1971), Oscar Zeta Acosta, *The Revolt of The Cockroach People* (New York: Straight Arrow, 1973), Ron Arias, *The Road to Tamazunchale* (Reno, Nevada: West Coast Poetry Review, 1975), Orlando Romero, *Nambé-Year One* (Berkeley, California: Tonatiuh International, 1976), Rudolfo A. Anaya, *Bless Me, Ultima* (Berkeley, California: Quinto Sol Publications, 1972), Alejandro Morales, *Caras viejas y vino nuevo* (Mexico: Joaquín Mortiz, 1975), Joseph V. Torres-Metzgar, *Below the summit* (Berkeley, California: Tonatiuh International, 1976), Rudolfo A. Anaya, *Heart of Aztlán* (Berkeley, California: Editorial Justa Publications, 1976).

[37] Guillermo Rojas, "La prosa chicana: Tres epígonos de la novela mexicana de la Revolución," *De Colores*, 1, No. 4 (1975), 43-57.

[38] Mariano Azuela, *The Underdogs*, trans. E. Munguía, Jr. (New York: Signet, 1962).

[39] See, for example, Juan Rodríguez' *Carta abierta V* (Los Angeles: Department of Ethnic Studies, Univ. of California, October, 1976), in which he says *Bless Me, Ultima*, among other novels, is a reactionary rip-off written to reap economic benefits (p. vii).

[40] Lomelí and Urioste, *Chicano Perspectives in Literature*, p. 40.

[41] Ibid., p. 40.

[42] Tomás Rivera, "Into the Labyrinth: The Chicano in Literature," *New Voices in Literature: The Mexican American* (Edinburg, Texas: Pan American Univ. 1971), p. 18.

[43] Forward to *The Road to Tamazunchale* (Reno, Nevada: West Coast Poetry Review, 1975), p. 7.

[44] Ibid., p. 7.

[45] Luis Dávila, "Chicano Fantasy Through a Glass Darkly," *Otros mundos, otros fuegos* (East Lansing, Michigan: Latin American Studies Center, Michigan State Univ., 1975), p. 247.

[46] Frank Pino, "Realidad y fantasía en *". . . y no se lo tragó la tierra,"* *Otros mundos, otros fuegos*, pp. 249-54.

[47] Ortego, "Chicano Poetry: Roots and Writers," p. 4

[48] *Floricanto en Aztlán* (Los Angeles: Univ. of California, 1971); *Nationchild Plumaroja* (San Diego, California: Toltecas en Aztlán Publications, 1972); *Timespace Huracán* (Albuquerque: Pajarito Publications, 1976). For criticism, see: Jesús Maldonado, *Poesía chicana: Alurista, el mero chingón* (Seattle: Centro de Estudios Chicanos, Univ. of Washington, 1971); Nicolás Kanellos, "La llorona de Alurista," *Otros mundos, otros fuegos*, 261-64; and Guillermo Rojas, "Alurista, Chicano Poet, Poet of Social Protest," *Otros mundos, otros fuegos*, 255-60.

[49] See, for example: Carlota Cardenas de Dwyer, "Chicanos: Their Prose y Poesía," *Review*, 4, No. 3 (1974), 51, and Guadalupe Valdés-Fallis, "Code-Switching in Bilingual Poetry," *Hispania*, 59, No. 4 (1976), 877-86.

⁵⁰Rafael J. González, "Pensamientos sobre la literatura chicana," *Mujer* (Cd. Juárez), 2, No. 1 (1972), 30. However, Tomás Rivera states that *la lucha* is one of three persistent elements in Chicano literature; the other two are *la casa* and *el barrio*, which are explained in "Chicano Literature: Fiesta of the Living," *Books Abroad*, 49, No. 3 (1975), 439-52.

⁵¹Sylvia Alicia Gonzales, "National Character vs. Universality in Chicano Poetry," *De Colores*, 1, No. 4 (1975), 10-21.

⁵²Sergio Elizondo, *Perros y antiperros* (Berkeley, California: Quinto Sol Publications, 1972).

⁵³Abelardo, *Bajo el sol de Aztlán* (El Paso: Barrio Publications, 1973), *Chicano: 25 Pieces of a Chicano Mind* (Santa Barbara, California: La Causa Publications, 1971), and *It's Cold: 52 Cold Thought-Poems of Abelardo* (Salt Lake City: Barrio Publications, 1974); Ricardo Sánchez, *Canto y grito mi liberación* (El Paso: Mictla Publications, 1971) and *Hechizospells* (Los Angeles: Chicano Studies Center, Univ. of California, 1976); Juan Felipe Herrera, *Rebozos of love/we have woven/sudor de quiblos/ on our back* (San Diego, California: Toltecas en Aztlán Publications, 1974).

⁵⁴See, for example, José Armas, "Entrevista con Octavio Paz," *De Colores*, 2, No. 2 (1975), 4-21, and Don Porath, "Existentialism and Chicanos," *De Colores*, 1, No. 2 (1973), 6-29.

⁵⁵See the introduction and chapters one and two of the Luis Valdez and Stan Steiner anthology, *Aztlán: An Anthology of Mexican American Literature*, and Philip Ortego's dissertation, "Backgrounds of Mexican American Literature."

⁵⁶Maldonado, *Poesía chicana: Alurista*, p. 3. José Armas also states in his editorial to the volume 1, No. 4 (1975) issue of *De Colores* that "the Chicano writer may eventually be like all other writers, producing mundane and general subject matter. However, the unique experience that went into the make-up of the Chicano will produce a unique body of literary work in this country that can only be relevantly and honestly be fully understood (at least for the time being) by Chicanos," (p. 5).

⁵⁷Guillermo Rojas, "Alurista, Chicano Poet," p. 255.

⁵⁸*El corno emplumado* (México), 25 (enero 1968), 6. Another parallel–between Rodolfo González' *I am Joaquín* and José Hernández' *Martín Fierro*–has been suggested by Gerald L. Head, "El chicano ante El Gaucho *Martín Fierro*: un redescubrimiento," *Mester*, 4, No. 1 (1973), 13-23.

⁵⁹Malcolm G. Scully, "Minority Literatures Gain a Slippery Foothold," *The Chronicle of Higher Education*, 29 November 1976, p. 3.

⁶⁰Gustavo Segade, "Toward a Dialectic of Chicano Literature," *Mester*, 4, No. 1 (1973), 4.

⁶¹Juan Bruce-Novoa, "The Space of Chicano Literature," *De Colores*, 1, No. 4 (1975), 27.

⁶²Hinojosa, "Mexican-American Literature," p. 423.

# Luncheon Presentation
# and
# Looking Back Remarks

# Faulknerian Techniques in Gabriel García Márquez's Portrait of a Dictator*

Harley D. Oberhelman

ABSTRACT

Gabriel García Márquez, the most widely read novelist in Spanish America today, owes a substantial literary debt to William Faulkner. With the publication of his most recent volumes, especially *El otoño del patriarca* (1975), that debt has been repaid and with abundant interest. Recent research dealing with García Márquez's early career as a journalist in Cartagena and Barranquilla confirms his early acquaintance with Faulkner and his world. Interviews confirm that the Colombian later began to read Faulkner seriously shortly before the publication of his first novel, *La hojarasca* (1955).

There are frequent examples of exterior relationships between the two writers; both created fictional settings, Yoknapatawpha County and Macondo, settings based primarily on their childhood memories of life in provincial, rural regions washed by the nearby waters of the Caribbean and the Gulf of Mexico. These societies both bear the burden of a historical past interrupted by civil wars whose memory still shapes the present. The characters of both writers represent the different levels within each society, and they speak a language which demonstrates a sensitivity on the part of both creators to the syntactical patterns, diction, and tone of their region. Certain incidents in García Márquez's works seem to be derived directly from Faulknerian sources.

*El otoño del patriarca*, García Márquez's portrait of a dictator, goes beyond the ruins of Macondo in its narrative structure and stylistic techniques. *Otoño* is a more mature, more complex, more Faulknerian novel. After all, a brilliant literary style is the real achievement of both William Faulkner and Gabriel García Márquez. They are regional writers who deal with universal problems. Faulkner views his created world with a sense of moral judgment. Likewise, García Márquez, in what may be the best of the current vogue of novels of dictatorship, attempts to wipe away the repugnant, dictatorial past, and allow the inhabitants of his fictional nation to celebrate the arrival of a new day of moral justice.(HDO)

*Grateful acknowledgment is made for research grants from the College of Arts and Sciences and for a Faculty Development Leave from Texas Tech University which in part supported this research project.

171

The 1973 Comparative Literature Symposium at Texas Tech University considered the impact of William Faulkner on world literature. Except for Robert G. Collmer's luncheon presentation, "When 'Word' Meets *Palabra*: Crossing the Border with Literature,"[1] no mention was made of the dramatic impact of Faulkner on contemporary Spanish American prose fiction, an impact which began in 1934 with the first Spanish translation of *Sanctuary*[2] and which continues unabated to the present. This study will focus only on the prose fiction of Gabriel García Márquez, the most widely read novelist in Spanish America today, and special attention will be given to his most recent novel, *El otoño del patriarca* (1975), one of the best of a recent series of Spanish American novels dealing with the theme of dictators and the political and social environments in which they wield their power. This may be an appropriate time to reassess García Márquez's debt to William Faulkner since in a number of interviews and public statements the Colombian novelist has affirmed that he has no immediate intention of writing more fiction and that he is leaving the field of creative literature until the moment comes when the resistance movement is able to destroy the military government of Augusto Pinochet in Chile. Until that moment arrives, the world will probably have to be content with García Márquez's political writings and social pronouncements.

The discovery of William Faulkner came as a dramatic revelation to the young Colombian journalist. The chaotic material which Faulkner shaped so carefully to create his own Yoknapatawpha County seemed to be lifted from the prime material of Colombian rural life. "Cuando leí a Faulkner, pensé: tengo que ser escritor," García Márquez related to Luis Harss.[3] Spanish American prose writers a generation before García Márquez—Horacio Quiroga, Mariano Azuela, Martín Luis Guzmán, José Eustacio Rivera, Rómulo Gallegos, and Ricardo Güiraldes, to name a few of the best known—were limited in their presentation of characters as types or as generalized symbols of social and economic abuses or geographical misfortunes. The result was a "depersonalization" of the human being as he faced overwhelming odds as a pawn of the Mexican Revolution, the unjust system of land tenure, or the impersonal forces of the jungle, the pampa, or the high sierra.

Between this earlier generation of Spanish American writers and the new generation of today's novelists stands a Lost Generation of North American writers whose works were widely read and translated in the decades following the First World War: John Dos Passos, Erskine Caldwell, Ernest Hemingway, John Steinbeck, and especially William Faulkner. At an earlier time when his relationship with the Peruvian novelist, Mario Vargas Llosa, was more felicitous, García Márquez discussed this Faulknerian influence in the following terms: "Yo creo que la deuda mayor que

tenemos los nuevos novelistas latinoamericanos es con Faulkner. . . .
Faulkner está metido en toda la novelística de la América Latina;
creo que . . . la gran diferencia que hay entre los abuelos . . . y nosotros, es
Faulkner; fue lo único que sucedió entre esas dos generaciones."[4] In the
same interview he clarifies this influence primarily as one of method: "Es
decir, nosotros estábamos viendo esta realidad y queríamos contarla y
sabíamos que el método de los europeos no servía, ni el método tradicional
español; y de pronto encontrábamos el método faulkneriano adecuadísimo
para contar esta realidad. En el fondo no es raro esto porque no se me
olvida que el Condado Yoknapathawpa [sic] tiene riberas en el Mar Caribe;
así que de alguna manera Faulkner es un escritor del Caribe, de alguna
manera es un escritor latinoamericano."[5]

There is no doubt that Faulkner was in the air as the new novelists of
Spanish America turned to the Lost Generation for method, for theme,
and ultimately for inspiration. What they most frequently found was disillusion, bitterness, and a loss of faith in the traditional pre-war values.
Faulkner's first novel, *Soldiers' Pay* (1926), is a prime example of the
disillusion faced by the returning soldiers. The fact that Faulkner soon
turned almost exclusively to Southern themes is of special importance
when the whole of his work is viewed vis-à-vis the new novel in Spanish
America. In a recent interview with Christopher Sharp, Mexico's Carlos
Fuentes suggests that Southern writers have a special role in the whole of
North American fiction. "Until recently, American writers never had the
chance to deal with a national failure. The American idea of success has
done a great deal to standardize American art forms. That's why I think
that for many years the most original American writing has come from the
South, where there had been a real sense of regional tragedy, and where
there was a need to reexamine the things that had been taken for grant-
ed."[6] Faulkner needed a locale in which to reexamine the South, its great
tragedy, and its system of traditional values; in 1929 he published two
novels, *Sartoris* and *The Sound and the Fury*, which delineated what was
to be the locale in almost all his succeeding works. He named it Yoknapatawpha County with its county seat in Jefferson. Ultimately the county
was to be the home of the Compson, Sartoris, McCaslin, Snopes, and
Sutpen family clans. Faulkner's creation was to win him the Nobel Prize
for Literature in 1950. While he will always be remembered as a novelist of
the South, it was his ability to transcend the regional and to penetrate
profoundly the universal problems of mankind, what he called "old
verities and truths of the heart" in his Nobel address, that made him a
great, and not just a good writer. On 6 July 1962, Faulkner died of a heart
attack shortly after the appearance of his last novel, *The Reivers*. He left
Yoknapatawpha in mid-air; *The Reivers* is a mediocre effort and certainly

not the "Doomsday Book, the Golden Book, of Yoknapatawpha County,"[7] which he had planned as a grand finale, after which he would break his pencil and quit.

A full generation after the birth of Faulkner in 1897, Gabriel García Márquez was born in 1927 in the dusty, northern Colombian village of Aracataca. After completing his secondary education at the Colegio Liceo Nacional de Zipaquirá, he began the study of law in 1947 at the National University in Bogotá and published his first short stories in the newspaper, *El Espectador*, the same year. His study of law was cut short on 9 April 1948, with the assasination of the Liberal leader, Jorge Eliécer Gaitán, and the subsequent "bogotazo" which led to the closing of the university and general chaos throughout the nation.

For most of the next decade García Márquez was to work in the field of journalism while continuing to write short stories and his first novel, *La hojarasca* (1955). His first stop was Cartagena; then in 1949 he moved to Barranquilla where he established contact with a group of intellectuals known as "el grupo de Barranquilla." These friends were to have a profound influence on him even after his departure for Bogotá in 1954 to resume work for *El Espectador*. As he moved to Rome as a correspondent for *El Espectador* and later to Paris, he continued to write fiction, but not without great economic difficulty due to the closing of *El Espectador* by the Rojas Pinilla dictatorship. *El coronel no tiene quien le escriba* came out in 1961, and *La mala hora* appeared the following year,[8] along with a short story volume called *Los funerales de la Mamá Grande*. After journalistic ventures in Bogotá and Caracas and a trip to the Iron Curtain countries to do a series of ten articles, García Márquez opened the Bogotá office of Fidel Castro's Prensa Latina, went briefly to Havana, and was sent by Prensa Latina to become assistant bureau chief in its New York office. He remained in New York only a few months, resigned from Prensa Latina, and made a trip to the South "en homenaje a Faulkner y con sus libros bajo el brazo."[9] Continuing with his family on to Mexico, García Márquez produced what was to become Spanish America's best selling novel, *Cien años de soledad* (1967). With its unprecedented success both García Márquez and his fiction have become the object of an avalanche of critical inspection and interpretation.[10] Various collections of short stories and newspaper articles followed *Cien años*, but an ardent public was forced to wait eight years before the appearance of the promised *El otoño del patriarca* whose theme and style are in many ways so different from his previous works that critics and readers alike have reached conflicting opinions regarding its merit, its method, and its literary value.

Shortly after the publication of *La hojarasca* in 1955 critics were quick to point out García Márquez's Faulknerian tendencies. There are frequent examples of exterior relationships between the two writers; both created fictional settings for much of their writing, settings based primarily on their childhood memories of life in provincial, rural regions washed by the nearby waters of the Caribbean and the Gulf of Mexico. These societies both bear the burden of a historical past interrupted by civil wars leaving memories that still shape the present. The characters of both writers represent the different levels within each society, and they speak a language which demonstrates a sensitivity on the part of both creators to the syntactical patterns, diction, vocabulary, and tone of their region. García Márquez's characters, however, speak a less regional dialect than do the inhabitants of Yoknapatawpha County. Still, in García Márquez's prose, the careful reader notes certain words and expressions heard only in Colombia and the Caribbean coastal region of South America.

There is in both writers a direct relationship between their short stories and their novels; often characters are first delineated in a short story only to reappear in one or more novels. Family clans dominate both regions. The Montiel and Asís families of *La mala hora* prefigure the Buendía dynasty of *Cien años de soledad*. Certain incidents in García Márquez's works seem to be derived directly from Faulknerian sources. Macondo's physical appearance with its wooden houses and zinc roofs is not unlike that of many Southern towns viewed by García Márquez on his journey through Faulkner country. In the last pages of *Cien años* García Márquez wipes Macondo from the face of the earth. It has not appeared in subsequent works. In the meantime Yoknapatawpha County stands in a kind of unfinished limbo. What Faulkner would have done to it in his "Doomsday Book" can only be left to conjecture.

In all of the critical discussion about Faulkner's influence on García Márquez it is necessary to proceed cautiously. The latter is sometimes understandably disturbed by the opinion that he is a mere imitator of Faulkner, and at times he refuses to discuss the issue. His affirmation that " . . . yo había publicado ya mi primera novela, *La hojarasca*, cuando empecé a leer a Faulkner por pura casualidad,"[11] is not supported by recent research covering the period 1948-1949 when he was living in Cartagena. Writing in *El Universal* on 28 July 1949, García Márquez laments the departure of a close friend, Ramiro de la Espriella, to study law in Bogotá in the following words: ''A nosotros—personalmente—nos va a hacer falta de la Espriella durante algunos meses, para hablar mal de André Maurois, para discutir sobre Faulkner y para estar de acuerdo sobre Virginia Woolf."[12] While he may not have read Faulkner prior to 1955, García Márquez was most certainly aware of his work as early as 1949, and a case may clearly be made for Faulknerian influence in *La hojarasca*.[13]

A definitive study of Faulkner's influence on García Márquez is yet to be done. Such a study is beyond the parameter of the present paper which will focus primarily on *El otoño del patriarca*. This Gargantuan picture of an unnamed patriarch who governs an unnamed Caribbean nation for an indeterminate time and who lives to an age between 107 and 232 years is a hyperbolic study of a Latin American dictator whose excesses are Rabelasian in character. As the novel opens vultures are circling the palace; cows munching velvet curtains are wandering through the vast rooms; the patriarch is dead. As his timid subjects enter the decrepit palace, there is an air of uncertainty since a previous "death" of the patriarch had turned out to be that of his perfect double, Patricio Aragonés. Since no one has really seen the man for many years, his identification is at first only provisional.

The six divisions of the novel are circular, each beginning at the point of the patriarch's death, and the last division is one long sentence running to fifty-two pages.[14] Within these circular divisions the details of the patriarch's rise to power are offered in fragmentary reminiscences by the patriarch himself and by a series of unnamed witnesses. Some of these witnesses only retell bits and pieces of legendary materials passed down from generation to generation since none could have been witness in the true sense of the word to events which took place over a hundred years ago. His birth as the bastard son of a bird woman, Bendición Alvarado; his rise to power with the support of the British and later the Americans; the disappearance of his favorite mistress, Manuela Sánchez, during an eclipse of the sun; and the death of his wife and son, Leticia Nazareno and Emanuel, who are torn to bits in a public market by trained dogs are events which gradually fall into narrative sequence as the past is recalled in fragmentary pieces. An additional technique is the interpolation of hyperbolic elements which give the work a tone of magical realism: the enlarged testicle of the patriarch which pains him throughout his life, his power to change the hour of the day, his influence on the hereditary process which causes cows to be born with the presidential brand, his secret ordering of the drowning of two thousand children who are innocent accomplices in the patriarch's rigging of the weekly lottery, and finally his sale of the Caribbean Sea to the Americans who transport it piece by piece to Arizona.

At first blush it is apparent that *El otoño del patriarca* is quite different from *Cien años de soledad*. It is a meditation on the solitude of absolute power, a theme suggested in the presentation of the figure of Aureliano Buendía in *Cien años* and in earlier writings. Instead of a fictional town such as Macondo or Jefferson, García Márquez has created an entire nation with a Caribbean setting, a nation whose capital is reminiscent of Havana or Caracas. There is no lack of models for his prototype of a dictator. William Kennedy traces the genesis of the novel in the following manner: "In 1968 when he began to write this majestic novel, Gabriel García Márquez told an interviewer that the only image he had of it for years was that of an incredibly old man walking through the huge, abandoned rooms of a palace full of animals."[15] Kennedy goes on to say that García Márquez, as he witnessed the downfall of Marcos Pérez Jiménez in Venezuela, mentioned to friends that he would one day write such a book. An earlier Venezuelan dictator, Juan Vicente Gómez, is almost certainly the principal model used for the novel's dictator. There is no dearth of models as one surveys the rest of Latin America, but the timeless, nameless, and imprecise qualities of the patriarch lift him from the realm of the specific and elevate him to the world of myth. There are antecedents to *El otoño del patriarca* in García Márquez's earlier fiction. The use of various narrators who recall the life of a person now dead is the method used in *La hojarasca*. The gross exaggerations of the short story, "Los funerales de la Mamá Grande," prefigure this most recent novel as do the fantastic, imaginative tales of the short story collection, *La increíble y triste historia de la cándida Eréndira y de su abuela desalmada* (1972). And, of course, the style of *El otoño del patriarca* recalls what Kennedy describes as "a densely rich and fluid pudding that makes Faulknerian leaps forward and backward in time. . . . making the novel a puzzle of pronouns, consistently changing narrative points of view in mid-sentence."[16] It is precisely this change of style that is the most Faulknerian aspect of this work of art.

Critics citing Faulknerian influence on García Márquez's earlier works always compared their created worlds, Macondo and Yoknapatawpha; their use of family clans and reappearing characters; their historical perspective, i.e., the burden of past history on the present; and, in the case of *La hojarasca*, the use of multiple points of view. But a point was always made that the styles of the two were vastly different. Kennedy, in an earlier study, quotes Gregory Rabassa's description of *Cien años* as " . . . classical, very clear. He doesn't fool around with syntax. . . . He uses the right word in the right place."[17] Kennedy conjectures that Rabassa will no doubt be the translator of *El otoño del patriarca*, a fact which has now become a reality in the form of a translation which has won acclaim both for the talent of the translator as well as for García Márquez.[18] Ernesto Volkening, writing in 1963, asserts that Faulkner and García Márquez can only be compared "en lo temático."[19] Where Volkening sees in Faulkner " . . . frases laberínticas, complicadas, interminables . . . " which he relates to Joyce's "intestinal" style, he finds that García Márquez uses "el giro breve, conciso, lapidar y cristalino que va derecho al grano . . . ."[20] With the publication of *El otoño del patriarca* it is necessary to reconsider the matter of style and Faulkner's possible influence.

Faulkner's better known novels are often described as "difficult" for the average reader. The some fifteen narrators of *As I Lay Dying* require constant shifts on the part of the reader to organize the sequence of events which describe the journey of Addie Bundren's body to Jefferson where it was her wish to be buried. *The Sound and the Fury*, although it uses only four different points of view, is immensely more fragmented and complicated. These novels retell the past, combining the traditional narrative with a stream-of-consciousness technique. The historical scope of *Absalom, Absalom!* (1936) is much greater in that it covers a historical period from 1817 to an ambiguous present. García Márquez was especially interested in *Absalom*, and its structure and technique are evident as possible models for several works, including *El otoño del patriarca*. In 1929 when *The Sound and the Fury* appeared Faulkner seemed to invite the reader to share with him in a search for order, truth, and significance. Much the same was in store for the readers of later Faulknerian novels. García Márquez first used this method in *La hojarasca*. In *Cien años* there is a sense of linear progression in story development, but many flashbacks are required to complete the picture of Macondo and its final destruction. *El otoño del patriarca* breaks what is a deceptively facile narrative style for what Seymour Menton calls "complejidad cronológica, narrativa y estilística."[21] The repetition of the verb "vimos" allows constant shifts in point of view, but first, second, and third person verb shifts make the task of the reader much greater as he sorts out chronology from such a multitude of material. Here one must recall Jonathan Yardley's description of Faulkner "con sus largas frases enredadas y cargadas con el peso de los siglos . . . ambos [Faulkner y García Márquez] buscan la verdad de la existencia humana por medio de la elevada realidad de la inventiva; a pesar de toda su experimentación y fantasía, ambos son—de todo corazón—notablemente tradicionalistas y fieles al arte del relato."[22]

In many of Faulkner's writings and in *El otoño del patriarca* the work begins at or near the end of the action, and flashbacks related by different narrators fill out the picture. Each point of view is incomplete; often it is the *memory* of the past as recalled in a distant present. Often there is an incompleteness at the end of the work, and the reader is called upon to "finish" the novel. The Civil War in Faulkner and the long dictatorship in *El otoño del patriarca* are the antecedents of a present sense of fatality. Time seems to stand still, or at least it seems to make futile circles which result in a chronological and spatial fragmentation. Clarity is achieved only after events pass into a distant historical perspective, only after the reader has had time to decipher their meaning. Timelessness also permits the characters and events to achieve universal meaning on a mythical level. In this way the regional characters of Faulkner and García Márquez become protagonists with universal problems and concerns. The patriarch is a prototype of the universal oppressor, and the impersonal "nosotros" becomes the voice of his victims.

Incidents derived directly from Faulknerian sources are almost totally absent from *El otoño del patriarca*. Only one event, the death and subsequent national tour of the body of Bendición Alvarado, the patriarch's mother, recalls the long journey of Addie Bundren's body in *As I Lay Dying*. The purpose of the two journeys is quite different, however. In Faulkner's work it is the desire of Addie's husband, Anse, to fulfill her wish to rest in the Jefferson cemetery. Bendición Alvarado's body is sent "para ser exhibida en las escuelas públicas de vereda, en los cuarteles de los desiertos de salitre, en los corrales de indios . . ." (p. 140). Miracles follow the body of Bendición; "la vimos abrir los ojos y vimos que sus pupilas eran diáfanas y tenían el color de acónito en enero y su misma virtud de piedra lunar . . . (p. 141). Subsequent efforts to have her cannonized and named a saint recall events of recent Argentine history following the death of Eva Perón.

Such an incident points out a basic difference between García Márquez and William Faulkner. Specifically it is "lo real maravilloso," the introduction in a natural and objective manner of improbable or miraculous events into a basically realistic narrative, that sets García Márquez apart from Faulkner.[23] While Faulkner frequently used shocking and appalling incidents in his works, only rarely did he allow his characters to act within the framework of the improbable or the supernatural. García Márquez believes that Faulkner's outlandishness is disguised as reality while in Latin America surrealism runs through the streets and comes from the very reality of life.[24]

A final comparison is necessary. Faulkner left as part of his legacy a moral tone and standard by which mankind could judge his characters and ultimately himself. His faith in man was evident in his Stockholm address when he insisted that "I believe that man will not merely endure: he will prevail." As one finishes *El otoño del patriarca*, Faulkner's words come to mind. The patriarch is a victim of the false sense of power which he himself has created. Ultimately he is described as "un tirano de burlas que nunca supo dónde estaba el revés y dónde estaba el derecho de esta vida que amábamos con una pasión insaciable que usted no se atrevió ni siquiera a imaginar por miedo de saber lo que nosotros sabíamos de sobra que era ardua y efímera pero que no había otra, general, porque nosotros sabíamos quiénes éramos mientras él se quedó sin saberlo para siempre . . . " (pp. 270-71). Even from the ruins of the patriarch's palace it is possible to hear "las campanas de gloria que anunciaron al mundo la buena nueva de que el tiempo incontable de la eternidad había por fin terminado" (p. 271). Man has prevailed once again.

*Texas Tech University*

## NOTES

[1] *William Faulkner: Prevailing Verities and World Literature*, Proceedings of the Comparative Literature Symposium, VI (Lubbock: The Texas Tech Press, 1973), pp. 153-64.

[2] William Faulkner, *Santuario*, trans. Lino Novás Calvo (Madrid: Espasa-Calpe, 1934), 271 pp.

[3] *Los nuestros* (Buenos Aires: Editorial Sudamericana, 1969), p. 396.

[4] Gabriel García Márquez and Mario Vargas Llosa, *La novela en América Latina: Diálogo* (Lima: Carlos Milla Batres/Ediciones Universidad Nacional de Ingeniería, [1968]), p. 52.

[5] Ibid., pp. 52-53.

[6] Christopher Sharp's interview with Carlos Fuentes was published in *W*, a supplement to *Women's Wear Daily*, 29 Oct. - 5 Nov. 1976, p. 9.

[7] Frederick J. Hoffman and Olga W. Vickery, eds. *William Faulkner: Three Decades of Criticism* (East Lansing: Michigan State University Press, 1960), p. 82.

[8] García Márquez refused to accept the first edition published in 1962 in Madrid since a proofreader made numerous changes in an effort to improve the style. Many words were also changed to more "acceptable" terms. The first edition of this novel which García Márquez was willing to accept was that done in Mexico by Ediciones ERA in 1966.

[9] Mario Vargas Llosa, "García Márquez: De Aracataca a Macondo," in *Nueve asedios a García Márquez* (Santiago de Chile: Editorial Universitaria, 1972), p. 140.

[10] García Márquez has published a collection of his earlier short stories with the ironic title, *Cuando era feliz e indocumentado* (Caracas: Ediciones El Ojo del Camello, 1973).

[11] Armando Durán, "Conversaciones con Gabriel García Márquez," in *Sobre García Márquez*, ed. Pedro Simón Martínez (Montevideo: Biblioteca de Marcha, 1971), p. 34.

[12] The text of this newspaper article is reprinted in an article by Jacques Gilard, "La obra periodística de García Márquez. Cartagena (1948-1949)," *Eco*, 29, No. 179 (Sept. 1975), 525-34. The article also contains a bibliography of García Márquez's signed newspaper articles published in *El Universal* during his 1948-1949 residence in Cartagena.

[13] An excellent study of *La hojarasca* which mentions affinities between the novel and Faulkner can be found in an article by Robert L. Sims, "García Márquez' 'La hojarasca': Paradigm of Time and Search for Myth," *Hispania*, 59, No. 4 (Dec. 1976), 810-19.

[14] The edition used for this study was published in Buenos Aires by Editorial Sudamericana, 1975. Subsequent references in the text of this paper are to this edition.

[15] *The New York Times Book Review*, 31 Oct. 1976, p. 1.

[16] Ibid., pp. 1, 16.

[17] William Kennedy, "The Yellow Trolley Car in Barcelona, and Other Visions," *The Atlantic*, 231, No. 1 (Jan. 1973), 57.

[18] Rabassa's translation is called *The Autumn of the Patriarch* (New York: Harper & Row, 1976), 269 pp.

[19] "Gabriel García Márquez o el trópico desembrujado," in *Nueve asedios a García Márquez*, p. 150. This article is reprinted from *Eco*, 7, No. 4 (Aug. 1963), 275-93.

[20] Ibid.

[21] Seymour Menton, "Ver para no creer: *El otoño del patriarca*," *Caribe*, 1, No. 1 (Spring 1976), 20.

[22] "Una obra maestra," in *Lecturas Dominicales*, a literary supplement to *El Tiempo*, 5 Dec. 1976, p. 5.

[23] For a more detailed discussion of magical realism see Menton, p. 27, n. 10.

[24] Kennedy, "The Yellow Trolley Car . . .," p. 53.

# Looking Back: Ten Years of Comparative Literature Symposia

Wolodymyr T. Zyla

Since this, the Tenth Annual Comparative Literature Symposium, is the last one under my guidance, perhaps I may be permitted to make a few general remarks about this literary project. It was organized *de novo* and almost *ex nihilo* by the Interdepartmental Committee on Comparative Literature, on my initiative, in February of 1968. At that time we responded to University President Grover E. Murray's question, "What can you do for your University to add to its excellence?" We considered that by conducting the Comparative Literature Symposia we would establish a new forum for worthwhile discussions which would broaden the perspective of scholars in various literary fields. From the beginning the symposium was designed to focus public attention on Comparative Literature and its goals and to stimulate a more intense interest in the study of literature at our own University. At the same time, we hoped to make, through our publications, some original contribution to the realm of literary study. The degree to which we succeeded in accomplishing our tasks must be evaluated by others. For me personally the symposium was a goal of my life to which I devoted all available time for ten years, hoping and praying for its success. It was my dream that one day this project would become a means whereby the University could attract students and faculty, and that it would become known not only in this country but also abroad. Now it seems to me that the groundwork for this has been laid and that the Comparative Literature Symposium is well established.

During my ten years as Chairman of the Symposium Committee as well as of the Interdepartmental Committee on Comparative Literature, I brought to this campus eighty prominent scholars from the United States, Canada, Great Britain, Poland, Yugoslavia, and Turkey. Among them were such outstanding personalities as the late Reverend William T. Noon, S.J., one of the greatest American Joyce specialists; Professor Cleanth Brooks, who is regarded as one of the country's leading literature scholars; Professor Norman Sherry, the outstanding Conrad scholar of Great Britain; Professor Francis M. Rogers, a student of the development of the Romance Languages and of medieval and Renaissance literature at Harvard University; Professor Anna Balakian, whose critical work in modern fiction has been widely acknowledged, and this year Professor Boyd G. Carter, the outstanding scholar of Spanish American literature, whom we honored by dedicating to him this Ibero-American symposium and its Proceedings. In addition, we brought to Texas Tech some forty guest panelists in an effort both to enhance the scholarly character of our discussions and further to enliven them.

From volume one through volume seven the Proceedings of the Comparative Literature Symposium were placed in 662 libraries throughout the world in order to stimulate the growth of comparative literature studies. As of now there are eight volumes of the Proceedings published—altogether 1,285 printed pages. The ninth volume's 1,023 page manuscript is in press, and we hope that this symposium will contribute a manuscript of some 324 pages. Thus when all volumes representing the ten annual symposia are published we should end with approximately 2,104 printed pages. Each comparative literature symposium involved many time-consuming activities which need not be enumerated here.

At this point I should like to express my appreciation and gratitude to all distinguished speakers and guest panelists who honored my invitations in the past decade and participated in the symposia. Thanks are due to the Texas Tech departments of Art, Music, Speech and Theatre Arts, The Museum of Texas Tech University and the University Library for their generous and most helpful cooperation. Allow me to thank all my colleagues at Texas Tech University who helped in different symposia by serving as speakers and panelists and by working on various committees; in particular I should like to thank Dr. Wendell M. Aycock, Dr. Carl Hammer, Jr., Dr. Norwood H. Andrews, Jr., Dr. Marion C. Michael, and Dr. Donald T. Dietz. My special thanks are also due to Dr. Lawrence L. Graves, Dean of the College of Arts and Sciences, for his assistance and cooperation. I am especially grateful to Dr. Grover E. Murray, former President, and Dr. M. Cecil Mackey, present President of Texas Tech University and Dr. J. Knox Jones, Jr., Vice President for Research and Graduate Studies, for their generous support over the years of the comparative literature symposia project.

Finally, I should like to congratulate Dr. Wendell M. Aycock, a new Chairman of the Interdepartmental Committee on Comparative Literature and to wish him all possible success in the difficult and challenging assignment. I sincerely hope that under his chairmanship the Comparative Literature Symposia will continue on a high level and will help develop the academic program in Comparative Literature at Texas Tech University.

*Texas Tech University*

## NOTES ON THE AUTHORS

Dr. John S. Brushwood is Roy A. Roberts Professor of Latin American Literature at the University of Kansas. He received the B.A. degree from Randolph-Macon College, the M.A. from the University of Virginia, and the Ph.D. from Columbia University. From 1946 to 1967, he was on the faculty of the University of Missouri, where he taught Spanish American literature and served a term as chairman of the Department of Romance Languages. His scholarly interests are Mexican literature and the Spanish American novel. *Mexico in Its Novel*, published in English in 1966 and in Spanish (revised) in 1973, is probably his best known book. His studies also include *Breve historia de la novela mexicana*; *Los ricos en la prose mexicana*; and, most recently, *The Spanish American Novel: A Twentieth-Century Survey*.

Dr. Boyd G. Carter, Professor Emeritus of the University of Missouri, 1976, Visiting Professor in the Department of Spanish and Portuguese of the University of Iowa, 1977, joined the staff of Texas Tech University in January, 1978 as Adjunct Professor. He has studied at the University of Toulouse, France, and he holds the B.A. from the College of William and Mary and the M.A. and Ph.D. from the University of Illinois, Idaho, Wyoming, Nebraska, Southern Illinois, Missouri and Coe College. His first job was with the Associated Press. In 1956 he was awarded the *Palmes académiques*. He is author, co-author or editor of, or represented in some twenty books (scholarly, texts and trade), among which are *Las revistas literarias de Hispanoamérica*; *Historia de la literatura hispanoamericana a través de sus revistas*; *Manuel Gutiérrez Nájera: estudio y escritos inéditos*; *En torno a Gutiérrez Nárrez Nájera y las letras mexicanas del siglo XIX*; *La 'Revista de América' de Rubén Darío y Ricardo Jaimes Freyre*. His other writings (studies, criticism, bibliography, features, short stories, poems) have appeared in more than fifty publications. For several years he has been a regular contributor to "The Hispanic World" of *Hispania*.

Dr. Frank Dauster is Professor of Spanish and Portuguese at Rutgers, The State University of New Jersey. A native of New Jersey, he received the A.B. and M.A. from Rutgers and the Ph.D. from Yale. Among his publications are *Breve historia de la poesía mexicana*; *Ensayos sobre poesía mexicana*; *Historia del teatro hispanoamericano de los siglos XIX y XX: Ensayos sobre teatro hispanoamericano*, and a study of the Mexican poet and dramatist Xavier Villaurrutia. He has also published several texts and has contributed to journals in the United States and Latin America. He has been Contributing Editor in Modern Drama for the *Handbook of Latin American Studies* since 1953 and is presently a member of the Advisory Board.

Dr. Angela B. Dellepiane is Professor of Spanish at the City College of the City University of New York and Professor of Spanish American Literature at the Spanish Doctoral Program of CUNY. A native of Argentina, she received the M.A. and Ph.D. from the Facultad de Filosofía y Letras of the University of Buenos Aires. She has taught at the University of Buenos Aires and Fordham University. Professor Dellepiane has published articles in both English and Spanish in various American, European, and Latin American journals. She is the author of *Presencia de América en la obra de Tirso de Molina*; *Ernest Sábato: El hombre y su obra*, and of an annotated edition of the "gauchesco" classic *Don Segundo Sombra*. She is interested in Surrealism in Spanish American literature and in Spanish American literature in Spanish American theatre. She has served as Chairperson of the Twentieth-Century Spanish American Literature of the MLA and is an Associate of the Columbia University Latin American Seminar.

Dr. Dick Gerdes earned the Ph.D. from the University of Kansas, and he presently teaches Spanish American Literature at the University of New Mexico. He is the author of *Julio Ramón Ribeyro y la narrativa peruana*, soon to be published by the Instituto Nacional de Cultura in Lima. He has published articles and reviews in *The American Hispanist*, *Arco* (Bogotá), and *Revista Interamericana de Bibliografía*. Future articles and reviews are scheduled to appear in *Kentucky Romance Quarterly*, *Latin American Theatre Review* and *Modern Language Journal*. He is currently directing a year-long lecture series on Hispanic Civilization in the Southwest, funded by the New Mexico Humanities Council.

Dr. Seymour Menton is Professor of Spanish and Portuguese at the University of California, Irvine. A native of New York City, he received the B.A. from City College of New York, the M.A. from the Universidad Nacional Autónoma de México, and the Ph.D. from New York University. He has taught at the University of Kansas, the Universidad de Costa Rica, the Universidad de San Carlos in Guatemala, and Dartmouth College. A specialist in Latin American prose fiction, he has published books on the Guatemalan novel (1960), the Costa Rican short story (1964), and the prose fiction of the Cuban Revolution (1975). His historical-critical anthology, *El cuento hispanoamericano*, is now in its fourth printing, having sold over 70,000 copies. His articles include critical analyses of *María*, *Los de abajo*, *La vorágine*, *Confabulario*, *Hijo de hombre*, and *Cien años de soledad*. Professor Menton has been editor of *Hispania* (1963-1965) and President of the American Association of Teachers of Spanish and Portuguese (1971).

Dr. Robert J. Morris received his A.B. and M.A. degrees at the University of North Carolina at Chapel Hill and his Ph.D. at the University of Kentucky. After teaching for three years at the University of Cincinnati, he came to Texas Tech University where he is presently an Associate Professor of Spanish and Portuguese. Professor Morris' research interests have centered around the contemporary Hispanic American theatre, particularly the Peruvian. He has articles and reviews appearing in such journals as the *Latin American Theatre Review*, *Revista de Estudios Hispánicos*, *Letras femeninas*, *Hispania*, *Romance Notes*, and *The American Hispanist* and a book, *The Contemporary Peruvian Theatre*. He is a member of several regional and national professional organizations, and the President of the Southwestern Council on Latin American studies.

Dr. Harley D. Oberhelman, Professor of Spanish at Texas Tech University, joined the faculty in 1958 after earning degrees in Spanish and Romance Languages at the University of Kansas. He is the author of *Ernesto Sábato*, "Education and the History of Knowledge in *Cien años de soledad*," "García Márquez and the American South," "José Donoso and the 'Nueva Narrativa,' " and other articles and reviews in journals such as *Hispania*, *Chasqui*, *Revista de Estudios Hispánicos*, and *Books Abroad*. In 1961 Professor Oberhelman was a Fulbright lecturer at the National University of Tucumán, Argentina. In 1970 he received the Standard Oil Foundation Distinguished Teaching Award, and in 1975 he was named a Piper Professor. During the 1977 spring semester Professor Oberhelman is the recipient of a Faculty Development Leave to do research on William Faulkner's influence on García Márquez.

Dr. Gregory Rabassa is Professor of Romance Languages and Comparative Literature at Queens College and the Graduate School, CUNY. He has also taught at Columbia University. He received the A.B. from Dartmouth College and the M.A.

(Spanish) and the Ph.D. (Portuguese) from Columbia University. He is author of *O Negro na Ficçao Brasileira* and the translator of several novels and short stories from Spanish and Portuguese. In 1967 he received the National Book Award for his translation of *Hopscotch*, by Julio Cortázar, and in 1971 was a finalist for *One Hundred Years of Solitude*, by Gabriel García Márquez. He was Associate Editor of *Odyssey Review* and has contributed to *The American Scholar*, *The New York Times Book Review*, *Saturday Review*, *The Nation*, *The New Yorker*, *Esquire*, *Playboy*, *Harper's*, *The Atlantic Monthly*, *Parnassus*, *The New York Review of Books*, *Centerpoint*, *Fiction*, *Tempo Brasileiro*, *Revista de Letras*, and other magazines and journals. He is chairman of the translation committee of the P.E.N. American Center and of the literature committee of the Center for Inter-American Relations. He served with the Office of Strategic Services in World War II. In 1965-1966 he was a Fulbright-Hays Fellow in Brazil.

Dr. Daniel R. Reedy is Professor of Spanish and Chairman of the Department of Spanish and Italian Languages and Literatures at the University of Kentucky. A native of Illinois, he received the B.S. from Eastern Illinois University and the M.A. and Ph.D. degrees in Latin American literature at the University of Illinois. As a Rotary International Fellow (1959-1960), he completed advanced studies at the Universidad Nacional Mayor de San Marcos in Lima, Peru. Before coming to Kentucky, he taught at the University of North Carolina and held a Visiting Professorship at the University of Kansas in Guadalajara, Mexico. His publications include *The Poetic Art of Juan del Valle Caviedes and Narraciones ejemplares de Hispanoamérica*. He has published articles in both English and Spanish in various American and Latin American journals. Professor Reedy is a Contributing Editor to the *Handbook of Latin American Studies*. His awards include a Fulbright Research Fellowship (1966-1967), a Social Science Research Council Award (1971), and an American Council on Education Fellowship (1975-1976). His current research includes aspects of literature of social commitment in modern Spanish America and the prose works of Julio Cortázar.

Dr. Sabine R. Ulibarrí is Professor of Spanish literature and Chairman of the Department of Modern and Classical Languages at The University of New Mexico. A native of Santa Fe, New Mexico, he received the B.A. and M.A. degrees from the University of New Mexico and the Ph.D. degree from the University of California at Los Angeles. His main field of interest is Spanish poetry, and he specializes in Twentieth-Century poetry. He has lived and studied in Mexico, South America and Spain. Professor Ulibarrí has published in the area of literary criticism pertaining to poetry. He also writes original short stories and poems in Spanish. His books have been published in Mexico, Ecuador and Spain.

Dr. Wolodymyr T. Zyla, a native of Ukraine, is Professor of Slavic Languages and Literatures at Texas Tech University. He received his B.Sc., and M.A. from University of Manitoba and his Ph.D. from the Ukrainian Free University in Munich. During the summer of 1965 he was Visiting Professor of Russian at the University of Texas at Austin. Dr. Zyla has been Chairman of the Interdepartmental Committee on Comparative Literature (1969-1976) and Chairman of the Symposium Committee (1968-1977). He edited ten volumes of the Proceedings of the Comparative Literature Symposium (beginning with volume V as coeditor along with Dr. Wendell M. Aycock). Dr. Zyla served for two years as President of the Texas Chapter of the American Association of Teachers of Slavic and East European Languages. He is the recipient of a grant from the National Endowment for the Humanities. Dr. Zyla has published many articles concerning Slavic literature and the study of names, and is the author of *Idejni osnovy Shevchenkovoho "Hamaliji"* and *Z istoriji ukrajino-znavstva i slavistyky v Kanadi.*